July, 1985

For my good friends,
Charles and Christine,
Good friends, also, of
Rogers and Tony.

Joey

×q lit crit 4

Critical Essays on Angus Wilson

Critical Essays on Angus Wilson

Jay L. Halio

G. K. Hall & Co. • Boston, Massachusetts

For Angus and Tony
and for Zack

Published by G. K. Hall & Co.
A publishing subsidiary of ITT

Library of Congress Cataloging in Publication Data
Critical essays on Angus Wilson.
    (Critical essays on modern British literature)
    Bibliography: p.
    Includes index.
    1. Wilson, Angus — Criticism and interpretation — Addresses,
essays, lectures. I. Halio, Jay L. II. Series.
PR6045.I577Z6   1985   823'.914   84-15841
ISBN 0-8161-8691-X (alk. paper)

This publication is printed on permanent/durable acid-free paper
MANUFACTURED IN THE UNITED STATES OF AMERICA

CRITICAL ESSAYS ON MODERN BRITISH LITERATURE

The new critical essays series on modern British literature attempts to provide a variety of approaches to both the modern classical writers of Britain and Ireland, and the best contemporary authors. The formats of the volumes in the series vary with the thematic designs of individual editors, and with the amount and nature of existing reviews, criticism, and scholarship. In general, the series seeks to represent the best in published criticism, augmented, where appropriate, by original essays by recognized authorities. It is hoped that each volume will be unique in developing a new overall perspective on its particular author.

Jay Halio's study of Angus Wilson includes his early reception by reviewers, three major interviews with Wilson, a major section on criticism of Wilson's individual works, and overviews encompassing several works or aspects of Wilson's works. A bibliography of Wilson's books is appended.

Halio's masterful introduction begins with an overview of Wilson's work and reputation, includes a substantial biography especially as it affects Wilson's writing, and finally provides a survey of the major scholarship and criticism on Wilson to date. Halio explores Wilson's place in the social revolution after World War II and his development as a liberal humanist. His picture of Wilson reveals not a static writer who repeats himself either in style or story line, but a novelist continually experimenting and evolving. Halio's biography provides a context for the social attitudes expressed in Wilson's fiction. In contrast with Wilson's evolving art as a writer, he is generally consistent in political and social views held throughout his lifetime. Halio's judgment and observations are backed by the personal interviews with Wilson published in the present volume. These include a recent interview published for the first time.

The division of the book into sections on reviews, interviews, and criticism affords us some of the reasons why Wilson's books were so immediately popular. Unlike the case with more obscure or complicated novelists, Wilson's books, while never facile or formulaic, could be understood by intelligent first readers without the painstaking scholarship that writers like Joyce demanded. Nevertheless, the reviewers chosen by Halio represent some of the finest British and American critics, and their assessments of the novels and short stories are often far more detailed and critical than initial reviews are apt to be of so valuable and public a contemporary figure as Wilson. It is natural that interviews might be important sources of both attitudes and artistry. The three published in the present volume span twenty years, the most recent with Jack I. Biles, published for the first time in the present volume. The last three essays in the volume are all original and represent the first major critical articles on *Setting the World on Fire* and Wilson's highly acclaimed biographies of Zola, Dickens, and Kipling. The volume should prove to be a valuable and permanent asset for critics and devotees of Angus Wilson.

Zack Bowen, GENERAL EDITOR

University of Delaware

CONTENTS

INTRODUCTION

Angus Wilson: An Overview

At a time when British novelists are discovering more and more ways in which to detach the novel from its traditional moorings, it may seem something of a paradox that some of the very experimenters were, a generation ago, in the vanguard of a movement in an entirely opposite direction. The period immediately following World War II was not a time of experimentation but just the reverse: in reaction against earlier twentieth-century writers, preeminently James Joyce and Virginia Woolf, novelists were "rediscovering" or otherwise championing the achievements of Trollope, Dickens, Dostoevski, and Thackeray from the previous century.

The days following the cataclysmic events of the War — not in the destruction of cities so much as the downfall of other, less tangible aspects of civilization — led writers to a renewed emphasis upon the social and moral content of fiction. If some like Alan Sillitoe extended, *mutatis mutandis*, the preoccupations and to a degree the social-realistic style of the fiction of the thirties, others like C. P. Snow went back further to the great nineteenth-century precursors for their models. Britain was undergoing a revolution in manners and mores but much more deeply in its social underpinnings. To some of us in America it may have been surprising, even shocking, that the great war hero, Winston Churchill, was so roundly defeated in the first postwar election. But to others, the election of Britain's first Labour government was already overdue.

It was partly out of this milieu of social ferment that Angus Wilson's fiction emerged or, to be more precise, was tempered. For Wilson still claims that the origins of his career as a writer are deeper and more personal. In a sense, it was an accident that he began writing at all, though he later recognized that the developing pattern of his life had actually been moving in that direction for some time, however unaware he was of it at first.[1] Recovering from a nervous breakdown, and finding his weekends spent in the country rather empty, he decided to spend the time writing short stories, since they could be conceived and completed within that short span. Before long he had a considerable number of stories and showed some of them to a friend. He in turn showed them to Cyril Connolly, who published the first of these in *Horizon*. Another friend at Secker & Warburg

1

thought a dozen or so would make a good volume, and the firm brought out *The Wrong Set* in 1949, despite conventional publishing wisdom which dictated that collections of short stories, since they did not sell well, was the wrong way for a writer to launch his career. But *The Wrong Set* did so well, both critically and financially, that a second collection, *Such Darling Dodos*, was published the next year, with similar results.[2]

Although he thus began his career as a successful short story writer, Wilson and others regard his eight published novels as his major contribution to fiction. Nevertheless, his early stories reflect the social, moral, and stylistic attributes of his fiction from which he has never fully departed. Early referred to as the second Evelyn Waugh because of his biting wit and social satire, he took for his targets in the first collection various kinds of "false innocence" preserved in such characters as Vi in "The Wrong Set," the two old ladies in "Raspberry Jam," or the young civil servant hero of "Crazy Crowd." In the second collection his targets, as in the title story, become the preserved innocence of "genuinely good, but blinkered" characters, such as the left-wing don and his wife. The attack, as Wilson later analyzed it, shifts to one not against *false* standards so much as against *insufficient* standards.[3] But in both collections, it appears now, Wilson was clearing the way for his major fiction, not only in the kind of apprenticeship writing he was doing (even though there is little evidence of the neophyte in those stories), but in purging himself of preoccupations that then seemed uppermost in his mind. At the same time, as critics like Edmund Wilson and others recognized, he was mapping out the contours, the hills and valleys, of the social revolution that had taken place in Britain and was continuing to go forward during the decades following the war.[4]

As he was soon to demonstrate in his novels, the older forms of fiction were not exhausted: the honed blade of the short story was still a serviceable instrument in the hands of a talented writer. Not the form, but the voice that brought the form to life, was the key to Wilson's success. He cannot claim the innovations of a writer like Lawrence or Chekhov, nor was he aspiring to any such achievements. It remained for other writers, such as Leonard Michaels and Donald Barthelme in America, or Jorge Borges in Argentina, to show the further developments possible in short fiction. But Wilson's ear for dialogue is matched only (to cite American parallels again) by writers like Philip Roth and Bernard Malamud, whose characters, however, are worlds away from his. His gift of mimickry — a lifelong trait — he put to good and spirited use. And while his stories cut right to the heart of the matter, they reveal an ambivalence that is also their trademark. Characters whom the reader may condemn on moral grounds, such as the dandified sponger or his ladyfriend in "What Do Hippos Eat?," can also arouse in the same reader much sympathy, partly as a result of the "preserved innocence" they retain, partly out of compassion for the plights into which they have propelled themselves from all too recognizable human weaknesses.

The accomplishments of the short stories are everywhere apparent in

Wilson's first novel, *Hemlock and After* (1952), which he wrote in the space of four weeks while on annual leave from the British Museum, where he was employed as a full-time civil servant. But the longer form enabled Wilson to explore more thoroughly those issues that concerned him now ever more deeply: the kinds of self-deception that even the most morally high-minded are liable to, or the conflicts of reason and emotion, specifically the use and abuse of power, that became an abiding motif. His second and third novels continue the theme of self-deception and the struggles to fuller self-awareness; in fact, taken together *Hemlock and After, Anglo-Saxon Attitudes* (1956) and *The Middle Age of Mrs. Eliot* (1958) form a kind of trilogy, although in many important respects each novel is different from the others. In every instance, however, the principal character is someone who, not as an adolescent or young adult, but as a mature person, comes face to face with truths about himself or herself that a lifetime has been spent avoiding. As early as these first novels, Wilson's refusal to repeat himself is noticeable: each form is different, and the particular circumstances of each hero or heroine's dilemma are far from identical. Bernard Sands quite suddenly recognizes the innate cruelty that is part of his nature along with the altruistic tendencies he prides himself on; Gerald Middleton discovers that the causes of his years-long depression need not be as crippling as he has allowed them to become; Meg Eliot finds that she can survive the collapse of her attractive and sheltered existence and, unlike her quietist brother, David Parker, go out and meet life head on — and enjoy it. If Bernard Sands dies before he can adequately come to grips with the truth about himself, his wife Ella recovers sufficiently from her paranoid depression to carry on his work afterwards.

Anglo-Saxon Attitudes is Wilson's most "Dickensian" novel, as many have recognized, and the debt is fully acknowledged.[5] It is also his most popular novel, doubtless because of the range of colorful characters — some of them quite seedy — that Wilson has included. In chronicling English society in mid-century (with several important returns to England of the 1920s and 1930s), Wilson became identified now not only with the advocates of the traditional novel, but with a rising group of novelists and playwrights grouped together as "The Angry Young Men." Wilson, of course, was neither as young as John Osborne, John Wain, and the others, nor as "angry": his motives and intentions in writing were quite dissimilar, although it might fairly be said that all of these writers in the 1950s shared a common antagonism against the hypocrisies and rigidities that still clung to much of British life. What distinguishes Wilson from the others is his liberal humanism; for underlying his attack on the follies and foibles of his characters, whether dodos or birds of another plumage, is the deeply felt — and conveyed — sense that life is worth living, that muddled as we often become, human endeavors are not despicable. Paradoxical as it may seem, this attitude, which colors all of Wilson's writing, is not inconsistent with a pervasive pessimism that also adheres to his work and that many early critics saw as its only salient aspect. Wilson's humanism is different from that of, say, E. M. Forster's, with which it has often been compared, and to which Wilson was himself earlier attracted. But later when he came to recognize Forster's patronizing attitudes, his basic disregard for the weak or unsophisticated characters in his novels, Wilson found them repugnant.[6] In his activist tendency (revealed most clearly at the end of *The Middle Age of Mrs. Eliot* or *As If By Magic*) Wilson also contrasts with his illustrious forebear.

Where *Anglo-Saxon Attitudes* cast its net wide, *The Middle Age of Mrs. Eliot* went deep, as Wilson developed his use of the interior monologue to fullest effect. But *The Old Men at the Zoo* (1961) came as the first big surprise to readers who were growing comfortable with Wilson's humanism and his wit. Not that either one is abandoned in this fourth novel; but political satire set several years in the future and having to do with the possibilities of Armageddon in the context of a community of naturalists and zoo keepers was not quite what people expected. If Jane Austen, George Eliot, and Dickens had been to some extent the guiding lights for his development as a writer up to then, Jonathan Swift, Aldous Huxley, and less importantly George Orwell became the major influences here. But "influence" is almost always a misleading term: whatever the models a writer may take, his achievement is measured as much, or more, by his departures from them, his transmutation of the basic materials, as by the inspiration they may afford. So it was with Wilson in *The Old Men at the Zoo*, an anti-utopian novel just as his *No Laughing Matter* would be an anti-*Forsyte Saga* saga. If Simon Carter, the chief character in the novel, shares with Lemuel Gulliver the dubious distinction of becoming first a vehicle for, then the object of, the author's satire, comparisons end there—except perhaps for the way both figures lose their compassion for human beings as such. Nowhere in Swift can we find the detailed and accurate descriptions of nature and wildlife that Wilson offers in this novel to develop his theme of the importance of the instinctual life among human beings as well as animals—and the depravities to which it may also be subjected.

By this time it was becoming apparent to anyone who would see—and many curiously would not, addicted to the labeling and pigeon-holing as they were—that Angus Wilson was not simply a brilliant neo-traditionalist but an experimenter who was determined not to repeat himself. As early as 1953 he had published, with Phillippe Jullian, an interesting *jeu d'esprit* called *For Whom the Cloche Tolls: A Scrap-Book of the Twenties*, which demonstrated his ability to mingle various kinds of narrative technique (not excepting the line drawings Jullian contributed) as well as non-sequential chronology in fiction.[7] Publication of *Late Call* in 1964, however, seemed a throwback to more conventional forms, especially to the techniques and themes of *The Middle Age of Mrs. Eliot*, the novel it most closely resembles, although there again important differences exist. Whereas each novel takes a woman as its protagonist, Sylvia Calvert is at some distance from Meg Eliot, not only in social class, education, and personality, but in age and outlook too. The social themes of the earlier novels reemerge, here in the focus upon one of England's "new towns" built after the establishment of the welfare state in Labour-dominated Britain. Of greater importance was Wilson's increasing interest in the idea of a kind of "secular grace" to go along with an emphasis on good works through which his characters might find their spiritual salvation. Though Wilson was, as he remains, an agnostic in matters of religion, he freely adapted the concept of secular grace in his work, to which critics have begun to pay greater attention.[8]

All of Wilson's accomplishments in fiction found their apogee in the masterpiece he had been pointing toward, it now seems, from the very beginning of his career. *No Laughing Matter* (1967) is more than a *tour de force*; it demonstrates more clearly than anything Wilson had done before the ways in which the protean form of the novel lends itself to both the experiments of the great twentieth-century writers and the traditional forms of narrative. It shows how within the broad confines of a novel other modes of fiction may be incorporated, such as short plays, parodies, and various sorts of pastiche. The result was clearly astonishing, from the opening pages of the Matthews family's excursion to the great Wild West Exposition of 1912, presented in cinematic-surrealistic fashion, to the quiet closing of events in which, for once, Wilson allows his characters to achieve something (instead of stopping short, as in his earlier novels, after insight has been attained but before the fruits of that hard-won insight have been reaped). If there had been any question about Wilson's stature as a major writer in the century, all doubt was now removed.

One of the signs of a good writer is the way he pays his debts to those who have been important in his own development. Always a "literary" novelist, Wilson has salted his books with frequent allusions to other writers. Often, his characters explicitly compare themselves with childhood heroes or heroines from their reading; or they attend plays by Ibsen or Osborne, plays that have a direct relevance to the themes Wilson is also using; or the situations they find themselves in have sources or analogues in farces by Feydeau or mythological adventures such as Phaethon's ill-fated chariot ride through the skies. Some writers acknowledge indebtedness more directly by discussing authors who have interested them over the years; their criticism thus reveals, as Wilson's has repeatedly done, preoccupations as well as interests that have a direct bearing on their own current work. Much more rarely writers go into the related but quite different genre of biography to show not only what impresses them, but what they consider ought to be more generally acknowledged by the reading public. In his biographies of Dickens (1970) and Kipling (1977) Wilson demonstrated, first of all, that his earlier study of Zola (1952) was not a fluke; that the abilities he had as a biographer were solid ones that could be, and were, used for further purposes. Although it would be too much to say that the vogue Dickens now enjoys is owing largely to Wilson's efforts (which include a number of critical lectures and essays as well as his book), it is certainly true that Wilson has been in the forefront of those who have helped to reestablish Dickens as the great novelist he is. Similarly, Wilson's recent efforts on behalf of the often misunderstood and misprized achievements of Rudyard Kipling have helped to recover some of his reputation as well.[9]

No Laughing Matter extended over three generations in time, as it traced the adventures and misadventures of the Matthews family. Where Wilson would turn next to extend the frontiers of his art was a good guess, but what emerged was, again, hardly the expected. *As If by Magic* (1973) is in many ways still his least understood (and for that reason probably his least liked) book. Referred to as his "global" novel,[10] it encompasses many of the known parts of the world, setting its scenes in various parts of Asia, Africa, and Europe. Not that Wilson was ever a parochial novelist in any of a number of possible definitions. His urbane protagonists are usually too well-traveled as well as cultured to be caught within the cosy confines of a regional novel or a narrowly focused one, for all of Wilson's admitted concerns with postwar England and its problems. *As If by Magic* does not leave those concerns behind, but seeks to expand their relevance to the much broader scope that such "global" coverage suggests. The settings in the novels of Graham Greene, a contrasting figure in many ways, differ in this respect, that (despite their vividness and diversity) they suffer from the very limitations the immediate environment can impose. In *As If by Magic* Wilson does not try to make the whole world one, but he does present the interaction of several cultures in illuminating and significant ways as his scientist hero, Hamo Langmuir, traverses the earth with what he at first thinks will be his population-saving new miracle rice hybrid. The cultures that interact, moreover, are not only geographical, but generational also, as the subplot involving Hamo's goddaughter, Alexandra, shows.

Having explored the reaches of time and space, where could Wilson go from there? *Setting the World on Fire* (1980) was one answer to that question, but it can hardly be his last. Without departing from the human landscape, which remains as always his chief object, Wilson now turned ever more closely to the world of art, the tensions inherent in any masterpiece that keep the work alive, and the effect such art has upon human consciousness. If in *Anglo-Saxon Attitudes* Wilson invented an important archeological excavation and a hoax (modeled both on the discovery of the Sutton Hoo burial ship and the Piltdown Man scandal), in this new novel he invented a mansion constructed in part by Vanbrugh and in part by Pratt, two quite dissimilar architects, whose opposing temperaments and attitudes are reflected in the characters of Piers and Tom Mosson, the chief characters in the book. Within the great hall of this mansion, which Wilson persuasively sets in the middle of Westminster, is a Verrio mural depicting the fall of Phaethon that has contrasting effects upon the two brothers, first as children, later as adults. The joys and fears of walking on cracked ice is a major theme, but the novel also brings out more strikingly than before the conflicts between reason and emotion, or freedom and order, that have informed all of Wilson's fiction and much of other literature besides. The final recognition is that order, of course, is essential — without it nothing stands or endures — but it must not crush the creative spirit by asserting its claims too early or too mightily.

Angus Wilson has been grappling with these contesting claims throughout his career, and that is one reason why his *oeuvre* defies easy definition or pigeon-holing. His early efforts to reestablish the values of the nineteenth-century novel were not simply an exercise in traditionalism but, in their own way, also experimentalist. For Wilson never intended that the Dickens novel, for example, should be revived as such. What he was trying to accomplish, and very largely did, was to show how the methods of older writers could be incorporated with later ones. Having succeeded there, as in *Anglo-Saxon Attitudes,* he then turned to other kinds of experiments so that in retrospect his work appears as a long series of attempts, most of them fruitful, to explore the boundaries of his art and, by so doing, not only keep the novel alive, but keep it vigorous and growing.

ANGUS WILSON, THE MAN

Writer, critic, biographer, teacher, president of literary societies, panelist, chairman of Arts Council committees — Angus Wilson has been and is everything that one might associate with the expression man-of-letters. Yet he hardly expected his life to turn out that way. Born in Bexhill on the south coast of England on 11 August, 1913, he was the youngest of six sons — but the next in age was already thirteen, and his parents were in their mid-forties. Though born in London, his father, William Johnstone-Wilson (Angus soon dropped the "Johnstone"), came of a well-to-do Scots family and liked to behave very much as the country gentleman, even after the family fell onto increasingly hard times following World War I. His mother, Maude Caney, was a South African whose parents were wealthy merchants; her inferior social standing was something William never forgot or allowed her and their sons to forget. The four oldest brothers were all in the armed services during World War I, and one of them was twice wounded. Angus grew up a lonely, sensitive, rather spoiled child, surrounded by older persons and often having to bear the role of mascot to his father. (To this day he hates to stay up after ten o'clock — a consequence of his father's late evening card parties at which he demanded his son's presence.) Playing on the south downs during the war years and listening to the talk among his elders fed his imagination and led to what he has called the "gothic" quality of some of his fiction.[11]

Heavily influenced by Freudian theory, Wilson attributes much of his later development to these alienating childhood years, to the family's shifting about from one small hotel or boarding house to another, trying to keep up the appearance of gentility while often at the edge of poverty. Many of the characters in his early fiction derive from persons he came to know in this environment, such as Mrs. Hennessy or Bruce Talfourd-Rich in "Saturnalia." After the war, one of his brothers set up a school, which Angus attended. The school was at another seaside town, Seaford, near Bexhill, and had a magnificent garden that may have sparked Angus's interest in what later became his chief hobby. Before these schooldays began, however, occurred a quite different chapter in his life, when he accompanied his parents on an extended visit to Durban, South Africa, where his mother's family still lived. A version of his experiences there among his mother's people, almost all of them of British origins, appears in the short story "Union Reunion." Although Angus must have felt as out of place there in many ways as he did with the adults he lived among in England, he also enjoyed a care and attention, especially from his "Kaffir," George, such as he had not known previously.

Returning to England three years later with his Durban accent, his sense of alienation deepened. In 1927, when he entered one of England's best public schools, Westminster, as a day boy, he was filled with trepidation against the prospect of bullying, but in fact experienced none. There he first met and formed what became a lifelong friendship with Perkin Walker, now emeritus professor of the Warburg Institute, to whom Wilson dedicated *The Wild Garden*. (In a memoir Walker speaks of this early friendship and his determination to protect Wilson from bullying and then not having to.)[12] When in 1929 Wilson's mother was stricken by a heart attack, her son got back to the hotel only just in time before she died. The event affected him so profoundly that he has never been able to introduce it in a direct way in his fiction, though much of his mother's pluck and some of her later devotion to Christian Science have provided attributes of characters such as Meg (in *The Middle Age of Mrs. Eliot*) or Jackie Mosson (in *Setting the World on Fire*). After her death, it was Perkin Walker's parents, among others, who became a kind of surrogate family for Angus, affording him his first exposure to a different sort of family life — sophisticated, cultured, politically left-wing — as opposed to the shabby genteel, raffish, and unintellectual life of the Johnstone-Wilsons. If he later satirized the insufficiency of the Walkers' standards in stories like "Such Darling Dodos," he has never forgotten the devotion they showed him at a time when he needed it greatly.

Westminster School was followed by Merton College, Oxford, which Wilson entered in 1932, thanks to a small income left him through his mother's bequest. An account of his life there appears in a collection called *My Oxford* edited by Ann Thwaite. Though he had a pleasant time and was graduated with a good degree in history, he never formed the sort of debilitating attachment to Oxford that some others have done who cannot feel really happy anywhere else. During these Oxford years Wilson further developed his acting abilities, begun at school, and even thought of making the stage his career. (His histrionic ability is everywhere apparent in his fiction.) But after a year or two of various odd jobs, including helping one of his brothers run a tea shop, he found a position that afforded him the kind of security he believed he desperately needed—working as a cataloger in the British Museum library. There he remained until the outbreak of war and his service, beginning in 1942, for the Foreign Office doing intelligence work.

Living in London and working at the Museum, engaging in political activities to prevent the war everyone knew was coming, dining out with friends, attending the theater—these and other aspects of those years provided the subjects and substance of many of Wilson's first short stories. By the time of Munich, in early 1938, he saw that political activity was futile; it was then, also, he must have glimpsed what he later referred to as the decline of liberalism in our time. But whatever his criticisms of those liberal attitudes and programs,[13] he has never abandoned his convictions as a social democrat, just as he has remained true to his ideas of liberal humanism. At Bletchley during the war where he then worked, a more personal crisis temporarily shattered Wilson's view of himself, causing him to spend long periods of introspection such as he had never done before. By then his father had died and with him went their very close relationship, leaving Wilson to search for some other. At the end of the war and his resumption of work at the British Museum (he was in charge of replacing thousands of volumes that had been damaged or lost in the bombings), he had suffered a nervous collapse and was trying various ways to help himself recover. He began writing his stories, at first as a means of diversion, but very soon with serious interest and remarkable skill.

In his interviews—for he is generous of himself almost to a fault—Wilson speaks openly and freely of his childhood and indeed of all periods of his life. What in others might appear egoism, in him is clearly an effort to understand himself and his work and share with others who may be interested in that understanding. For example, in one of his earliest interviews[14] he discusses the conflict he experienced as his books became more and more successful (*Such Darling Dodos* was a Book Society Choice in Britain). He was still working full-time at the museum and wanted to write a longer novel than he was able to do in *Hemlock and After.* Moreover, he had written a play and felt the demands of rehearsals would make life extremely difficult. He confronted the situation bravely, resigned from his safe, secure job as (by then) deputy superintendent of the Reading Room, and with a scant three hundred pounds in the bank went to live in Suffolk and became a full-time professional writer. His play, *The Mulberry Bush* (1956), was produced by the Bristol Old Vic and then invited to inaugurate George Devine's new enterprise at the Royal Court Theatre in London in April 1956. Successful in Bristol, it flopped in London, for reasons that still remain unclear. Soon afterwards, John Osborne and the new wave of playwrights began storming the West End and, except for a few television plays, Wilson has not attempted to write in that medium again.

He turned instead fully to writing fiction and, to help eke out his income, doing reviews for weeklies like the *Sunday Observer. Anglo-Saxon*

Attitudes appeared in 1956; his third collection of stories, *A Bit Off the Map*, the next year, and *The Middle Age of Mrs. Eliot* in 1958. By this time Wilson was earning a reputation, too, as a lively and knowledgeable speaker, and he was frequently invited by the British Council to give lectures abroad. It was on a trip abroad, in fact, during a stop at the Karachi airport, that he conceived the idea for his third novel, when he heard someone crying uncontrollably in a cloakroom and he wondered what would happen to him if he suddenly lost everything. The long flight over desert landscapes also influenced his conception of that novel and is recaptured in Meg's meditations during her trip with Bill, her husband, who is fatally wounded at Srem Panh Airport while trying to prevent an assassination. One of the reasons Wilson left the British Museum, he admits, is that he longed to travel more extensively, and he has done so ever since, often spending the winter months in places like Egypt or Sri Lanka, where he is able to enjoy the sun and warmth and the leisure to write.

His methods of composition are somewhat unusual, though he confesses to have got the idea partly from his examination of Zola's notebooks when he was doing research for his biography. Before attempting to write, Wilson fills up a number of notebooks with the details of a running debate with himself, trying to persuade himself of the truth of what he has imagined. If the initial impetus, as in the scene at Karachi Airport, is usually a visual image, scenes and characters and much dialogue are worked out painstakingly over months until he feels he has convinced himself and is ready to begin. Then he writes the novel in a single, rarely altered draft. The manuscript is afterwards typed, corrected, and sent off to the publisher. No revisions or alternate drafts are done, for they do not seem necessary; once the early spade work has been accomplished, the novel gets written directly. Wilson places great emphasis, therefore, on the gestation process which, for him, is much more than merely deep rumination. It is active and often arduous. Whether preparing his novel or writing it out, Wilson invariably sits in a camp chair out of doors, if possible, puts plugs in his ears to keep out distracting noises, and sets to work.

By 1960, owing to his growing reputation as a writer and speaker, Wilson was invited to give a number of lectures in the United States and elsewhere. Out of the Ewing Lectures delivered at the University of California at Los Angeles in 1960 grew a very personal account of his career as a writer, *The Wild Garden, or Speaking of Writing* (1963). Though favorably received in the United States, the book was less regarded in Britain, where "confessional" writing is considered bad form. Several years later, doubtless as a result of Wilson's success as a lecturer, he was invited to alter the course of his life again and become a university teacher. The occasion was the founding of the University of East Anglia, where Ian Watt, an Englishman who had spent many years teaching in America, headed the English Department. It was unprecedented in Britain at that time to have a professional writer join the ranks of academics, not to teach "creative writing" (which Wilson was not especially interested in doing), but literature. Wilson agreed on condition he would be required to teach only two of the three terms during the year (he later reduced his commitment to one term). On his impact upon academic life, his colleague, Professor Nicholas Brooke, has written glowingly, recalling Wilson's service also as the university's public orator.[15] In 1966 Wilson was given a personal chair, or professorship, at East Anglia, which he held until 1978, when he retired at the statutory age of sixty-five. His elevation to that rank is a sign of the esteem in which he was held, not least by his students, among whom are several novelists, such as Ian McEwan and Rose Tremain, who have begun to establish reputations of their own as writers.

In the fall of 1967, while a visiting distinguished professor at Berkeley, Wilson learned that his name would be on the Queen's New Year's Honors list in recognition of his many services on behalf of his country. A decade or so later, he was knighted. These honors are not tributes so much to the high quality of his fiction as to the many efforts Wilson has spent in a wide variety of related and unrelated activities; for example, serving as chairman of the National Book League for three years; working on a wide range of committees, such as those against apartheid or for the rights of homosexuals; traveling abroad on many British Council trips; organizing lecture tours within Britain; and so forth. Public-spirited, responsible, sociable, acute, he has been as he remains — a force to reckon with in his time, and the recognitions he has received are no more than his due.

THE CRITICISM

Although literary criticism in academic journals did not begin until a decade later, Wilson's books from the outset received considerable attention in the number and extent of their reviews. Several eminent writers and critics, such as Edmund Wilson, Ernest Hemingway, and Evelyn Waugh, marked him at once as someone to watch, and they have clearly been right. Comparisons to Waugh's fiction were almost as inevitable as they were immediate, and it remained for critics like Valerie Shaw to distinguish more accurately between Wilson's irony and Waugh's satire, or the important changes in English social life that were the targets of each writer's accordingly quite different attacks.[16] When his second collection of stories appeared, at least one reviewer, John Richardson, remarked on Wilson as a "potential novelist,"[17] although it was another two years before *Hemlock and After* appeared. The *London Times Literary Supplement* devoted a full page to review of this novel, as partial testimony to the emergence of an important voice in fiction, and his novels ever since have commanded long and thoughtful reviews in those pages and in major literary reviews everywhere. A sampling of reviews of his early work appears in this collection along with representative critical essays on specific novels or Wilson's overall achievement. Since space is limited, several significant essays not included are discussed in the context of issues raised by others that are reprinted.

A relevant example of the kind of review Wilson's novels receive is V.S. Pritchett's analysis of *Anglo-Saxon Attitudes* in the *New Statesman and Nation*. After duly noting the complexities of the plot, the use of symbolism, the varied characters in the novel, Pritchett gets down to Wilson's major contributions and originality and credits the author with revising the conventional picture of English character. Like the short stories, the novel broadens the picture by showing the "morbidity, madness, even sourness" that had earlier been ignored. But these qualities had to be introduced by someone with humanity, and Wilson does this. Moreover, he is subtle in presenting "the social foundations of egocentricity," as in the character of Mrs. Salad. Reviewing *A Bit Off the Map*, John Raymond praises Wilson's "benevolence towards his creatures," calling him a "neo-liberal" because he is humane in both his moral and his ideological perceptions — a rare combination. Believing in a multi-ideological society, Wilson allows his characters to act their ideologies, however distasteful they may be, or however foolishly or mechanically engendered. It is, Raymond argues, "the one great heartening paradox" of his work.[18]

A. O. J. Cockshut takes a different view of the matter in "Favoured Sons: The Moral World of Angus Wilson," the first essay to appear on Wilson's fiction in a literary magazine.[19] His starting point is the "hatred of humanity" frequently up to then leveled at Wilson's stories by reviewers (a charge that later critics radically revised and then dropped). Without subscribing to the charge, Cockshut argues that Wilson's conception of human nature is at least pessimistic. But curiously enough, Cockshut says, the treatment of a few characters, notably Bernard Sands and Gerald Middleton, contrasts with the general tone of "moral severity and aesthetic distaste" that pervades the treatment of others. Cockshut focuses primarily upon Bernard Sands in *Hemlock and After,* complaining of Wilson's readiness to indulge Sands for crimes or sins he would not dream of extenuating, let alone condoning, in others. He therefore concludes that Wilson is guilty of moral confusion, or at any rate the adoption of double standards. But, as others have said, Cockshut may be guilty of misconceiving the central irony in the novel and thus Wilson's point: since Sands is the only one who has claimed any moral superiority in the novel, the events which bring him closer to the failings of others, and to the shocking awareness of his own false motives, is necessarily more terrible.[20] C. B. Cox notes further that, for Wilson, Sands is justified insofar as he attempts to limit the effects of his own egotism and to avoid the excesses of others, like Mrs. Curry, an embodiment of evil in the novel.[21] Cox's full study of the ambiguities in Wilson's humanism appears in the chapter of a book that considers the humanist tradition in George Eliot, Henry James, E. M. Forster, Virginia Woolf, and Wilson. Like Cockshut, he focuses on *Hemlock and After* but first spends a good deal of time analyzing the ideas and attitudes in the short stories, where he differentiates Wilson's humanism from that of his forebears. Lacking, for instance, Forster's assurance, the stories reveal a "rage at human inadequacy." Where Forster is evasive, Wilson is "savage and uncompromising."[22] Since reality is his ideal, Wilson is particularly antagonistic to the poses and false assumption of roles that many people adopt to cover the absence of personality. Typically, self-pity blurs his characters' acceptance of reality—the only means through which they can recover their humanity—and irony is Wilson's chief weapon in the process of unmasking: nevertheless, he is not insensitive to the pathos these poor mortals arouse: his compassion for many of them, even some of the most befuddled or inept, is genuine. In all this Wilson fights against his own despair, trying valiantly—and in his novels, at last with some success—to find ways to rebuild an optimistic humanism.[23]

The first step, as Cox notes, is the recognition of the power of evil. *Hemlock and After* is primarily concerned with understanding the motives of human action; even where they may seem to be most altruistic, most pure, there may lurk base intentions, as Bernard finds to his horror and goes to his grave in despair. If his vision of despair is, as Cox says, something that "haunts the modern humanist,"[24] he need not be utterly shackled by it, as subsequent characters in the novels, like Gerald Middleton and Meg Eliot, show. Avoiding responsibility, or "traveling light," like Bill Pendlebury in *Hemlock*, is no solution; this is a criticism of Forster's *A Passage to India*, where Fielding uses the term Wilson has Pendlebury echo. "To travel light is not to live," as Cox explains.[25] Despite the loneliness which is fundamentally a part of the human condition, people can and should engage in relationships, even if they carry the risk of injuring or profoundly affecting others' lives. In *Anglo-Saxon Attitudes*, the vitality of Dollie Stokesay and Elvira Portway help Gerald Middleton overcome the paralysis of his will and get on to creative work, just as by accepting her own strengths as well as weaknesses Meg Eliot in the next novel recovers from her breakdown to resume leading a life of active involvement. In all of these early novels, Wilson offers no simple solutions to complex issues, and the ambiguities inherent in any human action must be faced. But facing them need not lead to a surrender of responsibility or, as in Bernard Sands's example, the acquiescence in despair.

A decade and a half later, writing from the vantage point of Wilson's subsequently published novels, Edwin Riddell challenged Cox's criticism of Wilson's attitudes and Bernard Bergonzi's similar insistence that Wilson is a practitioner in the central liberal tradition of George Eliot. Wilson deliberately destroys the base of security on which the liberal tradition is founded, Riddell argues, especially in a novel like *The Old Men at the Zoo*, which hardly depicts the "the familiar and secure world of Warwickshire countryside or Schlegelite Chelsea."[26] In such novels, Wilson tries to place his humanist outlook "in the universal reality of violence, death, and evil," an effort that demonstrates Wilson is more than a novelist of manners, and not of ideas, as Bergonzi maintained.[27] The central concern of Wilson's mature work is the problem "of relating the individual experience of liberals like Meg Eliot and Simon Carter to a world largely hostile to liberalism, to the experiences which have tended to the destruction of any kind of individual position."[28] If the success of such characters is limited, Wilson has nevertheless been able to define through them "a new status both for the individual in society and for the individual as a proper subject for fiction."[29]

Wilson's handling of his characters in his novels has led some critics, like James Gindin, to link him to the tradition of writers such as Trollope, Meredith, Hardy, and James, and in this century with writers such as Lawrence, Joyce, Fitzgerald, Cary, and Saul Bellow in what Gindin calls "the novel of compassion." Wilson is more an ironist than a satirist in Gindin's view; moreover, his irony qualifies, it does not destroy.[30] The problems of the remoteness, or isolation, and estrangement of the individual are found in all of the novels, including *No Laughing Matter,* where the range of Wilson's compassion is extended beyond that of his earlier work. Where art is used as a mode of perception, as in *The Middle Age of Mrs. Eliot*, Gindin sees the influence of Henry James.[31] The relation of Wilson's fiction to the traditional English novelists is treated at length in Ruben Rabinovitz's book, *The Reaction against Experiment in the English Novel 1950-1960.*[32] Recognizing Wilson's deep interest in Proust and his championing of contemporary writers like Lessing and Powell, who use contemporary settings and ethic in their work, Rabinovitz nevertheless regards Wilson as essentially a nineteenth-century traditionalist, a position that later critics like A. S. Byatt have found largely untenable.[33] In "Angus Wilson's Fiction and Its Relation to the English Tradition," Anna Katona notes the contradictory trends in Wilson's art and has attempted to isolate the "modern" and "contemporary" features in it, using the terminology of Stephen Spender's *The Struggle of the Modern*. If Wilson is a modern in his pessimistic view of "the whole modern industrial predicament" whose "universal greyness and doom" he depicts in his novels, he is also committed to the values of "order, duty and loyalty," which associate him with the ameliorating tendencies of contemporaries.[34]

From the beginning, analysis of Wilson's fictional method and techniques interested critics as well as his attitudes and ideas. In *The Writer and Commitment,* John Mander offers an extended critique of Wilson's short stories, noting their attempt to fuse the particular (specific references to an era) with the general (human nature). But the fusion is only rarely achieved: the great majority of stories are studies in psychology, "often of very great subtlety, but essentially ahistorical and independent of any particular social context."[35] When the fusion is achieved, as in "Saturnalia," its dialectical structure is mainly responsible — as opposed to the "simple parallelism" of stories like "The Wrong Set" or the early novels.[36] Using somewhat different terms, Malcolm Bradbury also perceives a mixture in Wilson's fiction — of moral realism and "gothic" sensibility inherited, in part, from Dickens. The combination encourages a kind of critical uncertainty: Wilson can be involved as much with his social grotesques as against them; his double attitude toward his material does not allow a simple response, and the shifting point of view he employs deliberately forestalls an easy identification with his characters. This disquieting effect, including his sense of social unreality, tending to surrealistic landscape and surrealistic society, contributes to a special kind of fantasy that is peculiarly his.[37]

Bradbury expands his analysis of this fictional method in "The Fiction of Pastiche: The Comic Mode of Angus Wilson," where he emphasizes the elements of self-doubt and self-mockery that are as significant in Wilson's work as the adult social seriousness he admires. The reason that Wilson's "apparently substantial and stable" novels do not "hold steady when we read them, but dissolve into a distinctive kind of grotesque" is that their moral toughness is tempered with an equally strong measure of malice, a combination that brings into question all motives, revealing none of them as "pure."[38] It is also a reason why the narrator, "moving between the creation of his characters and of a design and attitude which might contain them, tends to shift and increasingly to dissolve with the books, giving the writing an increasing flavour of mimicry or pastiche."[39] The pastiche and the "odd moral stance" point toward an "emptiness" at the center of all human action and the attempt to cope with it, as through a persistent theatricality. "Human life is a role or performance, society is a theatre, the masks and disguises are irrevocable and they are total. The self we live with is counterfeit, and in that situation the trickery reaches back to the narrator himself, who acts too, as creators must, but in so doing does not so much make a meaningful society and meaningful agents in it as mimic them both."[40] Wilson's need for a mode of writing that allows him a "high degree of social mimicry and involvement" while at the same time a means for "assertive control" was expressed in No Laughing Matter, of which Bradbury offers an extended and trenchant analysis, focusing especially on the "protean" mode of Wilson's narration and the very openly conceived theatrical metaphor.[41]

The questions of the nature of reality and of art and its relation to reality posed by No Laughing Matter have preoccupied other critics as well; in this respect, it has attracted more attention than any of his novels so far. In "Reality and Fiction: No Laughing Matter" Guido Kums explores several possible definitions of realistic in literary criticism and the complex self-reflexiveness of Wilson's novel. Despite lifelike characters, familiar historical events, and other specific details, the novel's formal aspects and techniques (such as "The Game" or the author's use of irony) undercut the impression of realism and raise the question of reality and its representation in fiction. Kums concludes that the two apparently contradictory aspects in the novel make it impossible to regard it as either a "purely subjective act of the author," an autonomous world he has created, or a "pure reference dependent for its meaning on a formerly given reality."[42] The way out of the dilemma, he argues, is to consider the polarities as two complementary aspects of language as the medium of fiction. Fiction may create a clear, coherent world which is also complete, but it cannot do so without the referential force inherent in language. Fiction thus may not offer us a "real" reality — something that may exist apart from itself — but "it gives us a certain reality, because the world of language is constituted by the elements through which we absorb and know reality: words, language, and ultimately the culture based on language in the widest sense of the word."[43]

Using a different approach, Herman Servotte shows how the themes and techniques of *No Laughing Matter* are so interrelated that the deep uncertainty about the nature of man is reflected in the novel by an equally deep uncertainty about the possibilities of technique in fiction itself. In spite of these uncertainties, or perhaps because of them, *No Laughing Matter* is a brilliant exemplar of modern fiction, one that emphasizes to the reader continually its "literariness." This awareness does not diminish the value of the genre; on the contrary, it enhances it, linking it to the great classical forms that never offered themselves as copies of the world but through their stylistic accomplishments as only what they were: creations of the imagination.[44] Similarly, Jean Sudrann notes how the characters in the novel keep asking "the same question: how do we know what is real? And the novel keeps answering: man makes his reality by self-conscious creation."[45] Nevertheless, it is also true that while fictions can help heal wounds and create meanings, "they remain . . . fictions: tools of life, not life itself."[46]

Although Wilson has on occasion rejected craftsmanship as the highest reach of novelist's art,[47] *No Laughing Matter* and the novels that have followed show him to be the conscious artist critics have more and more come to recognize. Here, his literary criticism plays an important corollary role, as Peter Faulkner and Kerry McSweeney have demonstrated in their extensive studies.[48] Like T. S. Eliot in poetry, Wilson in his novels has attempted to work out problems, such as the right blend of diversity and depth, that he sees confronting the novelist and that he discusses at length in his criticism. An early concern for evil in the English novel was the subject of his Northcliffe lectures and has interested many critics. Although John Oakland disagrees that Wilson, any more than Christianity, has been able to give an adequate account of evil,[49] others regard his lectures as excellent literary criticism, even if his own fiction does not entirely solve the problems he outlines, such as the need to wed a sense of transcendent evil (as opposed to issues of right and wrong) to the social novel of the English tradition.[50] McSweeney has edited a collection of Wilson's criticism which has been favorably received in reviews by such eminent critics as John Bayley in the *Times Literary Supplement.*[51]

As Angus Wilson's stature has grown, and as each book increases his stature, critical attention has grown as well, so that by now there is a considerable body of work, including a number of doctoral dissertations, devoted to his achievements. *Twentieth Century Literature* recently devoted an issue wholly to him and contains J. H. Stape's updating of Robert J. Stanton's *A Bibliography of Modern British Novelists* (1978). Like Peter Faulkner's "Select Bibliography," there are items both by and about Wilson, but Stape's differs in including many reviews of Wilson's latest work. The range and depth are impressive but hardly surprising. For there seems little question now that Angus Wilson is one of the century's preeminent writers, and his impact on the world of literature will be felt for many years to come.

University of Delaware   JAY L. HALIO

Notes

1. Angus Wilson, *The Wild Garden, or Speaking of Writing* (London: Secker & Warburg, 1963), p. 11.

2. Jay L. Halio, *Angus Wilson* (Edinburgh: Oliver & Boyd, 1964), pp. 8–9.

3. *The Wild Garden*, p. 28.

4. Edmund Wilson, "The Emergence of Angus Wilson," in *The Bit between My Teeth* (New York: Farrar, Straus, Giroux, 1965), pp. 270–73. This review originally appeared in *The New Yorker*, 15 April 1950.

5. See, e.g., Peter Faulkner, *Angus Wilson: Mimic and Moralist* (London: Secker & Warburg, 1980), p. 74, and cf. Betsy Draine, "An Interview with Angus Wilson," *Contemporary Literature*, 21, No. 1 (1980), 2–3.

6. See C. W. E. Bigsby, "An Interview with Angus Wilson," *Literary Review*, No. 28 (1980), 8–9, 13.

7. Faulkner, *Angus Wilson*, p. 48.

8. See, e.g., James Gindin, *Harvest of a Quiet Eye: The Novel of Compassion*, (Bloomington: Indiana Univ. Press, 1971), p. 286.

9. Cf. Alice Green Fredman, "Angus Wilson: Literary Critic and Biographer," *Twentieth Century Literature*, 29, No. 2 (1983), 206.

10. Margaret Drabble, " 'No Idle Rentier': Angus Wilson and the Nourished Literary Imagination," *Studies in the Literary Imagination*, 13, No. 1 (1980), 128.

11. These and other biographical details appear in various interviews, *The Wild Garden*, and Jay L. Halio, "Angus Wilson," *Dictionary of Literary Biography: British Novelists 1930-1959*, ed. Bernard Oldsey (Detroit: Gale, 1983), 15: 591–614.

12. D. P. Walker, "Talking about Angus Wilson," *Twentieth Century Literature*, 29, No. 2 (1983), 115.

13. Bigsby, "Interview," pp. 9–10.

14. Michael Millgate, "Angus Wilson," *Writers at Work: The Paris Review Interviews*, ed. Malcolm Cowley (New York: Viking Press, 1959), p. 255.

15. "Talking about Angus Wilson," *Twentieth Century Literature*, 29, No. 2 (1983), 133–36.

16. Valerie A. Shaw, "*The Middle Age of Mrs. Eliot* and *Late Call*: Angus Wilson's Traditionalism," *Critical Quarterly*, 12, No. 1 (1970), 9–10.

17. In the *New Statesman and Nation*, 40 (1950), 181.

18. V. S. Pritchett, "The World of Angus Wilson," *New Statesman and Nation*, 51 (1956), 532; John Raymond, "Mid-Century Blues," *New Statesman*, 54 (1957), 464.

19. *Essays in Criticism*, 9 (1959), 50–60.

20. Halio, *Angus Wilson*, p. 33.

21. C. B. Cox, "Angus Wilson: Studies in Depression," in *The Free Spirit* (London: Oxford Univ. Press, 1963), p. 134. Cf. his earlier essay, "The Humanism of Angus Wilson," *Critical Quarterly*, 3, No. 3 (1961), 235. This topic and others, including the title's allusion to Socrates, are fully discussed in Karin Wogatzky's monograph, *"Hemlock and After": A Study in Ambiguity* (Berne: Francke Verlag, 1971).

22. Cox, *The Free Spirit*, p. 118.

23. Ibid., p. 122.

24. Ibid., p. 135.

25. Ibid., p. 136.

26. Edwin Riddell, "The Humanist Character in Angus Wilson," *English*, 21 (1972), 47.

27. Bernard Bergonzi, *The Situation of the Novel* (London: Macmillan, 1970), p. 161.

28. Riddell, "Humanist Character," p. 47.

29. Ibid., p. 53.

30. Gindin, *Harvest of a Quiet Eye*, p. 296. Gindin's earlier study, "The Qualified Nationalism of Angus Wilson," appeared in his *Postwar British Fiction: New Accounts and Attitudes* (Berkeley: Univ. of California Press, 1962), pp. 145–64.

31. Gindin, *Harvest of a Quiet Eye*, pp. 296–97.

32. New York: Columbia University Press, 1967.

33. A. S. Byatt, "People in Paper Houses: Attitudes to 'Realism' and 'Experiment' in English Postwar Fiction," in *The Contemporary English Novel*, ed. Malcolm Bradbury and David Palmer. Stratford-upon-Avon Studies 18 (London: Edward Arnold, 1979), pp. 19–24.

34. Anna Katona, "Angus Wilson's Fiction and Its Relation to the English Tradition," *Acta Litteraria Academiae Scientarium Hungaricae* (Budapest), 10 (1968), 117.

35. John Mander, "The Short Stories of Angus Wilson," in *The Writer and Commitment* (Philadelphia: Dufour, 1962), p. 115.

36. Ibid., p. 127.

37. Malcolm Bradbury, "The Short Stories of Angus Wilson," *Studies in Short Fiction*, 3 (1966), 117–25.

38. Malcolm Bradbury, "The Fiction of Pastiche: The Comic Mode of Angus Wilson," in *Possibilities: Essays on the State of the Novel* (London: Oxford Univ. Press, 1973), p. 213.

39. Ibid., p. 213.

40. Ibid., p. 214.

41. Ibid., pp. 219 ff.

42. Guido Kums, "Reality and Fiction: *No Laughing Matter*," *English Studies*, 53, No. 6 (1972), 530.

43. Ibid., p. 531.

44. Herman Servotte, "A Note on the Formal Characteristics of Angus Wilson's *No Laughing Matter*," *English Studies*, 50, No. 1 (1969), 64.

45. Jean Sudrann, "The Lion and the Unicorn: Angus Wilson's Triumphant Tragedy," *Studies in the Novel*, 3, No. 4 (1971), 392.

46. Ibid., p. 398.

47. See, e.g., Jack I. Biles, "Some Words More, Some Years Later: A Talk with Angus Wilson," printed for the first time in this collection.

48. Faulkner, *passim*; Kerry McSweeney, "Angus Wilson: Diversity, Depth, and Obses-

sive Energy," in *Four Contemporary Novelists* (Kingston, Ontario: McGill-Queen's Univ. Press, 1983), pp. 10–53.

49. John Oakland, "Angus Wilson and Evil in the English Novel," *Renascence*, 26, No. 1 (1973), 24–36.

50. See McSweeney, "Angus Wilson," p. 26.

51. Angus Wilson, *Diversity and Depth in Fiction: Selected Critical Writings*, ed. Kerry McSweeney (London: Secker & Warburg, 1983); reviewed by John Bayley, "Life-Enhancing World-Views," *Times Literary Supplement*, 16 September 1983, p. 978.

REVIEWS

EMERGENCE OF ANGUS WILSON

Edmund Wilson*

After Evelyn Waugh, what? For anyone who has asked this question, the answer is Angus Wilson, whose first book, *The Wrong Set and Other Stories*, has just been published over here. In the England of Evelyn Waugh, everybody had plenty of money or managed to get the benefit of other people's having money; one was free to be as dizzy as one pleased, and the incidental brutality and swindling were hardly noticed in the general hilarity. In the England of Angus Wilson, the money has been giving out, and the clever upper-middle-class people are struggling, with a somewhat damaged dignity, to get hold of or to hang on to whatever income or position is attainable. In this struggle, though they keep up certain forms, they are always jeering and jabbing; they do not flinch from frank hatchet work. They all dislike one another, and the author dislikes the lot. It is hard to agree with the writer of the blurb on the jacket of this book that "beneath the surface brilliance of these stories there shines Wilson's deep compassion for humanity." Though he sometimes introduces a young person, unbroken to the ways of this world, who tries to take a stand against it, this character invariably turns out, like the girl in *Fresh Air Fiend*, to have played the role of a clumsy prig or, like the young men of *Crazy Crowd* and *Mother's Sense of Fun*, to succumb as helpless dupes. The gaiety is still going on that made the carnival of Evelyn Waugh — *Totentanz* and *Saturnalia* are among Mr. Wilson's titles, as well as *Crazy Crowd* — but, as the first of these stories indicates, it is now a dance of the dying.

This point is made by *Totentanz* explicitly, and the story differs somewhat from the others. (It seems to have been the last written, since it recently appeared in *Horizon* and has been added to those included in the English edition of the book.) Mr. Wilson has allowed himself here, with his vampires and ghosts and fantastic wills, a certain satirical and poetical extravagance. The other stories keep the rules of realism, and they almost achieve plausibility as pictures of certain strata of the England that has been trying to readjust itself after the efforts and privations of the war — for even when the stories deal with earlier times, they seem to reflect the mood of the present, with its exasperated snapping and snarling disguised as exquisite malice, its vulgarization of the cultivated and learned (academic careerists and frauds are a specialty of Mr. Wilson's), its cruelty of comfortable people deathly afraid of losing their comforts, its sexual life turning sterile in the instinctive biological fear that the nation or the class may not survive. Yet these stories are fundamentally satirical. There is evidently in Mr. Wilson a strain of the harsh Scottish moralist who does not want to let anybody off and does not care if his sarcasm wounds. This is nowadays an unusual element to crop up in a British writer. The school of smart fiction in England, though it cultivates bitter implications and sometimes invokes religion, has come to perfect a cuisine of light appetizing dishes, agreeable for one dinner and easily digestible, which — much though it would have surprised George Moore or Henry James if anyone had prophesied it to them — almost rivals that of the French in the early nineteen-hundreds. And it is true that Wilson's stories, too, from the point of view of neatness and brevity and of the avoidance of emotionalism, are products of the same cuisine; but they are carried to lengths of caricature that prevent them from being so pleasantly assimilable as the usual British product. The book becomes a sort of thriller, for one goes on from one horror to another, beginning to hold onto one's seat as one wonders what uncomfortable ignoble thing Mr. Wilson will think up next. Yet one shares in the malevolent gusto with which he invents detail, for he is a master of mimicry and parody and is as funny as anyone can be who never becomes exhilarated. It is rather like a combination of Sinclair Lewis with the more biting side of Chekhov, and Mr. Wilson's dreadful people may affect us in the long run a little like the caricatures of Lewis (the up-and-coming museum curator of the story called *Realpolitik* is an incipiently American type who might easily have been imagined by Lewis). We end by being repelled and by feeling that it is not quite decent to enjoy so much ugliness and humiliation. There ought to be some noble value somewhere. Sinclair Lewis at least opposes, and not always ineffectively, to his bugaboos of rascality and cheapness the good old American virtues, upon which he still counts. Chekhov, who, like Mr. Wilson, plays the clinician for a failing organism, is sad as well as sardonic and has some sense of a human dignity that he hopes will emerge from the mess. But the things worth saving in *The Wrong Set* have been degraded almost beyond recognition; the victims of the people who are getting on have sunk almost out of reach of pity.

This may seem too severe a line to take with a book of short stories, a first book by a writer of thirty-six; but the talent displayed seems so firm and bold, so rich in invention and wit, that it stimulates these comparisons. Mr. Wilson may be capable of a great deal more, and even in this little collection the impression he makes is formidable. He seems, for better or worse, to represent something that is quite distinct from the well-bred and well-turned entertainment that we have lately been getting from England.

[Review of *Such Darling Dodos*]   John Richardson*

Mr. Angus Wilson's field may be small but he digs it deep. *Such Darling Dodos*, his second book of short stories, is a proof of how hard he has worked on himself. The sharp and perceptive eye with which he is blest always saw through the veneers of pretence and manners to the evil and hypocrisy beneath. But now it penetrates even deeper. This new set of characters have many more layers and they are rounder. Mr. Wilson has also managed to extend his range in another direction; his pattern is now more varied. Short-story writers tend to repeat the same motif, changing only the colours. But in *Such Darling Dodos* all the designs are different. Far from remaining a black-and-white satirist, Mr. Wilson reveals himself in these stories to be a potential novelist.

Perhaps Mr. Wilson's greatest accomplishment is his ability to pounce on the telling *cliché* or the revealing quirk of speech. In a professionally charming don he observes: "his habit of pointing with his pipe and saying: 'Now hold on a minute. I want to examine this average man or woman of yours more carefully'; or 'Anarchism, now, that's a very interesting word, but are we *quite* sure we know what it means?' " Or of the old cissy with his Jane Austen speech: "I think it vastly disobliging in you, cousin . . . to be at so much pains over me." Yes, Mr. Wilson brings it off every time, but occasionally trips himself up in the process. His characters' *clichés* become his own. The Boots' Library Book, for example, is a sort of symbolical prop that recurs too often. Also he is inclined to indulge in semi-private jokes. His awful cosiness is often effective, but it can be overdone as in this description of a Christmas party in a Government office, for instance:

> . . . where the adding machines usually stood, ran a row of little pots of holly made so cleverly from tinfoil and decorated with little cut-out black cats in bedsocks. A whole collection of "In" and "Out" trays had been lined with paper doyleys and filled with every sort of delicious cake and sandwich — Thea's sausage rolls and Penelope's dainty bridge rolls filled with sandwich spread, Helen's raspberry fingers and little pyramids and chocolate powder and post toasties that Joan Fowler called "Coconut Kisses."

"It's worse than wicked, my dear, it's vulgar." The *Punch* joke still has a sting in it; we must congratulate Mr. Wilson on daring to risk that. We must congratulate him further for wearing his vulgarity so lightly and with such distinction. When too much English writing is dull, constipated and frightened, it is heartening to read something which is not. Mr. Wilson never hesitates to draw attention to social anomalies no nice person notices. Undeterred by sportsmanship or kindliness, he hits exactly where he likes and his blows hurt. Good taste and gentility are as roughly handled as hum-

*Reprinted with permission from the *New Statesman and Nation*, 40 (12 August, 1950), 181–82.

bug. One reason for the success of Mr. Wilson's attacks is his poisonous sense of humour. Another is that his enmities and loyalties are unpredictable. He is liable in the middle of an offensive to switch and rush to the defence of someone whose predicament has won his allegiance. For Mr. Wilson supports the true heart or "the good scout" as ardently as he fights the two- or three-faced and the hordes of the pretentious.

[Review of *Hemlock and After*]   L. A. G. Strong*

Mr. Angus Wilson has written an important novel on a major theme. It is also an exceedingly witty novel, the wit being of the kind that spits its victims instanteously and precisely as with a hatpin, not only epitomising but immobilising them. Indeed, in the first chapters the novel is brought almost to a standstill, Mr. Wilson having transfixed everyone with such deadly accuracy that their careers seem finished.

> Bill could not bear to see anything hurt; when anyone he came in contact with got hurt, he made a practice of moving on. He called it "traveling light through life."

> "Do they?" asked Bernard, with a special little smile of intimacy for the questioner, which he had perfected for use when he was out of temper.

> The stockbroker's wife, who had only recently graduated from the suburbs into tweeds. . . .

This finality of character-drawing is the only sign that Mr. Wilson is a short-story writer. In the short story characters must be epitomised; there is no time for them to develop. But this story, a novel in conception and structure, recovers quickly from its opening and is carried not only to a climax but an epilogue. Bernard Sands, fifty-seven, a writer with a Shavian reputation for mockery of established institutions, takes the constructive step of nagging the Government into endowing a country house where young writers can work. Unfortunately his victory accelerates a process of disintegration in his own character. This, and the fact that on the day of the opening ceremony he cannot make the optimistic speech which he has led everyone to expect, his enemies seize upon, to his great personal harm and the danger of his enterprise.

The disaster Mr. Wilson invites us to consider is the ineffectiveness of so much that is good in our time. Tolerance and philosophical wisdom are no match for fanaticism or even for single-minded, biological pursuit of an aim. Sonia's snobbery and zeal to advance her husband are more effective

*Reprinted with permission from the *Spectator*, 189 (18 July, 1952), 110.

than Bernard's moderation or the basic human decency which Ella salvages from her neurotic retreat. Mr. Wilson's diagnosis is more grievous than Yeats's: his best not only lack conviction but are undermined by destructive weaknesses — in Bernard's case, a repressed homosexual urge — whereas his worst are not so much full of passionate intensity as unable to escape their Gadarene journey. What is more, when the law at last catches up with them, its punishment gives their vices fresh scope. In prison Mrs. Curry and Ron do very nicely.

Mr. Wilson's character-drawing is first-class. So are his phrasing and his dialogue. Where, judged by the highest standards, this impressive and frighteningly intelligent novel falls short is in the selection of the characters and the refusal or failure to sound a positive note. There is a little too much perversion to the square foot: even though Mr. Wilson understands what is behind a middle-aged urge towards youth, he gives us rather more of it and other tendencies than statistics would lead us to expect. Is he under any obligation, after so masterly a diagnosis, to suggest a remedy? Maybe not, but it is a tribute to his power that we would like one from him.

The World of Angus Wilson   V. S. Pritchett*

It is "our life" (says one of the characters in Mr. Angus Wilson's brilliant and ambitious new novel), that lies between ourselves and reality. *Anglo-Saxon Attitudes* is a novel about the conscience as it worries two generations of a middle-class family whose ample money comes out of steel and whose brains have gone into the academic world and popular politics. The title comes from Lewis Carroll who noticed — and who with better reason? — that the attitudes of the Anglo-Saxon were peculiar; they are formed by an incalculable mixture of going one's own gait and contorting oneself in the gymnasium of the English moral sense. Morally the English are liable to picturesque outbursts of self-deception: being intelligent, they are very conscious of this and if this is decadent it is also very interesting. When they say (as they have often said during the last thirty years), "What right have we to judge him or her?," they know quite well that they are going to be led to awful questions, the conundrum of the greater or the lesser evil, the blandishments of the wider view, and so on. The countrymen of Lewis Carroll and George Eliot are born worriers; the relieving thing about them is that they are also an awkward squad, bad at drill, prone to brutal jokes, underhand tricks, romantic sensuality, poker-faced wangling and the smug exploitation of lucky accident. Show me a Puritan and I will (thank God) show you a rogue. At the back of the lives of Mr. Angus Wilson's characters

*Reprinted with permission from the *New Statesman and Nation*, 199 (18 October, 1957), 521–22.

there is a dirty Anglo-Saxon trick — scabrous, silly, but rich in moral provo-cation. What more could we, who live on moral tension, desire?

As far as his novel is concerned, this angry practical joke is a useful device. It is full of symbolism which is a bore, but it has enabled Mr. Wilson to begin with some excellent comedy about academic life among historians and archæologists. As far as the general theme is concerned this joke is no more than a Gibbonian footnote — at least, I hope no more is intended. When the novel opens in the present day, the historians can still be set quar-relling about the discovery of a phallic object which was found in the coffin of the Saxon Bishop Eorpwald when he was dug up in 1912. It has not greatly disturbed the layman to suppose that Christians may have lapsed into paganism: after all, pagans had already lapsed into Christianity. But the Eorpwald discovery had sent one poor scholarly lady out of her mind: she connected it with Baltic trade and, thence, fatally, to the "wider view". There is more than a hint that the original discoverer, the eminent Lionel Stokesay, became very odd afterwards and certainly morally senile. He be-gan to talk like Ramsay MacDonald. The probability is that people who take the wider view are covering up.

In the opening chapter of *Anglo-Saxon Attitudes* we are to understand that the Eorpwald row has died down and that it remains open only in the minds of cranks. On the other hand, the central character of the book, Gerald Middleton, a sixty-year-old historian who was Lionel Stokesay's dis-ciple and his son's friend, becomes suspiciously irritable when the subject is reopened. For him, it reawakens what he is least inclined to examine: the errors of his life, the failure to go the full length of his talents, above all the failure of his will. He is a true Anglo-Saxon: he has a romantic sense of fail-ure as well as a romantic sense of success. (I am not sure that Mr. Angus Wilson is with us here.) At any rate, Mr. Middleton thinks — and so does Mr. Wilson — that he has sacrificed reality or truth to "his life." For Middleton has the strongest reasons for suspecting that a serious fraud was committed by Stokesay's famous, destructive, sadistic and short-lived son at the time of the discovery. Middleton has kept silence in the interests of the old man's reputation. Moreover, Middleton's great love was for the younger Stoke-say's wife. Romantic situation! In these terms, Middleton's silence is a symptom of his general moral guilt and weakness, which make him accept a bad marriage instead of a difficult love; which force him to prolong the marriage for the sake of his children whom he nevertheless alienates and who are not going to respect him later; which drives his mistress to drink while he plumps for urbanity, compromise, rational marital arrangements, the limitation of his talents, intellectual indolence and picture-collecting — which is unbecoming in a scientist and a scholar. (Puritanism will out: en-joyment of the arts by people with private means is morally suspect.) Middleton is saddled with money as well and has really bought his way out of his troubles — as many do who have no money — and now, at sixty, iso-lated by his habit of refusing life, he is left to look back upon the ruins of his life and to see his children infected by his mistakes. In the end, he gets a second chance. Or, rather, he makes it for himself. It is not a chance of reconciliation or of love — that is too late — but of acting with moral courage and of asserting his will to the full — when he's old enough to command with authority in any case. . . .

Such a collection of characters is promising, especially when they are vividly realised and morally involved. Mr. Angus Wilson understands this and dives into their lives with alacrity and intelligence and sympathy. He is garrulous and epigrammatic but he moves quickly and at the right moment from person to person. The novel is closely patterned; indeed, one of its great pleasures is in its construction. But he is a personal novelist, filling out his characters by opinionating and also, of course, taking from them some of their autonomy in so doing. In this he is like D. H. Lawrence and not like George Eliot, our great duty-monger. He has no great care for style, is more for English truculence than English urbanity. He is wicked in epigram though less sharp in his satire in this novel than he was in his short stories. He succeeds in the portrayal of character, is rather parsimonious of scenes (there is more opinionating reminiscence and talk). There are one or two very good scenes, of course. The ghastly party at the end of the book is a brilliant piece of work and contains some delightful culture snobbery; the happy family dinner which is broken up when Dolly gets drunk is wonderful, surprising and rather moving. And any place where Larrie the Irish spiv turns up, is packed with interest. Larrie and Vin are masterpieces of original observation and though I don't care for the melodramatic motor accident — a very odd fantasy to occur to a writer so on the spot as Mr. Wilson — the whole business of Larrie's hysteria is absorbingly done.

In every generation one or two novelists revise the conventional picture of English character. Mr. Wilson does this. There was morbidity, madness, even sourness in his stories — precisely qualities which our sociable tradition eschewed. They needed to be introduced by someone with humanity. We needed to recover our broadness without losing our moral sense. He has also bedded out in our rank social soil some of the hot-house blooms of our Dickensian tradition. Mrs. Salad, for example, is a perennial London joy: "Now the cyclermums is as delicate as my sister's skin. Her husband wouldn't have her wear a soiled garment not a day longer than was needed. Spurgin's Tabernacle they was." This poetic old dear is nastier than Mrs. Gamp, for she is close to crime and is thoroughly shady. She was — she is — a lavatory attendant and no shame to her; but that is a life, not a fantasy. Mr. Wilson is subtle in conveying the social foundations of egocentricity. Mrs. Salad is not a middle-class joke. He has given his people moral natures. He sees England with what looks like a foreign eye. That, for me, is an important virtue in a novel which, in any case, impresses by its range and its power of stating issues.

Dodos on the Wing   Kingsley Amis*

In this latest volume Mr. Angus Wilson has switched his faintly alarming attentions from Chelsea and North Oxford to the coffee bars and new housing estates that are widely held to typify the postwar era. As before, his subject is most often the explosions and embarrassments touched off when people of differing class, training or culture are made to confront one another. *A Bit off the Map* shows us a pampered young Jewish sensitive uneasily involved with a grubby but twee floosie, a "county" vicar's daughter married to a village shopkeeper, a mandarin-level critic trying to be urbane to a lacquered Teddy boy. This last encounter is a high point in the title story (one of the three longer pieces in the book), which is a brilliantly funny satire on Soho geniuses. The stars of the group are the philosophaster Huggett ("he says real genius means Will Power") and the novelist-to-end-all-novelists Reg ("we'll light such a blaze that all their nice little civilised fire-engines won't be able to put it out"). The climax, whereby it is the bewildered Teddy boy who proves himself the genuine Outsider by slugging a helpless dotard, comes not as an arbitrary resolution but as a stroke of ironical justice.

In this story, as in most of the others, Mr. Wilson wields his precision instruments with all the skill that distinguished his earlier collections; in fact one detects occasionally a ruthless farcicality which gives them an added cutting edge. The most conspicuous novelty, however, is to be found in another of the longer pieces, "More Friend than Lodger." Here the author's absorption in social collisions operates at reduced volume, and this is perhaps connected with the fact that this time the reader is never led to wonder, as he has to rather too often even with Mr. Wilson at his liveliest, whether people like this do actually exist and whether, if they do, they talk as they are shown to. On the contrary, the charmingly catty, animated and devious heroine-narrator of this story is real in every phrase, especially when one of her little verbal squibs fails to go off or her sophistication is momentarily holed, and her accounts of her pedestrian husband and snobbish-fake lover throw as plausible and clear a light upon her as upon them. And she differs sharply from the protagonists of Mr. Wilson's existing novels in never taking herself seriously. The outlook is bright.

*Reprinted with permission from the *Spectator*, 199 (18 October, 1957), 521.

Mr. Wilson's People   Frank Kermode*

Mr. Angus Wilson now writes long novels, and his latest[1] seems to be his best. Yet his world remains a small one. To define his area of interest by

*Reprinted with permission of the author from *Puzzles and Epiphanies: Essays and Reviews 1959–1961* (New York: Chilmark Press, 1962), pp. 193–97.

negatives: the people he is concerned about are not young, not poor, not happy and not common (this last is an old-fashioned word, but he gives it a new smartness). His young people are nasty and dreary — petty criminals, homosexual prostitutes, espresso layabouts and the betrayed; self-pitying children of ladies and gentlemen, all united by an unreasoning though not baseless contempt for their elders, with their obsolete kinds of guilt and archaic ethical standards. If they are more serious they remain odious, self-deceived and unprincipled, priggishly hating the intellectual and social ideals that gave a dowdy interest to the lives of their parents; as Mr. Wilson, with all possible cruelty and yet with compassion, explained in his superb story, "Such Darling Dodos." All this is in the mind of the widowed Mrs. Eliot as she studies the new world in which she must find a way of living. Youth treats her very badly.

> Her own generation's determination to ignore age barriers was the first blow in a battle to end the long tyranny of respect for elders. That battle was now over, and youth could afford to look down on middle age. In the end, however, she decided that it was a retrograde step. Her generation had treated people as individuals, not bothering about age; these young people were returning to a seclusion as narrow as the "secret lives" of youth in Victorian times.

And a whole episode is written into the book to show that this is true.

This horrible modern war between old and young provides Mr. Wilson with his nightmare images of family life — the mean, loveless loyalties, the fumbling anxieties of parental tenderness, the distortion of sex, all the myriad middle-class defensive poses, all the peculiar terrors and queernesses. Beyond the pale the poor pass their weird, morally indifferent lives, sometimes salty, sometimes prim; and the common adorn their hideous houses with dreadful furniture, betray their ignorance of the mandarin dialect and call each other by their appalling Christian names. But it is not by their attitudes to the poor and the common that we must judge Mr. Wilson's people; they themselves might do it, but their concept of snobbery is too subtle for general use. We have other standards provided; for example, the series of ladies, declassed, ageing, disreputable, who have rather gay names like Polly and Dolly and demonstrate the severe terms upon which life may be restored to dying dodos. And we have Mr. Wilson himself.

For this author is always there at the centre of his anxious, thoroughly known world, alert and probing, magnifying the cruelty and qualifying the compassion, as if every caressing hand contained a tiny razor, bound in with surgical tape. His people are introspective, they speak in a self-critical dialect which is so ironical that inverted commas are always sprouting round their key words; but Mr. Wilson is there to look even more deeply within, to expose their faults of discipline like a spiritual director in some modern Port Royal. A man speaks to his mistress on the telephone, and then rejoins his wife: "She was in an ostentatiously calm and efficient mood that allowed her to exercise all the tyranny of fussing without being accused of it. 'That was Elvira,' said Robin, who used sincerity to his wife as his only protest against her existence." She *is* accused of it; and if he thinks he can exploit sincerity, he's wrong. In order to go on doing this and other things, Mr. Wilson eschews any new-fangled "point-of-view" fictional methods; he must be there, minutely dispensing justice among his people.

Yet it seems that he himself thinks they matter only in so far as they are "real." This is curious; in the earlier novels, and most damagingly in *Anglo-Saxon Attitudes*, there is an evident clash between fantasy and "neo-realism," and the academic world of Middleton is surely no more like the "real" thing than Lucky Jim's. I don't mean that historians do not cherish high disinterested standards or that a betrayal of these could not be used as evidence of a deep moral failure; but only that the whole situation as presented is like nothing on earth. Yet *Anglo-Saxon Attitudes* is patently an attempt to achieve the sort of accurate panoramic view of a social landscape that one associates with earlier and less fantastic fiction. There is a queer contrast between the characters and the workaday machinery of exposition, with all its cinematic transitions, flashbacks and flatly offered information — for instance, the self-portrait of Middleton in the first chapter: "An ex-professor . . . a   sensualist . . . an   aesthete . . . a   sixty-year-old failure . . . of the most boring kind, a failure with a conscience. His heavy, handsome dark face flushed with disgust. . . ." There are obvious ways in which Mr. Wilson resembles George Eliot, and this is one of her kinds of failure; the plot, too, of this book, with all its conscientious archæology, turns out to be not like *Middlemarch*, with its conscientious medicine, but like *Felix Holt*, with its conscientious law.

The new book, though it does not abandon the idiom of Mr. Wilson's people, is in the matter of plot a new departure, very simple and very effective. It has to do with "personal loss, man's universal tragic predicament." First we see Mrs. Eliot, quite rich and happily married, in her "amusing," "intelligent" world; she sits on committees and collects porcelain. Then her husband is killed trying to stop an obscure political assassination; we observe her suffering and her attempts to find, in a peculiarly difficult world, the kind of life that will match her loneliness and comparative poverty. A twin narrative relates her brother's troubles; he loses the friend with whom he worked and lived, and this death is slow and agonizing. In the third book of the novel the narratives merge. Working slowly, accumulating observations in which time will induce a design, Mr. Wilson constantly invites one to judge him by the novelists he himself admires, especially Jane Austen and George Eliot. He shows his heroine losing her own world and her illusions, suffering in the world of the young, the common, the poor, seeking to understand what killed her husband, remembering the pleasure and the guilt of her marriage. She cannot live quite alone, and we follow her path from one old friend to another, discovering their inadequacies and her own; steadily she retreats into childhood and a period of illusory happiness with her brother David. He runs a not-common nursery garden and is every kind of snob, especially the ethical kind; but they mitigate each other's suffering very successfully until their association declares itself to be merely evasive, a regression from actual pain into a false childhood irresponsibility.

The details are skilfully correlated, and although the subject and the method of the book require audaciously long passages of authorial comment, the language always keeps on the right side of banality. Indeed, Mr. Wilson remains as acute as ever when analysing the motives of his people. Here an unlovable lawyer (Donald) rejoins the widowed heroine and her brother: "Her hardness is hysterical, he thought. She needs some gesture of affection to steady her. He found physical contacts difficult, but he took her hand and pressed it. Oh dear! she thought, if only he would laugh a little to ease the atmosphere. Donald came back with a light grey overcoat, a black hat, umbrella and wash-leather gloves." This is fine enough. But there is something finer; in a magnificent page Mr. Wilson both transcends himself and justifies his claim to belong to a great tradition of moralizing novelists. He is describing the last evenin g together of the brother and sister. They sit reading — they are working on a study of the early novel — and two happy, inattentive answers he makes to apparently innocent remarks convince Meg that her brother is not interested in their book except as an excuse for keeping them together. When the customary hiss of a syphon tells him she is going to bed, he, as usual, reaches out his hand over the back of his chair- — for he now touches her as easily as in childhood — and she does not take it. Next morning she comes down to breakfast ready to go away.

Later come the explanations — they were reading books they'd enjoyed together as children instead of leading their proper lives, his of self-denial, hers of loneliness in the real world of poverty, politics, bullets. But the sudden richness of that page, in which the accumulated power of the previous 400 is suddenly fully employed, sets one searching for noble comparisons. Mrs. Eliot, with whom it was previously possible to feel a little bored, suddenly grows big enough to inhabit successfully all the space Mr. Wilson provides for her, with a completeness like that of Gwendolen Harleth, or better, perhaps, of Dorothea Brooke when she meets her husband on the stairs at the end of the fourth book of *Middlemarch*. And for the first time one of the not-poor, not-common people really experiences, and can be seen to experience, a "universal tragic predicament." This enactment of Mrs. Eliot's necessary choice entitles us to call *The Middle Age of Mrs. Eliot* — for all that it may lack the glitter of some of his earlier work — Mr. Wilson's most distinguished performance.

Note

1. *The Middle Age of Mrs. Eliot* (London: Secker & Warburg, 1958).

Powers That Be   Anthony Burgess*

. . . [C. P. Snow and Angus Wilson] inherit the nineteenth-century tradition and are, on the whole, satisfied with it. This doesn't mean that their aims are identical or even similar. Whisper the name of Dickens, one of Mr. Wilson's masters, and Lord Snow (as C. P. Snow) will say this: "Dickens was like a mimic in a bar. As Frank O'Connor says in *The Mirror in the Roadway*, there is 'a flight to the periphery of the story,' where he is happy with the characters which, he knows from trial and error, he can mimic without thought and make his audience respond." Lord Snow is not happy about mimicry: "The danger is, it is too satisfying; it is too satisfying even when there is no audience: it gives one the slightly inflated feeling that there is nothing left to say." Now, here is the very great difference between the two authors. Mr. Wilson is a superb mimic; he glories in taking people off, and much of our pleasure in the performance derives from the pure virtuosity. The setting of *Late Call* is a New Town. St. Saviour's Church in Town Centre doesn't look at all ecclesiastical, and of its vicar the chief male character remarks: "You never get any of this dry-as-dust theological stuff from him that's done so much to keep people out of the churches. Quite the contrary. Last Easter he gave a sermon on the eleven plus." But this Easter he slips a disc and, says his wife, "We had to take what the archdeacon could send us at the last moment." The substitute is an aged Scot who preaches like this:

> Said the one carlinwife to the other, "Aye, Annie," says she, "I've been aye doing so muckle guid, I've no had time to set me down and mind who I am." Ah! And she can sit on her buttie to all eternity, for buttie's all she'll have — there'll be no living soul to save. Is there nothing we can do to help us to God's Grace? Indeed there is. . . . Go out, not into the busy clamour of getting and spending, nor even into the soothing clamour of good works. No, go out into the dreadful silence, into the dark nothingness. Maybe ye are no but a wisp of straw, but if you go out to face the fire . . . then indeed may you be visited by that Grace which will save your soul alive. And now to God the Father. . . .

Writing this sermon must have been great fun, and Lord Snow may well regard it as an act of self-indulgence, but Mr. Wilson seems to me to be using our delight in it to sneak in an important theme which could not properly be stated with austere directness. His book is about a retired hotel manageress who goes to live with her widowed son, a secondary modern headmaster greatly devoted to good works and serving on committees and the production of plays like *Look Back in Anger*. His world is the familiar Pelagian one of salvation through action; it is necessary to oppose to it the

*Reprinted with permission from *Encounter*, 24 (January 1965), 71–76.

Augustinian one of salvation through grace. Sylvia Calvert, the mother, cannot herself articulate the discomfort (admittedly qualified: this is a novel about a real person) she feels in her new environment. It is enough to say that she is the only one of the congregation to say to the preacher: "Thank you very much. I shan't forget what you said." The preacher shuts his eyes "against the sun and her talk" with his "Ah! Good! It's all old stuff, I'm afraid", and the theological clucking has led to the laying of a necessary intellectual egg.

"A flight to the periphery" — it's a disturbing phrase. There is a sense in which all genuine fiction represents such a flight. All of Dickens' novels have a hard centre but, by an artistic paradox, we can only come to know it after vigorous and joyful no-hands cycling round on the perimeter. A technique of pushing outwards produces, all art being an illusion, an illusion of closing in. Aldous Huxley was right when he said that it isn't a matter of *cogito ergo sum* but of *futuo ergo sum* or *caco ergo sum*. Naturally, there are dangers on the periphery, and Mr. Wilson bravely courts them. Immediacy sometimes means nothing more than topicality. The Festival of Britain and "Jolly D!" date *Hemlock and After*; the Piltdown hoax dates *Anglo-Saxon Attitudes*; *Late Call* will need annotation one of these days — Elsie Tanner's column in the *TV Times*, Beatle haircuts, the CND. Mr. Wilson is always up-to-date, and critics in the popular papers are praising him for it while the rest of us merely worry. But in his best book he dives straight into the future. The beauty of *The Old Men at the Zoo* derives from the creation of new myths, not the exploitation of existing ones. And yet where Mr. Wilson deprives himself of living models for his impersonations, he is led — still concerned with the brilliant performance — to the making of grotesque dolls and ventriloquist's dummies. The crazy *dénouement* of *The Old Men at the Zoo*, with its near-cannibalism, Europe victorious over the UK, proposed gladiatorial displays in Regent's Park, is the price we pay for the absence of today's papers and tonight's television programmes. I personally prefer to pay it.

But the sharpness of Mr. Wilson's compassion for his characters is moving precisely because of the strict contemporaneity of its images. *Late Call* takes bigger chances than the other novels: it plunges into a world which Mr. Wilson knows to be heartbreakingly ephemeral, out of which the deracinated Sylvia Calvert chooses some of the rags which clothe the emptiness of her retirement. She is fat and has high blood pressure and can no longer manage an hotel; her husband, ranker-officer in the First World War, subsists on ancient anecdotes, the odd flutter, loud and obscene grouses about the decay of the times. Her son's with-it house is equipped with thermostats and an unintelligible labour-saving kitchen. She can escape into *Maigret* on the telly or a nice historical novel from the library (plenty of opportunities for mimicry here). But the only true escape is into country untamed by the New Town, where a farm cat slinks by with a half-dead rabbit in its mouth and a tree is struck by lightning. There is no timeless image for the new: the new is the here-and-now, the totally contemporary, with the jargon of the bowling-alley and the Pelagianism of the church you'd hardly know for a church:

> . . . it was just a big room with everything very simple and quiet, especially the thin slotted glass windows through which the sun poured with a lovely sky-blue light. She picked up a card and read the prayer that was printed on it — "help us to avoid the easy jibe, the grouchy mood, and the martyred smile. Help us to forget ourselves in doing what we can for others and in doing it cheerfully. . . ." It all seemed sensible enough; lots of people found a great deal of comfort in religion.

INTERVIEWS

Angus Wilson: The Art of Fiction

Michael Millgate*

A London apartment in Dolphin Square, just downriver from Chelsea. Dolphin Square — and this came as something of a surprise — is a huge block of service apartments, with restaurant (where we ate lunch), indoor swimming pool, shops, bars, etc. — the layout and décor of this part strongly reminiscent of an ocean liner. The apartment itself, on the ground floor and looking out on the central court, was small, comfortable, tidy, uneccentric; there were books but not great heaps of them; the pictures included a pair of patriotic prints from the First World War ("The period fascinates me"). For Wilson it is just a place to stay when he has to be in London: his real home is a cottage in Suffolk, five miles from the nearest village ("I find I hate cities more and more. I used to need people, but now I can be much more alone"). The electric fire was on, although the late September day was fine and quite mild. Wilson explained that he had just got back from Asia — Japan (where he had been a guest of honor at the P.E.N. Conference), the Philippines, Cambodia, Thailand — and found England cold.

Although one does not think of Wilson as a small man, he is rather below the average height. His face is mobile but somewhat plumper than in most of the published photographs, the hair white at the front shading to gray at the back, the forehead lined, the eyebrows rather prominent, the eyes pale gray and serious — but not solemn: Wilson's manner has a liveliness and warmth that is immediately engaging. He talks quickly, confidently yet unaffectedly, eagerly — obviously enjoying it. The conversation before and during lunch was mainly about Japan — it had been his first visit to Asia and he had clearly been impressed — and about other writers. Now, after lunch, Wilson agrees to talk about himself.

INTERVIEWER: When did you start writing?

WILSON: I never wrote anything — except for the school magazine — until November 1946. Then I wrote a short story one week end — "Raspberry Jam" — and followed that up by writing a short story every week end for twelve weeks. I was then thirty-three. My writing started as a hobby: that seems a funny word to use — but, yes, hobby. During the war, when I was working at the Foreign Office, I had a bad nervous breakdown, and after the war I decided that simply to return to my job at the British Museum would be too depressing. Writing seemed a good way of diversifying my time. I was living in the country and commuting to London then and I could do it at week ends. That's why I started with short stories: this was something I could finish, realize completely, in a week end.

*Michael Millgate's interview with Angus Wilson from *Writers at Work, The Paris Review Interviews*, ed. Malcolm Cowley (New York: Viking, 1959). Reprinted with permission of the *Paris Review*.

INTERVIEWER: Had you never thought of becoming a writer before that time?

WILSON: No, I never had any intention of becoming a writer. I'd always thought that far too many things were written, and working in the Museum convinced me of it. But I showed some of my stories to Robin Ironside, the painter, and he asked if he could show them to Cyril Connolly, who took two for *Horizon*. Then a friend of mine at Secker and Warburg said, "Let us have a look at them," and they said that if I gave them twelve stories they would publish them. This was *The Wrong Set*. They told me there wasn't much sale for short stories and so on, but the book was surprisingly successful both here and in America. After that I went on writing—reviews, broadcasts, more short stories. The thing grew and grew, and when I came to write *Hemlock and After* I had to do it in one of my leaves. I did it in four weeks. But when I wanted to write a play—that was a different matter. I knew it would take longer to write and that I'd have to revise it, attend rehearsals, and so on. And I was still a full-time civil servant at the British Museum. Now at the age of forty-two I no longer wanted a permanent job. It meant giving up my pension, and that isn't easy at that age. But so far I haven't regretted it.

INTERVIEWER: Do you find writing comes easily to you?

WILSON: Yes. I write very easily. I told you *Hemlock* took four weeks. *Anglo-Saxon Attitudes* took four months, and an awful lot of that time was taken up just thinking. The play—*The Mulberry Bush*, the only thing I've rewritten several times—was different again. My latest book of short stories, *A Bit Off the Map*, took longer too, and my new novel is proving a bit difficult. But I'm not unduly worried. When one starts writing it's natural for the stuff to come rolling off the stocks—is that the right image?—rather easily. And, of course, the fact that it comes harder doesn't necessarily mean that it's worse. When Dickens published his novels in serial form he always added in his letter to the reader: "I send you this labor of love." After *Bleak House* he couldn't; it hadn't been a labor of love. But the later Dickens novels are certainly none the worse for that.

INTERVIEWER: Do you work every day?

WILSON: Goodness, no. I did that when I was a civil servant and I don't propose to do so now. But when I'm writing a book I do work every day.

INTERVIEWER: To a schedule?

WILSON: Not really. No. I usually work from eight to two, but if it's going well I may go on to four. Only if I do I'm extremely exhausted. In fact, when the book is going well the only thing that stops me is sheer exhaustion. I wouldn't like to do what Elizabeth Bowen once told me she did—write *something* every day, whether I was working on a book or not.

INTERVIEWER: Do you usually work on one book at a time?

WILSON: Oh, yes. I've never worked on more than one book at a time, and I don't think it would be good.

INTERVIEWER: About how many words a day do you write?

WILSON: Oh — between one and two thousand. Sometimes more. But the average would be one or two thousand.

INTERVIEWER: Longhand, typewriter, or dictation?

WILSON: Longhand. I can't type. And I'm sure it wouldn't work for me to dictate, though I did think of it when I was doing the play; it might help with the dialogue. But the trouble is I'm too histrionic a person anyway, and even when I'm writing a novel I act out the scenes.

INTERVIEWER: Aloud?

WILSON: Very often. Especially the dialogue.

INTERVIEWER: Do you make notes?

WILSON: Books of them. The gestatory period before I start to write is very important to me. That's when I'm persuading myself of the truth of what I want to say, and I don't think I could persuade my readers unless I'd persuaded myself first.

INTERVIEWER: What sort of notes?

WILSON: Oh, notes about the ages of the characters, where they live, little maps, facts about their lives before the book starts. Names are very important to me, too. Look at these notes for *The Mulberry Bush*, for example. There are statements of themes, like this: "James and Rose are the core of the tradition." And questions — I'm always asking myself questions — like "What are Kurt's motives here?" I set myself problems and try to find ways out of them. Then the thing begins to take shape — this note, for example: "The first act ends in row between Ann and Simon." Then comes the first version of the first act. It's the same with the novels: I write notes like "But this isn't what the book is really about. What it *is* about is . . . ," and so on.

INTERVIEWER: Why do you feel the need for so many notes?

WILSON: Two reasons. To convince myself, as I said before. And to keep a kind of check on myself. Once one starts writing, the histrionic gifts — the divine passion or whatnot — are liable to take control and sweep you away. It's a matter of setting things on their right course. Then it's much easier to write as the spirit moves.

INTERVIEWER: Do you do careful or rapid first drafts?

WILSON: Oh, I only do one draft. I never do any other. I correct as I go along. And there is very little correction; the changes in the draft are mainly deletions. Occasionally a new paragraph goes in. Take the end of *Hemlock*, for example. It's rather a Dickens ending, accounting for all the characters. At the end I found Ron's mother, Mrs. Wrigley, wasn't accounted for, so I put in the paragraph about her. It's rather like Dickens at the end of *Dom-*

bey and Son. After he'd sent the manuscript to his publishers he sent them a note: "Please put in a paragraph about Diogenes the dog: something on these lines. . . ." I like to have everyone accounted for, too.

INTERVIEWER: What is the difference for you between a short story and a novel?

WILSON: Short stories and plays go together in my mind. You take a point in time and develop it from there; there is no room for development backwards. In a novel I also take a point in time, but feel every room for development backwards. All fiction for me is a kind of magic and trickery — a confidence trick, trying to make people believe something is true that isn't. And the novelist, in particular, is trying to convince the reader that he is seeing society as a whole.

This is why I use such a lot of minor characters and subplots, of course. It isn't willful love of subplots for their own sake, willful Victorianism, but because they enable me to suggest the existence of a wider society, the ripples of a society outside. And more important is this thing about fiction as trickery. The natural habit of any good and critical reader is to disbelieve what you are telling him and try to escape out of the world you are picturing. Some novelists try to make the magic work by taking you deep down inside one person. I try to multiply the worlds I put into the books — so that, like the ripples of the stone thrown into the brook, you feel the repercussions going farther and farther out, and at the same time bringing more in. The reader is more inclined to believe in Gerald and Ingeborg because someone so different as Mrs. Salad is affected by them. I've always thought this had something to do with the endings of Shakespeare's tragedies. An entirely new lot of people come in — Fortinbras in *Hamlet*, for example, and it's the same with *Macbeth* and *Lear*. You believe in the tragedies more because these others from outside confirm them. The worst kind of nightmare is the one where you dream you've woken up and it's still going on. The third reason for all the characters is the Proustian one, which seems to me very good, that the strangest and most unlikely lives are in fact interdependent. This is especially true in times like our own when the old boundaries and demarcations are becoming blurred.

INTERVIEWER: What about short stories?

WILSON: You can't do this sort of thing with short stories. They have a kind of immediate ethical text. Many of mine have punning titles. I take a platitude — "the wrong set," for example: the point is that no one knows what the wrong set is, and one person's wrong set is another's right set. And you get the pay-off, which is something I like. A play is rather like this, but has more depth. And plays and short stories are similar in that both start when all but the action has finished.

INTERVIEWER: I think you've seen what Frank O'Connor said about *Anglo-Saxon Attitudes* when he was interviewed for this series. He criticizes your "exploitation of every known form of technique in the modern novel" — techniques taken, he says, from the cinema and from *Point Counter Point* — and the whole modern tendency to concentrate the action of a novel around the actual moment of crisis instead of covering a longer period and "demonstrating the hero in all his phases." *Anglo-Saxon Attitudes*, he says, "would have been a good novel if it had begun twenty years earlier." I'm sure you will have something to say to this.

WILSON: Yes, indeed. I thought his remarks very curious. He implies that I'm in the twentieth-century experimental tradition. It's very flattering, of course — "every known form of technique in the modern novel" — but I wasn't aware of using any techniques, except that the book was concerned with echoes of memory. I think the reader should be unaware of techniques, though it's the critic's job to see them, of course. O'Connor seems not to have noticed that the techniques used in *Anglo-Saxon Attitudes* are not just flashbacks as in the cinema, nor just episodic as in *Point Counter Point* — I've recently reread that and can see no shape in it at all. If you examine the flashbacks in *Anglo-Saxon Attitudes* — and they took me a lot of trouble, I may say — you'll see that it is an ironic picking up of phrases. Marie Hélène says, "Life consists, I believe, in accepting one's duty, and that means often to accept the second best." This leads Gerald to remember his courtship of Ingeborg: he accepted the second best then, and it has ruined both his life and hers. This is an ironic comment on the cynical realism of Marie Hélène. It's not just cinema, you see, it's very carefully planned, though I say it myself.

INTERVIEWER: What about O'Connor's remark that it should have started twenty years earlier?

WILSON: If it had started twenty years earlier it would have been a simply enormous book — a kind of chronicle novel, I suppose: *The Story of a Disappointed Man.* Where O'Connor goes wrong is in thinking that I'm concerned at all with the hero as such. I'm only concerned with the hero as an illustration of the inevitability of decline if life is denied. After all, there's a definite statement in the book: Gerald's life goes wrong in two ways — with the historical fraud, and with his wife and children. And when he tries to "face the truth" — in the conventional phrase — he can do this in relation to the fraud all right, but he can't remake his life with his wife and children. This shows up the platitude of "facing the truth." Gerald is only freed in that he faces the *result* of his *not* having faced the truth — he accepts his loneliness. A matter of theoretical morality can be put right, but this can't be done where human beings are involved.

INTERVIEWER: Other people besides O'Connor have commented on certain technical similarities between your work and Huxley's. I gather you don't feel you owe him any particular debt?

WILSON: Consciously, of course, I'm in great reaction against Huxley —

and against Virginia Woolf. But I read them a great deal when young, and what you read in adolescence can go very deep. I've been much more influenced by Dickens, Proust, Zola. And the ceremony in *Hemlock* is obviously influenced by that scene in *The Possessed* where the poet, who is Turgenev, comes in and makes a fool of himself. Zola has certainly influenced me a great deal in the form and shape of my novels. From Proust I get the feeling about paradox and the truth of improbability — especially the latter.

INTERVIEWER: Are your characters based on observation?

WILSON: Oh, yes. I don't see how else you can do it. But not taken from life. Every character is a mixture of people you've known. Characters come to me — and I think this is behind the Madeleine business in Proust — when people are talking to me. I feel I have heard this, this tone of voice, in other circumstances. And, at the risk of seeming rude, I have to hold on to this and chase it back until it clicks with someone I've met before. The second secretary at the embassy in Bangkok may remind me of the chemistry assistant at Oxford. And I ask myself, what have they in common? Out of such mixtures I can create characters. All my life I've always known a lot of people. Some say my novels are narrow, but I really can't see what they mean. I thought they were pretty wide myself.

INTERVIEWER: Some people think you have an unnecessarily large number of vicious characters.

WILSON: I really don't know why people find my characters unpleasant. I believe — perhaps it would be different if I were religious — that life is very difficult for most people and that most people make a fair job of it. The opportunities for heroism are limited in this kind of world: the most people can do is sometimes not to be as weak as they've been at other times. When Evelyn Waugh reviewed *Hemlock and After* he was very percipient about techniques, but described the characters as "young cad," "mother's darling," and so on — terms it would never occur to me to use. I told him I thought the people he described in those terms had behaved rather well. Terence — the "young cad" — is on the make, certainly, but he behaves rather well in spite of that. And Eric does half break away from his mother — which is quite an achievement in the circumstances.

Of course, all my characters are very self-conscious, aware of what they are doing and what they are like. There's heroism in going on at all while knowing how we are made. Simple, naïve people I'm impatient of, because they haven't faced up to the main responsibility of civilized man — that of facing up to what he is and to the Freudian motivations of his actions. Most of my characters have a Calvinist conscience, and this is something which in itself makes action difficult. The heroism of my people, again, is in their success in making a relationship with other human beings, in a humanistic way, and their willingness to accept some sort of pleasure principle in life as against the gnawings of a Calvinist conscience and the awareness of Freudian motivations. These people are fully self-conscious, and the only ones who are at all evil — apart from Mrs. Curry, who is something quite different, a kind of embodiment of evil — are those like Marie Hélène and Ingeborg who substitute for self-awareness and self-criticism a simple way of living, Marie Hélène's hard and practical, Ingeborg's soft and cosy. They accept a *pattern* of behavior and morality instead of self-awareness. Characters can be heroic even though they can squeeze only a minimum of action out of the situation. That is how I see it, anyway, though I realize some people might find my characters rather inactive.

INTERVIEWER: I noticed earlier that you sometimes seem to speak of your characters as existing outside the novel — the kind of thing the Leavises so object to. And Elizabeth Sands makes a brief appearance in *Anglo-Saxon Attitudes*.

WILSON: Yes, my friends have criticized my putting Elizabeth Sands in there — "Hugh Walpole," they say. I told E. M. Forster this and he said, "Ah yes — but Balzac too, you know." I'm on Leavis's side really, but he always writes as a critic, never as a creator. And the writer can't visualize his characters within a framework, although the creation of a work of art demands putting them within a framework. The use of a character for artistic creation is one thing; the author's knowledge of that character is another. Otherwise you'd remove the element of choice, which is the essence of the creative act. What if George Eliot had seen *Middlemarch* whole, in a lump? There'd be no choice. At some point she must have imagined what Mr. Casaubon's housekeeper was like and decided to leave her out. It's not instantaneous vision, and I don't think Leavis himself would expect it to be. Of course it was self-indulgence to bring Elizabeth Sands into *Anglo-Saxon Attitudes*: I felt that many people would like *Anglo-Saxon Attitudes* better than *Hemlock and After* — and for the wrong reasons — and I wanted to show them that the worlds of the two books were the same.

INTERVIEWER: You think *Hemlock and After* has been underrated?

WILSON: Yes. I think that in the long run *Hemlock and After* is a better book than *Anglo-Saxon Attitudes*, if not so competently carried out. *Hemlock* is both a more violent and a more compassionate book. I know this is a sentimental cliché, but I do feel toward my books very much as a parent must toward his children. As soon as someone says, "I *did* like your short stories, but I don't like your novels," or "Of course you only really came into your own with *Anglo-Saxon Attitudes*" — then immediately I want to defend all my other books. I feel this especially about *Hemlock and After* and *Anglo-Saxon Attitudes* — one child a bit odd but exciting, the other competent but not really so interesting. If people say they like one book and not the other, then I feel they can't have understood the one they don't like.

INTERVIEWER: The publisher's blurb for your new volume of short stories, *A Bit off the Map*, begins: "In an England where the lines of class and caste are becoming blurred and the traditional values have lost much of their force, the characters in Angus Wilson's new stories seek — sometimes cheerfully, sometimes with desperation—to get their true bearings on the map of society." Wouldn't this comment apply pretty much to all your books?

WILSON: Yes, I suppose it would. But you'll realize when they appear that each of these stories is designed to show a specific example of such blurrings of the class lines and of the false answers people provide today to get back some sense of position in society. These new stories are all satirical of the old philosophies which have now become fashionable again — neo-Toryism, Colin Wilson's Nietzscheanism, and so on — of people seeking after values which now no longer apply.

INTERVIEWER: Do you think of yourself primarily as a satirist?

WILSON: No, I don't. Satire for me is something more abstract — *Animal Farm, Erewhon*, that sort of thing. I'm much more traditional than that — which is why I was so surprised at Frank O'Connor's putting me with the experimental writers. I've deliberately tried to get back to the Dickens tradition. I use irony as one main approach, perhaps overdoing it. It's been said that too much irony is one of the great dangers of the English tradition, and perhaps I've fallen into that trap. I don't think of *Point Counter Point* as satire: it's comedy of manners — and you could call my work that. But satire implies an abstract philosophy that I don't have; there's nothing I want to say in the way that Butler wanted to say something about machines, for example.

INTERVIEWER: In writing about Anglo-Saxon attitudes, then, you aren't seeking to change them?

WILSON: Oh, no. I don't think it's the novelist's job to give answers. He's only concerned with exposing the human situation, and if his books do good incidentally that's all well and good. It's rather like sermons.

INTERVIEWER: Isn't a sermon intended to do good?

WILSON: Only to the individual, not to society. It's designed to touch the heart — and I hope my books touch the heart now and again.

INTERVIEWER: But you definitely don't think a novelist should have a social purpose?

WILSON: I don't think a writer *should* have anything. I have certain social and political views, and I suppose these may appear in my work. But as a novelist I'm concerned solely with what I've discovered about human emotions. I attack not specific things, but only people who are set in one way of thinking. The people in my books who come out well may be more foolish, but they have retained an immediacy toward life, not a set of rules applied to life in advance.

INTERVIEWER: What do you think, then, of the "angry young men?"

WILSON: Of course they don't really belong together—though it's largely their own fault that they have been lumped together. They thought popular journalism was a good way to propagate their ideas, and the popular journalists themselves have naturally written of them as a group. The only thing I have against them — while knowing and liking them personally — is the element of strong self-pity, which I do think is a very ruinous element in art. Whatever they write about — when Osborne writes about his feeling for the underprivileged, for example — you get the feeling that they are really complaining about the way *they* have been treated. And, apart from Colin Wilson, they are so concerned to say that they won't be taken in — we'll be honest and not lay claim to any higher feelings than those we're quite sure we have — that one sometimes wishes they'd be a bit more hypocritical. After all, if you think of yourself in that way you come to think of everyone else in that way and reduce everything to the level of a commercial traveler talking in a bar, knowing life only too well — and in fact people are often better than they make themselves out to be. Their point of view is Iago's, and Iago disguised a very black heart — I don't accuse the angry young men of being blackhearted, of course — beneath his guise of a cynical plain man's point of view. It isn't quite good enough for serious artists.

INTERVIEWER: What do you feel about writing for the stage? Do you feel the novelist has anything to learn from it?

WILSON: Yes. One learns a great deal about what can be omitted, even from a novel, because the play is such a compact form. The best modern plays — by Tennessee Williams, John Osborne, and so on — have tremendous and wonderful power. But the play of ideas — Ibsen and so on — is a little too much at a discount these days.

INTERVIEWER: Do you intend to write for the stage again?

WILSON: Certainly. I want to try to produce more purely theatrical emotion. And I hope to do that and still try for the ideas and the wit of dialogue that I think I got in *The Mulberry Bush*, which seemed a little untheatrical to some people. I want to get more theatrical power, not to write like Williams, but to bring back something of the Ibsen and Shaw tradition.

INTERVIEWER: What about the cinema?

WILSON: I should be only too pleased if my books were turned into films, but I can't imagine myself writing original film scripts — I don't know the necessary techniques, and I rarely even go to the cinema these days. When writing a play you have to realize that the final production won't be only your own work. You have to cooperate with the producer, the actors, and so on. And I'm prepared for that. But in the cinema the writer is quite anonymous, and I feel — for good reasons or bad — that I must be responsible for what I've written and collect the praise or blame for it. Once a book is done I don't care what other people do with it. *The Mulberry Bush* is being televised soon, and the producer rang me up to say it would have to be cut to ninety minutes. I told him to go ahead and do what he wanted: he knows television and I don't. But I couldn't have made a sketch of *The Mulberry Bush* and let it be played about with, if you see the difference.

INTERVIEWER: What plans do you have for the future?

WILSON: I'm in the course of writing another novel. And, as I've just said, I want to do another play. Then I want to do a book of literary essays on nineteenth-century writers, about whom I have a lot to say that I think hasn't been said. And I want to do a book — not fiction — about the home front during the 1914 war. Of all the terrible things that have happened in my lifetime I still think of the trench warfare of the 1914 war as the worst. And the home front was in the strange position of being concerned and yet unconcerned at the same time. The predicament of these people seems likely to connect closely with the predicament of many of the characters in my novels: Bernard Sands and Gerald Middleton, for example, are both concerned with tragedy yet become observers of it by their withdrawal.

INTERVIEWER: Would you say something more about your new novel?

WILSON: I'm sorry, but I don't like to talk about my books in advance. It isn't just that any short account of a novel seems ridiculous by the side of the real thing. But, as I've said before, fiction writing is a kind of magic, and I don't care to talk about a novel I'm doing because if I communicate the magic spell, even in abbreviated form, it loses its force for me. And so many people have talked out to me books they would otherwise have written. Once you have talked, the act of communication has been made.

An Interview in London with Angus Wilson
Jack I. Biles*

Jack I. Biles, of Georgia State University, interviewed Mr. Angus Wilson on December 24 and 28, 1964. Angus Wilson's *Anglo-Saxon Attitudes* (1956) is one of the most highly regarded novels to come out of postwar Britain, and *The Middle Age of Mrs. Eliot* (1958) was awarded the James Tait Black Memorial Prize for its year. A short story writer as well as a novelist, Mr. Wilson is also a student of the novel. His study of Emile Zola was published in 1952, and he is especially interested in Dickens and Samuel Richardson. Angus Wilson's most recent novels are *Late Call* (1964) and *No Laughing Matter* (1967).

WILSON: I'm living in Suffolk, as you know, and among our new universities which have started quite recently, there is one at Norwich, called the University of East Anglia. That began a year ago last fall, and I was asked if I would participate in this. Norwich is about forty miles away, and

*Reprinted with permission from *Studies in the Novel*, 2 (Spring 1970), 76-87.

I go once a week in the summertime and in the autumn — not in the winter, because that's when I go to Morocco to write. But in the summer and in the autumn, I go once a week and I teach at Norwich. It is a completely unusual appointment in this country. It's never been done before.

I don't teach creative writing, because I don't truly believe that this is something that can be done, although I'm very happy to discuss anything that the students write. But what I try to do is teach particularly the novel. This overlaps beyond English literature; for example, last term I taught Dostoevsky and Dickens together, and next year I'm going to teach four French novelists of the nineteenth century and four English together.

As to the question of teaching the novel, I enjoy it enormously, I must say. My first professor — he's now unfortunately left — the person who organized it all, and did it very well, is called Ian Watt. He wrote a book, *The Rise of the Novel*, which is quite good. It is very good on Richardson and is very good on Defoe as well and on the rise of the novel.

One of my specialties is Richardson. I gave the Leslie Stephen lecture a couple of years ago on Richardson, and I'm very, very much interested in him. Oh, it might well interest you, if you can get hold of them: I did, in fact, give at the London University what are called the Northcliffe Lectures. I gave four lectures on evil in the English novel. I gave them first in full form at University College, London; then, I did a shortened version for the Third Programme of the BBC, and these were reprinted in *The Listener*.

BILES: Would you comment on William Golding?

WILSON: I admire his work enormously. When I was in the States, he wasn't so very well known — that was in 1960 — and I spoke about him in every lecture, all over the States. He once said to me, "You know, I don't know why you were so mad about it." I admire his work very, very, much, and I was shocked to find it wasn't so well known as it should be, then.

BILES: But it is, now.

WILSON: I know it is, now. I think that the paradox of what has happened to the English novel is something which is very difficult to understand for — I wouldn't say American people, but for Continental people. I have had a lot to do with Continental novelists, and I have traveled a lot in Europe (that doesn't mean the Soviet Union, but Western European countries: France, Germany, Italy, etc.), and a person who doesn't spend much time reading English writers really finds it difficult to understand what the situation is with the English novel.

We had a very important experimental period in matters of language, in the discussion of the components of the personality, in trying to discover the various effects that Jung and Freud had on the way of looking at people, etc., during the 1920's and 1930's. The heyday for this was obviously with Joyce and Virginia Woolf, and my own belief is that they did absolutely magnificent work.

Well, now, when the war was over — perhaps I should say before the war started — I think some English novelists, particularly those who were Catholics and therefore had a concept of the personality which denied this dissipation which seems to be involved in the writing of somebody like Virginia Woolf — people like Evelyn Waugh and Graham Greene — necessarily found themselves writing in a more traditional form, because they had a more traditional view of the personality through their Christian beliefs.

And after the war this spread, I think. A novelist like Snow and, to some extent, I myself, Amis, and others, have felt since then that the traditional novel still has much to offer. Man's relation to society was not given its place in novels like those of Virginia Woolf — a weakness of Woolf. The weakness of Virginia Woolf is not any kind of stated social belief, but the unstated social acceptance of the society in which she lived; in a way, it was her *strength*, because it allowed her to forget about society and examine the personality as a kind of metaphysical unit. English society was changing very greatly in 1945, and it has been changing really very much ever since then; you know, this book of mine [*Late Call*] is much concerned with that. These changes led us to revive, in some degree, the traditional forms, I think.

Now, just at that very time — of course, by accident, for they had not been so much in touch with experimental writing of the 'thirties — people in France (Camus, Sartre, and others) came round to being interested in those things which had been the prepossession of English and American writers in the 1920's and 1930's. For example, when I was a young man, in the early 'thirties, I used to read all of Dos Passos; now, I can remember being absolutely amazed in 1948 or 1949 to hear Sartre speaking of Dos Passos as some completely new kind of influence, you see, and he wrote his books with this feeling.

Well, now, to me . . . I don't say it was "old hat," but it was something that I had absorbed quite a long time before. The Continental novel — first of all, the existentialist novel, then the *nouveau roman* — with Grillet, the German writer like Günter Grass, all these people have been very much concerned with verbal experimentation, with the breaking down of the personality, with interior psychology, with symbolism, and so on. Therefore, inevitably, they have begun to feel that the English novel is "neo-traditionalist," to say the least of it, and possibly rather old-fashioned.

A very disturbing situation sometimes occurs, one which I intensely dislike. On the few occasions when I have had to do with Iron Curtain countries — for examples, in Poland and at that congress in Leningrad, where I went with Bill [Golding] — I have found that we, the English novelists, who, on the whole, write in more traditional forms, appear on the Continent to be holding our brief for the ghastly qualities of social realism, because the Russians spend so much time attacking "avant-garde," experimental writing as being decadent. I spent quite a lot of time in Russia making it clear that any traditionalism that there is in England is a completely

"neo-"traditionalism and has nothing to do with remaining absolutely im-
bedded in this detestation for experiment, as such.

Well, now, why I think that Bill has been such an extremely valuable
influence in the English novel — and a very great novelist — is that he has, so
to speak, seen before any of us did that there was a need for a new approach
to experiment. Golding's novels have a very close story form, a narrative
form. Into that narrative form, which was, after all, rather dissipated by
people like Joyce and Virginia Woolf and revived, if you like, by people like
Snow and me, into that narrative form Golding has put all sorts of new
experiments of language, treatments of language that are completely new,
discussions of personality, examinations of personality, particularly by paradox. *The Inheritors*, which is my favorite novel of his, uses this paradoxical form, so that it is only at the end that you see what you've been up to, or
what he's been up to. All this has poured again a new experiment into the
traditional forms that we have revived, and this, I think, is a very great
achievement, indeed.

You know, he is a master of language. We haven't got anybody else at
the moment writing the novel with anything like his control of language
and, particularly, of the concrete detail. This is interesting, because here is
someone like Grillet, whose main concept is that we should try to fix our
eyes upon snails that you come across in the track or a dead mouse, or whatever it is, and to get rid of this kind of anthropocentric approach to the
universe we should give absolute value to them. Perhaps because (very typically of the French) they are so frightened of anything they feel might not be
"modish," there is no narrative to carry you along this. The boredom of this
kind of almost pre-Raphaelite detail is stunning; whereas, Golding has this
same marvelous eye for detail, but the narrative form and the impulsion of
all he had to say, of the symbol, and of the great concern — if not for
people — for men's souls, are so great that they rush you through what could
perhaps be boring detail, if it were given another way.

Handling detail has always been the greatest difficulty, I think, of the
novelist. When I was a boy, I used to read Walter Scott. How was it — perhaps, when you get older, you can't do it — when I was a boy, I could read
those descriptions of Scott, those minute descriptions, and somehow they
came together and made a whole? But if I read Scott now, far from making
a whole, those details of, say, costume obstinately remain apart and I can't
form any kind of image from them; *this* I feel with Grillet's experiments,
but with Bill never at all — all the same wonderful detail is there, but it coheres all the time. Partly the power of his symbolism, I suppose.

It means, of course, that it is no longer necessary to apologise to Continental writers for our traditionalism, because one can always point to Golding and say, "Well, this isn't so," and they *do* see. He works in forms which
are acceptable to them because of the great use of symbol, and so on. His
work is more acceptable, for example, than Iris Murdoch's work, because
Iris is a philosophical person, mainly interested in philosophy. In a way, I

doubt if she should write novels at all, though some of her novels had richly alive characters, certainly in the early days and even up to *The Bell* [published November 1958]. The later novels have become the use of almost mathematical symbols; the characters have lost all life and they are just moved about.

BILES: You seem to suggest that this flattening out of her characters has become a progressive degeneration. How do you see her book, *The Italian Girl*?

WILSON: Entirely symbol. This book is entirely thin, the people have no existence, and she is really only interested in moving them about as you would move logical propositions about. She's a linguistic philosopher, and there it is.

But Bill has this wonderful thickness which is, you know, the quality of the traditional novelist, as I see it, with this wonderful power of experimenting with words, with an interest in the dissection of the personality, and also a strong metaphysical sense, a sense of symbol, metaphysical symbol.

I have only two [adverse] criticisms [of Golding's work], but I think they are important and I think they come deep out of the kind of person he is. I have praised his work for many years, but we somehow just didn't meet. Then we met and we are very close to each other. We were, with John Lehmann [Bernard Wall and Kate O'Brien were the other members of the British contingent], the three English delegates in a tight-pack visit to Russia which extended over about a fortnight. I saw him every day, all the time, so that, in a sense, I did get to feel that I knew something about him.

There is something that makes for great strength in Bill's work; it is not cluttered up with a lot of "peripherals," as Snow would call them, details of the kind that I get into my work. But it makes for a certain weakness whenever he has actually to localise. The failure — oh, but I don't think it was by any means a serious failure — the comparative failure of *Free Fall* was, I think, that suddenly here he felt a need to introduce people in circumstances, people in actual life, and the truth of the matter is that he doesn't really care enough about all that for this to come in.

If Bill wants to experiment in the direction of something like *Free Fall* again, this is up to him; just as, if I want to write a symbolic, abstract novel, this is up to me. A novelist has his own right, and he knows best what he's doing. But one sees his strength — shall I put it that way? — one sees his strength in the direction of . . . well, particularly a work like *The Inheritors*, something which allows him not to pay any concern to the social externals but to pay great concern — and here he is absolutely marvelous — to the purely physical externals of life.

The island in *Lord of the Flies*, the small piece of geography in *The Inheritors*, the little rock universe of *Pincher Martin*, really nobody *can* give you an actual geographical sense in the way that he does. I'm sorry that hasn't been stronger in the last two novels. Even in *The Spire*, though the cathedral is there, I feel the novel is not quite a tight enough unit, as the earlier ones were. His great strength is in giving a book a concrete quality, which I think is absolutely marvelous. It is there in a great deal of *The Spire*. In *Free Fall* it isn't, it's dissipated, and that is one of the difficulties of the book, along with the fact that with that dissipation comes a demand for a kind of social externality which I just don't think he cares about.

The other criticism I would make, the other great danger he has — we all have dangers — is one which, so far, has really been a strength. This is the tour-de-force quality of the books. It is such a teetering-line strength that one wonders how he can control it so marvelously as he does. So far, I think, this has been an entire strength. Where it goes wrong — and this was getting to be true of *Free Fall*, I suppose — sometimes one has a slight feeling that one is toppling on the edge of a brilliantly constructed edifice, like *Free Fall* and *The Spire*. It depends so much on this [control]. And I think that I should mention that with his next novel there may be less of this precarious feeling of something built on an absolute tour de force.

I think that Bill is a person — I think he would say it himself — who is more interested in things than in people.

BILES: He says this.

WILSON: I think this is quite markedly the case. I think that he is immensely pessimistic. I'm, in a way, a pessimistic writer, but he's a much more pessimistic writer.

I remember I wrote a little book about my own approach to writing and this book I sent to Bill. It was very badly received here, because in England, you know, you must never say it; and it was attacked violently as being a terrible thing to do, to write about yourself.

BILES: You are referring to *The Wild Garden*, of course.

WILSON: Yes, that's it. This was thought very, very shocking and in terribly bad taste in England; therefore, it was very, very much attacked.

I sent it to Bill, and I remember he wrote me a very nice letter. Obviously, he had found it very interesting. His comment was, to me, terribly interesting, because it wasn't how I had seen it really and yet I saw what he meant. He said, "How incredibly tough the human psyche is, to survive. And how long before it realises that it must evaporate." This is, in a way, his whole feeling; that the personality is, in a sense, the thing that we must be rid of, that we must dissolve. Now, I have really rather the opposite view. As you see, what I feel, in a book like *Late Call*, what I want, what I love, is the capacity of the human individual to survive its circumstances.

BILES: Did you know that Golding worked on three different novels and threw each one aside in frustration before he wrote *The Inheritors*? For all it's a pun, that is surviving circumstances, I'd say.

WILSON: This is something so utterly unlike my own career. You know, I've never worked and discarded. I think I wrote a chapter of a novel that I didn't do, and otherwise everything I've done has been just as it came. So, I don't understand this kind of thing, but many writers do work this way. It's only when they've discarded a number of things that they really realise where they are.

Also, I can see that this might happen, particularly when you have had a very successful book and you're now asked to follow up with another. This is the moment when intense pressure comes upon you. And one has ideas. You know, lots of ideas fly out which, afterwards, you feel you didn't really want to expend yourself on. The pressure is great.

BILES: The pressure must be tremendous because, whatever you do, they're going to say that it isn't as good as the last one.

WILSON: The pressure is all the time on writers. I can't emphasize this enough. But, after you have something successful . . . I had a very clear idea after *Anglo-Saxon Attitudes*. That was the greatest success. Then *Mrs. Eliot* went all right, didn't it, but it was a decline. Then, really, when it came to *The Old Men at the Zoo*, it was very badly received here, indeed. And now, suddenly, that's shut up again with *Late Call*.

BILES: *Late Call* is getting good reviews?

WILSON: Tremendously good reviews. It has been put [recommended for Christmas giving] by all the selectors, and so on.

Well, now, what happens is that after a book has been a failure your concern is, the feeling is, that there are critics there ready to write you off altogether. But when you've had a success, there is also this tension, because you know that there are a lot of people who are already beginning to say that the book wasn't as good as people made out. And they are waiting to have their say at the next one. All this is very bad and shouldn't affect a writer, but I don't myself believe that there are any writers who are not affected by this.

BILES: Yes. That almost has to be the case.

WILSON: Well, now, it doesn't have to be, but it is.

BILES: What you said about *The Middle Age of Mrs. Eliot* is very interesting to me. I quite realized that I was swimming against the current when I chose *Mrs. Eliot* as the book to use in my seminar rather than *Anglo-Saxon Attitudes*. *Mrs. Eliot* is quite different from the rest of your books.

WILSON: Yes. Well, it's nearer to *Late Call* than anything else. Oh, it's quite different.

BILES: Just take the matter of our great interest in Dickens, which I share. You see, the Dickens shows in *Late Call*. You understand what I mean.

WILSON: Yes, it does.

BILES: But, it's hard to find Dickens in *Mrs. Eliot*.

WILSON: No, it's not there. If it shows influence — which it does — *Mrs.*

Eliot is a book which, I think, shows the influence of Virginia Woolf and probably of George Eliot, in a way, on my work. And Jane Austen, too.

BILES: Jane Austen. And Samuel Richardson.

WILSON: Yes, yes. Richardson and Jane Austen *very much*.

BILES: Yes, very strongly. But, you never mention Henry James, this is curious.

WILSON: I admire much of James very much. Particularly *Portrait of a Lady*, which I love dearly. Odd, but it hasn't influenced me really. Funnily enough, *Portrait of a Lady* comes to me as an echo of *Daniel Deronda*, which, in its turn, is an echo of Lovelace and Clarissa. I *feel* that's the thing.

BILES: You're a great Richardson man, but what about Fielding?

WILSON: Well, Fielding is a very good man and a very nice man. I like *Tom Jones*, you know. *But*, just *because* Fielding was the very ordinary good-hearted man of his time, he accepted life on its surface, I think *very* much. He had no capacity, for example, to see that women were more than they were [permitted to be] in his age, as Richardson *did* see. Fielding had no instinctive understanding as Richardson, despite his Puritanism, did about the strange tensions between Puritanism and lust. Life was altogether a much simpler affair for Fielding. I love him as a person, but I can't regard him as a very penetrating novelist.

BILES: Back to your books, let me raise one adverse criticism, if it *is* adverse. One thing that I am most often asked by students is . . .

WILSON: In *Mrs. Eliot*, you're speaking of?

BILES: Yes, even in *Mrs. Eliot* specifically, but also generally. The question comes up constantly: why does Mr. Wilson deny the consolations of religion to his characters?

WILSON: Because I'm not a religious man.

BILES: Well, I know you're not. Of course, *you're* not, but many people *are*.

WILSON: Yes. But what *would* one say to that? What would you *say*? One might ask why does a religious novelist — whom shall we say? Charlotte M. Yonge — give the possibility of freedom of thought to her characters? I mean . . . it doesn't occur to me to . . . I don't know how.

I've had religious characters in my books, quite a number of religious characters, as a matter of fact. There is — now we come to speak of it — in *Mrs. Eliot*, there is a character, Gordon, who is a religious man who dies. You speak about the comforts of religion: he specifically does die in the comforts of religion. He's an attempt on my part to be sympathetic to a religious figure. But not *wholly* sympathetic, although I prefer him to the character of David. Gordon has but a certain kind of egotism; however, he's a man who dies *in*, certainly *in*, the comfort of religion.

Religion doesn't play a very large part in my books. It comes in a certain amount, you know into *Late Call*. There is a good emphasis on grace as opposed to works and so on, but seen in a secular sense. I'm interested in the concept of grace. The kind of writer that I suppose is my father is E.M. Forster, who is essentially not a religious writer at all but is very much concerned with religious concepts in a secular world. How does one apply this? Because it is no longer possible to feel that works are sufficient.

Now, this doesn't mean to say that I don't think there is a very great deal to be done. Given the world as it is now—Bill Golding and I argued about this—given this situation of the vast amount of poverty and hunger and so on, in Asia and elsewhere, I think that good works have a very high place in our ethical code. Still, I always come back to the question that J.S. Mill asked himself at a certain point: "If, in fact, everything that I want were socially carried out, what would life be like?" There must be something else to life than this.

I would answer this, as Proust would have done, in terms of art. I would also say that I do believe that there is some kind of grace which some people acquire in life in a mysterious way which has nothing to do with works whatsoever. But I would not be able to give this necessarily a transcendental, let alone a Christian, basis.

BILES: You know how minds tend in the academic literary world to run to metaphor or symbol. You have gardens all over the place; so, one says, "Well, where is the serpent?"

WILSON: Yes, yes. Well, my essay on evil shows that I'm very well awake to the concept, to a Garden of Eden—and to a serpent, surely. I think I'm a person deeply imbued in theological concepts—strangely enough—but having no declared religious conviction, simply because I have never received any.

I was saying this to Jack Priestley the other day. His new book is all about the relation to dreams to . . . he's concerned with some union, some future state. I said, "Well, this may all be true, but I've never had any experience of this kind; therefore, it's not for me to discuss it." "That you noticed," he said very quickly. "Well, maybe you have had it, but you haven't noticed it." I think this idea of a grace which is so vague that the recipient doesn't notice it is rather improbable.

BILES: Speaking of religion and of writers brings Graham Greene almost automatically to mind.

WILSON: Ah. Well, I frankly think that his religious views are very unattractive. To me. I think that the concept of the saved sinner and the lost good man is a vile one, frankly. As a rationalist and a person who has liberal views about society, I *detest* the concept. Of course, we know that there are many people who are counted sinners by the world who are good people. But it's the idea that if you had this particular grace, you're a Catholic; then, if you are a murderer, you are somehow saved, in a way. But a rationalist good man is not. This concept is to me very unattractive. And wrong-headed. And foolish.

I think a lot of his work is really awfully dotty, and it's very interesting to think that he has such wide readership. You know, he is read by vast millions for whom grace and works must be something quite remote. Certainly the concept, as in *Brighton Rock*, of Pinky as the *damned* person who is more important because he is a Catholic, even though he's damned, than Ida, who is a good woman, but because she's not a Catholic, you see. This kind of value or this set of orders would not be accepted, I think, by most of his readers.

I can't help thinking that what has made him so popular is that he was the first person to write about the "anonymous man." Pinky, Scobie, all these people, are *failures*. And in our contemporary society for a long time, especially in the 'thirties and onwards, there have been in all our building of status and hierarchy, and so on, vast numbers of people who feel themselves to be what I would call "the failed man in the mackintosh." It's this that Graham Greene put at the center of his work and it's this, I believe, that has made his appeal rather than his religious views.

But I also think that his writing in his early days — *Brighton Rock* is a striking example to me and, also, *The Power and the Glory* — is immensely powerful and most moving, simply because of the great, great capacity that he has to build up tension and pursuit. One of my greatest [*i.e.*, favorite] novels is Godwin's *Caleb Williams*, and Greene has all Godwin's understanding of the idea of pursuit and the anxiety you can engender. This he does marvelously, but I do feel in the more recent works, and in particular in *The Quiet American*, a sort of wrong-headed nonsense taking over that has destroyed this tension and power. And he is a *very bad* playwright. Just without any doubt at all. Just that.

BILES: In the English novel during the last thirty years or so, there has been an ever-increasing emphasis upon religion, or religiosity, and, simultaneously, upon sex. This may be a trap for the unwary, but one remembers the ancient conception, depending on the Scriptures, of sex as the type of sin. Would you comment?

WILSON: I think we are all brought up, all of us, deeply in the Christian tradition of life, even the most rationalistic of us. My chief hostility to Christianity, which does confuse sex with sin, is just this, and I feel extremely strongly against this confusion.

But I would also go on and say something more than that. I would say that what I find disturbing is the *treatment* of sex, and this is what I detest in Lawrence. What I find disturbing in the treatment of sex — it is one of my objections to *The Spire* — is, and it is certainly true, that sex, when it comes into novels where people have a deep concern for religious matters (I hope I have avoided this myself, but I may not have done), sex too often tends to take on what I would call a ritualistic flavor. I detest this approach to sex.

I think that there is in religion a deep ritualistic element as regards sex. If you want religion and sex to combine, as Lawrence wanted, or to make sex into a religion, you have to turn it into a ritual. My own belief as a humanist and a rationalist creates a great detestation of this, because I think that sex, if it means anything — and I think it means a lot — must be a matter of not only loving but of liking. Jack Priestley was saying this the other day and I think it's very good. Now in ritual, there is no liking. In Lawrence, there is really no liking; there are, oh, many, many statements about warmth, but the warmth is due to some kind of egotism or battle between the two egos. There's no liking; the whole thing is reduced to a ritualistic fight.

Sex is so frequently like this for all sorts of reasons to do with our civilisation, but one should try to find one's way to portraying warmth in this matter. That warmth can be only if you treat sex — I try to treat it so in my novels — as part of society and not as a thing in which two individuals remain, as it were, in an empty cellar carrying out their ritual of sex. This isolation is what I hate in Lawrence. I find it a bit, occasionally, in Bill's work. I object to the cutting off from the whole of the rest of mankind. I think sex, to have its meaning, should make people more part of society and not be a kind of ritual that is performed somewhere all away from the rest of mankind.

BILES: You mean it is human, a kind of common denominator of humanity?

WILSON: I think so. You see, if you look at all the eighteenth-century novels which have this tremendous emphasis upon sex — things like *Les Liaisons Dangereuses* or, more particularly, Sade's work — you will find that sex there is treated entirely as some kind of secret ritual. This, I think, is finally destructive of human beings; this is my fear.

I agree with you about the association of religion and sex in the novel since the 'thirties. It is much due to Lawrence's influence, and my objection to this is the danger of its turning sex into a ritual indeed and dehumanizing it.

BILES: Do you think that, aside from Lawrence, there is something in the world, the *Zeitgeist*, which has caused this great upsurge of concern specifically with religion in the novel? Or do you think this is Lawrence's influence again?

WILSON: I think that's in E.M. Forster. It starts there, in the most liberal and the most rationalistic writers, like Forster and Virginia Woolf. Well, I come back to that quotation I made from Mill, that any thinking, rationalist person, however he may consider that his concern is for society and for the amelioration of society and so on — I, personally, think that many questions to do with poverty, and race, etc., at the present time are the foremost questions which we've got to deal with — nevertheless, all this comes back to this thing, supposing the world was all right, what? This drives you back to some kind of concern with religion, with grace. I don't believe this necessarily involves forfeiture of rationalism. Take E.M. Forster in *A Passage to India*; he never gives up one minute of his rationalism, but he does suggest that there are forces which are more than immediate good works and social intercourse.

Some Words More, Some Years Later: A Talk with Angus Wilson

Jack I. Biles*

BILES: I want to quote briefly from an exchange between C. S. Lewis and Kingsley Amis and get you to make whatever comment you will about it.

LEWIS: I've never started from a message or a moral, have you?
AMIS: No, never. You get interested in the situation.
LEWIS: The story itself should force its moral upon you. You find out what the moral is by writing the story.
AMIS: Exactly, I think that sort of thing is true of all kinds of fiction.

WILSON: I would say that my initial impulse for writing — these things are very hard to trace back absolutely, of course — insofar as I've ever been able to trace it back in novels it has been a visual one, a sudden thing that I have seen which has set my mind moving.

For example, *Late Call*. I remember driving out in the country past the new towns, which are the center of *Late Call*. Those towns were started up for surplus London population after the war [World War II], and I saw a very big, stout woman — very towny looking, Londony looking — leaning over a fence, looking out over the countryside, miles and miles of empty countryside, as it must have seemed to her, at any rate. And she looked so desolately sad. And my mind dwelt on that and then went back to the problem of the lostness of a town person in the country, of the inadequacy of a new town to provide what such people needed, and also of the lostness of old people in new surroundings — especially, old people in new surroundings — and so set me off on the business of finding origins. And again and again, so far as I remember.

I do remember when I first went to Japan. We flew for the first time over the desert, and there was a German gentleman who explained to me about the desert, but it absolutely. . . . Even his persistent voice disappeared altogether; all I saw was the desert. All I could see was this endless mound of desert, which I'd read of but never had visualized what it would be like. And when we got to the Bangkok airport, with the extraordinary

*Prepared specifically for this volume from an interview in Ann Arbor, Michigan, 17 November 1979, and published here with permission of the author.

contrast, the fantastic flurry of life that was going on, the heat and the glitteringness, and so on. These set up in my mind that passage of Mrs. Eliot's journey. These are some of the kinds of ways that things begin.

But as to the moral, this would come to me as I begin to think about the story. I'm not in agreement with what they're saying in one respect; that is to say, I start to write rather late in the order. I plan the whole novel very fully before I start to actually write it; therefore, I would say that I do know what the plot and the moral are going to be. And I do very strongly believe that the plot and the moral are closely connected. I don't know how one could devise a plot without it becoming apparent to him that he was saying this or that about man's future or man's nature or society or whatever it is. The plot is for me something which is a statement, but the original impulse is a vision.

BILES: You have said, like Amis, that you get interested in the situation, talking about the desert, talking about the Bangkok airport.

WILSON: Yes, especially visually, *visually*.

BILES: Well, this I'm glad you said, because in that interview with Malcolm Bradbury you said something that wasn't clear to me, when you said that it all has to do with a vision. Now, I understand what you meant by a *vision*, that you didn't mean some revelation.

WILSON: Oh, no, no, no. With the visual, yes, yes. Very much with the visual. I mean, Proust speaks as though he got it from the smell or the taste of something. I can't say I ever have; it's been the vision.

BILES: You have said a fair amount, certainly to me, about the de-emphasizing of ideas and morals and whatnot, that such should not be emphasized in a novel.

WILSON: Yes, I do believe that. It seems to me that what one is doing is to try to draw, first, one's self into a particular fictitious projection of life, an arranged and imagined projection of life, which is made up of experience, of fantasy, of what one has read, all mixed together. One is trying to draw one's self into that; then, one is trying to draw the reader into it. And the most off-putting thing I can think of would be for the reader to be told early on in the book, "I'm trying to draw you into this, because I want to make you into a good Catholic or I want you to become a good Communist" or whatever other kind of purpose the book may be supposed to have. Indeed, it would be for *me* intensely off-putting if I had the purpose of my book, in that kind of inverted commas way, in my mind all the time. I just couldn't do it.

But I do realize, for example, if I take the novel which I've just finished — which is naturally very fresh in my mind — the whole plot, the situation, the scene, the vision came first. Then came gradually the plot. I took a long time, I extended it too far, cut a lot out, and so on and so on. But as it went along, I realized that I was writing about the conflict in life between two points of view which I might call the baroque and the classical. I have two brothers, one of whom represents order and the classical; the other of whom is a theatrical producer who represents baroque and fantasy. And they are very loving brothers, but their failure to unite does let in the terrorists, let in anarchy. As a lover of Rudyard Kipling, as you know, my great fear in life is anarchy. And I suppose that was apparent to me before I actually started writing the book, but I didn't sit all the time there thinking, "What have I got to say about anarchy, what have I got to say about order?" No, on the contrary, I was thinking, "What would Piers say to Tom at that point?" It's what's happening in the book.

BILES: You would disagree with Doris Lessing, who thinks that novels should not only be didactic, but also should be even propagandistic, polemical?

WILSON: Well, yes. Also, I was thinking of her when you were talking about vision. My difficulty with a lot of what they now in America, I discover, call "post-modernist" writing is that they are concerned — rather as Wells seems to me to have been, in his early days at any rate — with some kind of apocalyptic future. Although, as I think I've said to you before, Jack, as I get older I get more and more concerned with artifacts and nature and less with man, I still remain a humanist. And if we're not concerned with human beings, I really can't be concerned with some creatures that I've invented the name of and call JigglyJowls that live in a planet called MoongieBoo. I mean I just can't do that.

BILES: You still take the view — you haven't quite said this — but, it is your view that character is the single most important thing in the novel?

WILSON: Yes, I would certainly say so.

BILES: You said to Malcolm Bradbury that some part of the world is mysterious. You were talking about coming to an understanding of people and one's self, and relationships, but that some part of the world is mysterious. Would you speak to "mysterious"?

WILSON: I would like to say that I would become worried in any of my novels, if I felt that I really knew *all* about the characters or *all* about the situation. Life as one knows it contains all sorts of unknowables. Sometimes, later in life, you do learn them, and one is very surprised to learn what really was the situation. Sometimes you never learn them. But, behind all activities, behind the interplay of human beings, behind one's relationships with people, there is a vast mass, as it seems to me, of the mysterious. And I would expect to want that to be in my books, because that would be the only way that I would feel that I was being true to life as I experience it. If I really thought when I finished a book — or a story, even, but stories are rather different — but if I really thought when I finished a novel that I'd said everything that could be said about all the people in that book, I would know I'd made a mistake, because they weren't real people.

BILES: You mean not merely unknown, but unknowable?

WILSON: Unknowable, probably because unknown to the people themselves. Are you asking me now do I believe in a transcendent world? Then, I have to say that I have no evidence one way or the other, I remain an old-fashioned agnostic. I'm interested when I'm pushed down to it to the degree to which I have to say I am a humanist and an agnostic, because, on the whole, these are the parts of my equipment which I've played down in recent years because they imply a certain kind of dogmatic ethic which, as you know, I feel uncomfortable with in Forster.

Only once and that is in *A Passage to India* does Forster realize that his agnosticism doesn't only mean what he doesn't choose to state, but it also means what he really doesn't know and it may not mean that he's accepting religion but it does mean also that he's not refusing it. And when you get the boom in the caves then he, for once, strikes a note which I find very believable and very moving, because he is saying, "Yes, it may be a bit more than I had ever supposed."

BILES: What I had specifically on the top of my mind was that you said you never would want to know everything about a character. This reminds me of Iris' [Murdoch] talking about wanting the character to get away from authorial control. You're suggesting that some part of the character is simply unknowable; you cannot know everything about any one individual.

WILSON: I think this is absolutely true; nor do they know themselves.

It used to be said by Thackeray — the trouble with Thackeray is he's always so whimsical and playful — I think it was about *The Newcomes*, about Clive Newcome's mother-in-law. Thackeray used to say, after the book was finished, "Of course, you don't realize she really drank." Now, that's very whimsically put, but it's always been very much attacked, and people have said he tried to believe that the novel had life outside the art shape which it had. I think he was right, if he did believe that; I think it does have life outside that. But, on the other hand, the author is concerned with making the shape.

BILES: I had a most interesting talk with Beryl Bainbridge about that which is real and that which is fantasy, or at least that which is not real. She said several times with great conviction, looking out her window at the street, "That's *not real*, that's fantasy; what is in my novel *is real*." And we went round and round about how fiction, which manifestly is not real, *could* be real, and she insisted. She talked about the autobiographical cast of her writing and she said, "This is more real, to me at any rate, than that out there."

WILSON: Yes, I'm trying to think about it. It seems an interesting statement. As I write my novels, they are the most real part of the world that there can be, but if you ask me about the novels when they're finished, no, not at all. If I read *Anglo-Saxon Attitudes* or *The Middle Age of Mrs. Eliot* or any of them now, I think either they're rather good or I don't. Usually, I do. But, I don't really think, "Ah, this is my real world."

It's when I'm *writing* them that I think this is the *only* world, but that doesn't mean to say there isn't another whole world which lives with me every day, which is my life as it has gone along. Well, when I think, Jack, for example, of what I've never put into my books: I've never put my mother into my books, I've never put Tony [Garrett] into my books, I've never put my Oxford days into my books. I mean masses of my life which are vital to me aren't there at all. But while I'm writing the books, if you ask me what is real life, I would say, "This book here." And if that's what Beryl Bainbridge means, I would agree with her, but if she means that the whole of one's life is in one's books, then I am afraid I don't think so.

BILES: I'm going to quote you against yourself.

WILSON: Yes, please do.

BILES: I don't know offhand where I got this, but I've got it quoted: you said that Realism, reality, is something much more fantastic than the social-realistic surface of a novel.

WILSON: Oh, I really, truly believe that. I'm not at all worried about that being quoted. No, indeed. I think this is so. I have to explain that when I first started to write, I think I must have said this in print somewhere, but it's very important. You know Dickens has been vital to my life. If one single writer has been vital, it has been Dickens. There are others who were very important, like Richardson and Kipling, but Dickens is vital. And I was very much concerned with the Modernist movement, as it's called, I think. The anti-Victorian sweep of those Modernist writers had dismissed Dickens along with all the other Victorian writers as traditional realists. And I was concerned to rescue the whole Dickensian thing, which is reality taken and transformed into something extraordinary, as opposed to inquiries into the mind and strangeness of shape, as with James and Virginia Woolf.

And that was the moment when Snow and others were writing on a fundamentally realistic basis, and so I was associated with some kind of traditional realist movement, which I *don't* really feel any attachment to. My movement is not traditional realist whatsoever, but, on the other hand, I do believe in starting from real life. The thing that I've tried to put into my work — which I think Dickens had in his work and which I find in the great works of Dostoevski — which I find lacking in the modern novel is what I would call the staging. I think I've said this to you: here is the stage and the play goes on in the front and, meanwhile, there are these ballets being danced in the back. This is why my books have so many characters in little groups.

They give this feeling which I think one's life has as it goes along that here you are and you're living your life and this is your plot, but suddenly a person who has his ballet that he's doing all the time — and he'll go on doing it after you're dead — is drawn into your plot and he comes to the front of the stage, as far as this plot goes. To give the feeling of life as it really is, I want to have the narrative and the plot running in front and these other groups working all the time.

The greatest example of that and the greatest, finest novel of that kind is *Bleak House*. *Bleak House* has influenced me enormously again and again and again, and it is this that I have striven to do. Perhaps I do see the novel as much more than many people do. Perhaps because of my capacity to use dialogue, I do see it as being connected with the theater. I see the novel being shown on a stage, really.

BILES: Is it reasonably accurate to equate what you call "ballet" with "habitual action"?

WILSON: Habitual action performed as a concentric thing, done by the people as something which is the absolute center of their own life but, of course, not the center of other people's lives. This is partly why I was interested when you said Beryl Bainbridge's statement: she speaks as though this is unreal outside and this is real that goes on here in my books. Yes, I see the force of that, but I think that while I'm writing a novel — and this I've tried to incorporate by all these subplots — I'm very well aware that, yes, this is my reality but there are twenty-four other realities going on just within one hundred yards away.

BILES: Charles Snow once defined realism as "the writer's shaping his material in the way that he thinks corresponds to reality." And as I said to him, then that would make fantasy reality.

WILSON: Yes, you're quite right. It's a rather unsatisfactory definition of reality there, I'm afraid; at least, I would say so. I think that reality — you know, we've been talking all the time about this — reality is much more strange than that implies. Yes, indeed, you do arrange and shape what is before you in order to correspond with reality, but you realize that reality. . . . Goodness. I mean, Zola worked out all this complicated, Darwinian scheme of heredity and so on, but his actual novels — especially the good ones — it's as though it had all been thrown in the air and everybody was doing a Bacchanalian revel.

I don't feel happy with this whole attitude, as in the new novels of Doris Lessing that I've been reading about and all this even with Vonnegut. I don't really feel happy with that world. That seems to me as though when suddenly confronted with what is a very frightening world, they've simply taken flight and fled. And they've said, "Look at the Space Age, we can do *it*, we don't have to think about all that, because we can invent planets."

BILES: I've asked many novelists whether there be such a thing as fictive truth, and, if there be, how valuable it is. And I always use the obvious antithesis of Plato's barring the poets because they didn't tell the truth and Aristotle's saying that poetry is truer than history because it talks about what might be, instead of merely about what has been. Then, I come back and quote Joe Gargery—I'm really quoting you, of course—"lies is lies," which, of course, is twaddle. It ain't so.

WILSON: Some lies are beauty.

Is there such a thing as fictive truth? My answer to that is "Yes, certainly." I've already said that my mind is open to the transcendent; this may be my version of the transcendent. I don't know. But, I'm quite sure that a world in which poetry is denied, as Plato would want to do, would reduce human beings so greatly that they would reach ultimately, they would become, something of the likeness of automata.

What I hope great fiction does, what I hope all art does is to . . . if I said this: I've been looking a lot at paintings, because there are wonderful paintings in Cleveland and wonderful paintings in Toledo, and I've been there thinking that looking at paintings has the most strange quality. And the same is true of reading really good books. We went to see *The Alchemist* the other evening; the same is true of seeing a good performance of a play. You rest yourself and you blow yourself up at the same time. Man needs some rest from the constant grind of the working out of order and disorder in the world in which he lives, but that rest is at its greatest and finest— apart from pure, natural sleep, which is a different thing—that rest is at its greatest when it also explodes him. You know all this drug stuff, if you like, exploding the mind. Great art *does* explode the mind, but it also rests you from daily life; it does them at the same moment. I should think this must be the nature, if they have any reality at all, of mystical visions: that they totally transform, they blow you out of the art of real life, but they also give you a total rest from real life as it is, which is absolutely necessary to human beings. I'm now talking about the value of art, not for the creator, but for the reader, for the watcher, for the audience.

BILES: I was very much struck when you were speaking of painting. I have never had much patience with Salvador Dali, but I went to the City Museum in Glasgow, where that incredible crucifixion painting is, and it had a great effect upon me. I thought of that when you were talking about painting. Let me go on just for a second here and quote from Brigid Brophy's superb novelette called *The Adventures of God in His Search for the Black Girl*, a wonderful work. God says that He is a fictitious character and "As such, I have of course my own validity. . . ." Subsequently, an "idle-minded bystander" pontificates, "Fiction isn't true." And God responds, "Neither is a string quartet."

WILSON: Yes, yes. This is the *right* answer.

BILES: A phenomenal answer, an indisputable answer.

WILSON: People who say that they're reading a book or going to look at a picture to take themselves out of themselves are usually despised as though they were escapist. I don't think it's wrong to say that, but only if they realize that they're going to be let in for something else which is even more frightening and powerful and demanding than the thing they've been let out of. It's a double action: it releases you but it releases you into something which demands enormously of you, if it's any good.

BILES: In an issue of *Studies in the Literary Imagination* that I am working on at present, there is an essay by John Atkins in which he says—and this I want you to react to—"the novelist is not concerned with making a system for us," some kind of philosophical grouping of ideas, "and it would be false for us to divine a system. The novelist works in hints and suggestions." Now, that wouldn't be true of Doris Lessing or Graham Green.

WILSON: Well, Graham Greene is preaching a moral, which is another matter, isn't it? It's often really very splendidly done. Would you just read his last sentence again?

BILES: "It would be false for us to divine a system from the novels. The novelist works in hints and suggestions."

WILSON: Yes, and yet, you see, I think of a novelist like Dostoevski—who has been a very powerful influence on me—who had insane ideas mixed up with wonderful ones. One of the excitements of reading his novels—as well as the apprehension of life which is there from moment to moment—is that you begin to realize the total extraordinary scheme this man has. And so, with some novelists I think it is true, even though you may end by thinking the man's mad, the revelation of what great scheme he's built up for the universe is a very exciting one.

BILES: I've asked a substantial number of authors, "Why do you write?" and the reply has been some variation of *compulsion*, because I can't help it, I'm driven to it. In, I guess, every case; if not, very nearly that. And almost without exception, they have said, "I've done it since I was a child." You have *not* done it since you were a child.

WILSON: Never wrote a word. This is not true; I wrote two little things for school magazines. One of them was discovered lately at the request of my brother who was the headmaster when I was about seventeen. Otherwise, I never wrote anything at all till I was—I have to be careful about this— thirty-five or thirty-six, I'm not quite sure which. Not a word.

And I don't know that I do have a compulsion to write. I don't know that I do. I get ideas in my head, but—maybe I am different here—it would be very easy for me, since I enjoy so much of other things. . . . I mean, if suddenly at that moment someone came in and gave me a ticket and full arrangement to go and see the rococo sculptures and architecture in Brazil, which is something I've always wanted to do, I suspect that novel might go out of my mind fairly easily. So, there is a difference there.

BILES: Michael Moorcock asked you whether at this stage of the game you still ask yourself why you write, and you said you didn't know why.

WILSON: I don't know that I do know why. Well, I do know one reason, that I do it for a living. But, if I go beyond that? After all, there are other things that I do for a living: quite a lot, probably more.

I have enjoyed the process of writing novels, although it's painful so much. And I've made so many new schemes and so many new shapes have come, that when a shape arrives I think, "I must follow this up. Think of the excitement that I had in those other books. Who knows what this may produce?" So, that's really what it is. But I do think that I'm different in many ways.

One hesitates to start claiming differences to other writers, but the thing I do think I'm different in is the way in which each one of my novels is so totally different to the others. There are points at which you could say, "Ah, yes, this is an Angus Wilson novel." It's to do with the dialogue and the kinds of characters, but the themes, the settings, the subjects. It's been one of the reasons, Jack, quite frankly, I think, why my novels have not monetarily worked out as well as many others. Because people like to read the same. Just as they think, "He's so marvelous about middle-aged women," the next thing he's writing about an imaginary war in a zoo. Students liked that, "He's the man who writes about imaginary wars." Next, I write about an old lady retiring from a hotel. And my new novel is primarily concerned with theatrical production, opera, and architecture. And everything is different.

So, to some extent, I think I have a sense of compulsion that I'm not to repeat the same book again. There are marvelous and great, great writers who have been like that [compulsive], but what they *are* doing is almost like doodling, in the sense that they can't bear not to do it. And that's not true with me. If anyone said to me now, "I think you did such a good book about a middle-aged woman, write another book about a middle-aged woman," I should know that that was sheer nonsense from my point of view. But it might be that I suddenly was obsessed with the demand, the need, to write a novel about what it seems like to be a cat, and in the book there turned out to be a magnificent portrait of a middle-aged woman, that would be the way it would come. I don't think I would find it easy to repeat.

BILES: There was last year in the *New Review* a symposium on the state of fiction. Well, you wrote for that. Some people said foolish things and some people said sensible things. I want to quote one thing Kingsley Amis said, "the available wit and imagination goes not into the 'straight' novel but into the genres, the thriller, science fiction and various forms of fantasy."

WILSON: Yes. I thoroughly disagree with him. I think him a very good writer, as you know. I think he's a magnificent craftsman and a man of great intelligence, but I think he is a man who — I don't know for what reason — has evaded writing the novel he could have written. I don't know, but I think he could have written a big novel about English society which would have been one of the best we've had, and I don't think that has happened. Therefore, I think he makes this great thing about genre novels partly because he believes the day of the great novel is dead; hence, he thinks that the only thing people *can* do is to settle into genres.

I know he hates Dickens and it might be that he would hate quite a lot of the great authors. He doesn't like people trying to do big, gigantic things. His feeling is that what is needed is careful craftsmanship. And he's quite right, there's a lot of sloppy writing. And the way you'll bring that about is to confine yourself to a small thing like a detective story or a mystery story. He has produced some marvelous books in the course of doing that: a marvelous ghost story, a very good detective story, and a fantastically good bit of — you could call it science fiction — about the castrato singer. Marvelous.

BILES: Just wonderful. Among his very best work.

WILSON: These are frightfully good books, but they, in a sense, suggest that if you want to be really good at your craft you must settle to the little things and beware of trying to be a Dostoevski or a Dickens. I'm afraid my impulse is a different one. I, perhaps, don't care for craft so much. I have a problem with Kipling here. He was a great craftsman, but the work I like of his is not the great craft; it's the great art. And *I'm* always being asked to make a talk about the craft of Kipling; then, at the end of it, people say, "You seem to have spoken about the art, but you don't say exactly how he organized his sentences, and so on." And all this about the craft! I'm afraid my craft has to look after itself!

So, I would really very strongly disagree with Kingsley's statement, because I believe that the novel still can and *will* produce some great works. But, if we suddenly say that we're going to confine ourselves only to genre novels, then we have as good as said that we should paint only miniatures and so on.

BILES: Is there a point in being a second-rate writer? I mean this: if one *could not* be first-rate, if one could not be better than fourth-rate, isn't it still better to write second- or third- or fourth-rate novels than not to write at all? If one cannot be first-rate, should he simply not write at all, or is there a point in being something less?

WILSON: That's a very important point which comes up, naturally enough, in creative writing teaching, which I've done a certain amount of, a little in England and more in America. One is inevitably brought up there with people who you see have got some talent, but they're never going to be very good. Should one dissuade them? My feeling is certainly not. First of all, I should think it is a very pleasant thing to be able to write books that you enjoy writing and which sell well. If you can do that, that's marvelous. Now what about a more difficult case, that of the person who enjoys writing but who is not only not going to write good books but is not even going to write books that will sell at all? I don't know why one should dissuade him.

The only thing, and it is perhaps snobbery on my part, but I don't think it is; it's almost a religious thing: that I would certainly urge people to go on writing but only if they feel all the time that they are trying or believing that they can do something better than they did before. But, just to sit there being very happy that they're turning out the same thing! This may be snobbery, but I cannot bear the idea of people writing as if it were as you do knitting. But I would urge people to write on all levels. I love lots of historical novels and things of this kind which wouldn't be regarded as grand art at all. And great credit to people who can do that, even if they don't make money. I tell you what I think I'm getting at is that sometimes when you have to do with people who are wanting to be creative writers, you discover that they aren't really very good and why they are not very good. What they are doing is some kind of obsessive little thing which keeps them feeling that their egos are superior to the egos of the rest of the people around them. And this, I doubt, should be encouraged.

BILES: I was sure you would be distressed when you thought about the situation of the writer—and Kingsley Amis may be one—who will settle for less than the best he could do.

WILSON: Yes, but I think Kingsley certainly would say that he settles for the best craft that he can do and that people by trying to settle for bigger things write worse. So, this is the problem there.

There's a lot of sloppy writing in Dostoevski, but then I would rather write sloppily like Dostoevski than I would to do something perfectly. Of course, I think this is my point, Jack, really here, that I suspect that all the people that I have respected in this life—not all that I have loved—have sometimes been pretentious. You've got to be pretentious to manage anything.

CRITICISM

Angus Wilson

Ian Scott-Kilvert*

There is a well-known chapter in Henry James's biography of Haw-thorne which describes the drab uniformity of American nineteenth-cen-tury social life as James saw it, and laments the absence of those institutions and class distinctions which offer the novelist his richest opportunities. In America, Henry James argued, there was no court, no country houses, no cathedrals, no thatched cottages, no public schools, no Epsom, no Ascot! There was not enough show of externals or diversity of manners to make the writer's task interesting. And Professor Lionel Trilling has remarked that the novel was born in response to snobbery, which is a simpler way of say-ing, as he goes on to explain, that its characteristic function is to record the great expectations of human society — love, money, power and the rest — and to penetrate to the truth which lies behind the illusions. The novels and stories of Angus Wilson are set, one might say, in the bombed-out sites of that stately English social order of James's vision, but this is the kind of fic-tion and these are the critical counters which come to mind in discussing his work. It is he who has pursued more closely than any of his contemporaries or successors, the conception of the novel as a comic or satirical criticism of manners expressed in naturalistic terms.

He made his debut at a moment when the scene was uncommonly bare of new talent. The year was 1949 and the most promising names in English fiction still appeared to be those of writers such as Anthony Powell or Henry Green who had begun to publish in the previous decade. No new figure of importance had appeared during or immediately after the war, and most of the younger writers who were to make their mark in the 1950's were barely out of their teens. Mr. Wilson thus stands between the two generations, though in fact rather closer to his seniors. Born at the beginning of the First World War, he is old enough to remember the inter-war years at first hand, and his satire derives much of its bite from the transformation he has wit-nessed, often a painful process, of the England of his youth into the England of his middle age.

*Reprinted with permission of the author from *Review of English Literature*, 1, No. 2 (1960), 42–53.

His first book, *The Wrong Set*, made an immediate and a surprisingly powerful impact, surprising, that is, for a collection of short stories, which in Britain rarely reach a wide public. Everyone was well aware by this date, of course, that the British middle class, for so long nurtured on low domestic wages and a host of unconsciously assumed privileges, had received the shaking-up of a lifetime, but the effects of this social upheaval had still to be made articulate in fiction. Here was a new writer, backed by many years of observation (for Mr. Wilson did not begin to write until his mid-thirties), who brought this situation into a sharp if disagreeable focus. The tone of the book besides ushered in a new climate of feeling, already hinted at in the plays of Tennessee Williams, and characterised on the writer's part by a peculiar blend of compassion and disgust, a sense that it is weakness and failure which makes people interesting.

In his early work Mr. Wilson is first and foremost a satirist who excels, in Mr. Cyril Connolly's phrase, in jugular vein, a ferocious chronicler of self-deception in its most up-to-date aspect and vocabulary. His wit draws a great deal of its force from his mastery of dialogue and of the slang of carefully differentiated social groups: no modern writer has succeeded better in capturing the idiom and accent of our everyday talk. He has an unerring ear for the betraying cliché or trick of speech and he makes this a wonderfully sensitive instrument of characterisation. The prime object of his attack is the façade of middle-class values and manners, the hollowness of the respectability, the decorum and the apparently "progressive" virtues, which can mask hypocrisy, meanness, immaturity exhibited to a pathological degree, and, above all, cruelty.

His satire is closely woven into the fabric of family life with its demands and conformities, which so often conceal the bitterest resentments. It is as if he were conducting the reader around some trim rockery or herbaceous border, which turns out on closer inspection to be planted with nothing but mandrakes and toadstools, docks and darnels. He writes of lonely children who compensate for the absence of their parents' love by weaving dangerous fantasies, of men and women who feel themselves slipping in their jobs, their love-affairs, their social standing, of the embittered, the misfits and the lost. He is a master of the waking nightmare and one of his favourite themes is the "how did it all happen?" type of story, in which a household is introduced in quite normal terms, and is gradually revealed as nothing more than a whited sepulchre. *Ten Minutes To Twelve*, for example, opens with an imperious ultimatum penned by an elderly business tycoon to his board of directors of his company, but we learn a few pages later that his family has been keeping him under mental observation for twenty years and that the memorandum has just been handed to his nurse.

Each of Mr. Wilson's first two books of stories, *The Wrong Set* and *Such Darling Dodos*, deals in the main with the psychological casualties of middle-class life over the last twenty years, with those who have failed to respond to change or to discover the truth about themselves. The stories are crammed to the brim with realistic detail and yet remarkably economical in their structure, for if Dickens and Zola are Mr. Wilson's masters in his passion for life-like observation, he has also learned from Ibsen: he chooses expertly the moment at which the accumulated tension of years past is on the point of exploding, he is skilful in exposition and possesses a sure sense of climax. He handles his material in two quite distinct modes, the one realistic and closely observed, the other melodramatic. A story such as *Realpolitik*, in which a young, ambitious, thoroughly philistine director of an art gallery takes the measure of his genuinely cultivated but ineffectual staff, is a good example of his "documentary" style. The other approach is seen at its best in stories such as *Saturnalia* or *Union Reunion*, which display a thin veneer of refinement cracking in an outburst of vulgarity or hysteria. At its worst it can involve him in the sheer nastiness of *Raspberry Jam*, in which insanity and cruelty are piled on each other apparently to create an effect of horror for horror's sake.

Mr. Wilson has been described, in ironical terms, as a "humane killer," since his thrusts, although well-directed, are anything but painless. They hurt, as they are intended to do, and not only hurt but degrade, and yet he is evidently a writer who is emotionally involved with his victims. His satire does not attempt the farcical and exuberant invention of Evelyn Waugh, nor the intellectual acrobatics of Nigel Dennis. He does not invite us to laugh at the misdemeanours of some unassailable comic villain such as Basil Seal or Captain Mallet. We are intended to take Mr. Wilson's offenders more seriously, but it is difficult to rouse ourselves wholeheartedly against them. They yield to temptation so easily, betray themselves so inadvertently, in short are so obviously vulnerable, that the reader's feelings are divided between pity, amusement and contempt. The appeal of these early stories depends to a great extent on the skill with which Mr. Wilson holds the balance between these emotions.

Such Darling Dodos, which appeared in 1950, confirmed the impression of Mr. Wilson's mastery of this rather restricted field, but his first novel which was published two years later is an altogether more ambitious venture. In *Hemlock and After* he aims to prove himself not merely a collector of middle-class museum pieces, but an author capable of organising his creations into a social perspective. And since the book takes for its central theme a writer sitting in judgment on his own kind, it is noticeable that he abandons here his hitherto rather ambiguous attitude as a satirist and allows his sympathies to become much more explicit.

The central figure is a distinguished literary man in his public and his private character. Bernard Sands is a successful novelist in his middle age and a well-known figure on left-wing platforms, a kind of English counterpart of André Gide. He sets the seal on his public career when he succeeds in nagging the government of the day into financing a typically "progressive" project, the establishment of a Georgian country house, Vardon Hall, a retreat for young writers. On the private side the picture is less reassuring. As a friend puts it, "Bernard needs a growing mind to play sand-castles with," and he has allowed himself latterly, for the sake of his "fuller development" to indulge in the homosexual attachments to younger men which he had repressed in his earlier career. In consequence his wife has undergone a nervous breakdown several years before — and here Mr. Wilson explores a situation he had already sketched with great skill in the story *Et Dona Ferentes* — while his son and daughter are resentful and embarrassed at their father's abnormalities. The Vardon Hall scheme is opposed by a local resident, Mrs. Curry, who has unsavoury designs of her own on the property. Through her sinister activities as procuress to Sands's neighbours she is gradually revealed as a ludicrous yet menacing figure of evil, an archpriestess of perversion who diffuses her corrupting influence far and wide through the twin agencies of pandarism and blackmail.

Shortly before the opening ceremony at Vardon Hall, Sands witnesses the arrest of a male prostitute. He is appalled by the sadistic thrill which the episode excites in him and overwhelmed by a sense of guilt. He proves quite incapable of formulating the optimistic statement of ideals which is expected of him, and produces an apologia for decadence — "No culture that doesn't accept its own decadence is real" — which baffles and dismays his distinguished audience and comes near to wrecking the entire project. It is an astonishing climax to the book, but it *is* a climax, to which the title offers a clue.

The title harks back directly to the closing words of Socrates's defence at his trial: "If you say to me, 'This time we shall let you off, but on one condition, that you are not to inquire or speculate in this fashion any more. . . .' — then you must know that I shall never alter my ways. . . .," words whereby, in effect, he rejected the noble Athenian lie (or decent English pretence) and chose instead the poisoned cup of freedom. Vardon Hall confronted Sands with a particular moment of choice, but a similar situation might have arisen at any time in his life. He is a man whose honesty is always likely to spell danger, whose moral frontier also is always perilously exposed: a little later, for example, despite his tolerance of homosexuality, he does not resist his wife when she presses him to denounce and thus cause the suicide of an acquaintance who is attempting to seduce a fifteen-year-old girl.

Hemlock and After is a satire on contemporary corruption, spiritual, intellectual and moral, but a satire in which society is seen neither whole nor steadily. As in his later novels Mr. Wilson musters a large cast of some thirty characters, but for all its apparent variety it is drawn here from two well-defined groups, the professional middle class associated with the world of art and letters, the teaching profession and the civil service, and a parasitic underworld of casual delinquency and organised vice, which battens on the lusts and hypocrisies of its superiors. Two subjects dominate the book. The first is the distaste, and in a sense the unfitness of the liberal intellectual for making his ideals effective. This is a theme which lies at the heart of all Mr. Wilson's writing, and here he sees deeply into the moral inertia to which the liberal humanist is especially prone. The best, as he portrays them, not only lack conviction, in Yeats's phrase, but their virtues are apt to be inseparable from fatal weaknesses. "Although I know *their* motives to be wrong," Sands confides to his wife, "I cannot fight them while I am unsure of my own."

The second theme is concerned with the nature of homosexual attachments in contemporary society. No English novelist has come to grips with this subject more frankly: Mr. Wilson handles it with complete assurance and his understanding of the problem prevents him from softening the outlines. It is a repellent picture which he offers, made a good deal worse than it need be, he implies, by the existing state of the law, a picture of relationships dominated by self-seeking, insecurity, malice and, above all, fear. The sector of London literary and artistic life which he sketches is seen almost exclusively in these terms and the very clarity of its presentation makes for an obsessive effect. The peculiar horror of this world depends perhaps on its secret society-like character, which embodies its own code and cryptic vocabulary replete with double meanings. At any rate its repulsiveness is an integral part of the novel's design: a very different type of homosexual relationship, free of these corrupting factors, is described at length in *The Middle Age Of Mrs. Eliot.*

To all appearances the hero of *Hemlock and After* is dragged down by his association with these elements. He dies with his reputation far from vindicated; the Vardon Hall scheme stultifies itself; Mrs. Curry, even after the law has caught up with her, finds plenty of scope for her activities in prison. Yet something of what Sands has upheld with such difficulty survives, and is summed up by his wife in the final paragraph: "Doing doesn't last, even if one knows what one's doing, which one usually doesn't. But Bernard *was* something to people — lots of people — me, for example — and that has its effect in the end, I think. . . ."

Hemlock and After is the most topical of Mr. Wilson's novels and it possesses an urgency of statement and a dramatic impetus which the others lack. Its most obvious weakness lies in the incongruity of its characterisation. The author attempts a variety of modes which differ too sharply to be brought into a common focus. The professional men and the juvenile hangers-on are for the most part carefully drawn from life. Mrs. Sands suggests a Virginia Woolf character, while the egregious Mrs. Curry, after a brilliant start, finally topples over into absurdity. It is true, of course, that the various classes, especially in this kind of society, may intersect at the most unexpected levels, but Mr. Wilson lacks the unity of vision of a Proust to make these sinister juxtapositions sufficiently plausible.

His next novel, *Anglo-Saxon Attitudes*, is cast in quite a different mould, more expansive in design, more genial and relaxed in tone and covering a wider social canvas. "I see somebody now," says Alice in *Through the Looking-Glass*, peering at the Anglo-Saxon Messenger in the distance, "but he's coming very slowly, and what curious attitudes he goes into!" In these "attitudes" Mr. Wilson has hit on an extremely apt symbol for the curious Anglo-Saxon habit of going through contorted moral gestures, while at the same time pursuing (rather slowly) one's own inclinations. This time his hero is a distinguished mediaeval historian, Gerald Middleton, who has never quite fulfilled his early promise, and the plot is concerned with the consequences of the two-fold lie with which he has lived for forty years, and which has inhibited the proper expression of his gifts. While he was an undergraduate his admired teacher, Professor Stokesay, had made the sensational discovery of a phallic pagan image, buried in the tomb of a seventh-century East Anglican Bishop. Middleton has long entertained a nagging suspicion that this object was "planted" as a malicious hoax by the Professor's son, Gilbert, a brilliant contemporary of his own, later killed in the Great War, but loyalty has kept his lips sealed. Meanwhile he has married an ogress of sentimentality, a Junoesque Danish blonde, fallen in love with the younger Stokesay's wife and carried on an affair with her for years, before finally sacrificing her to his family obligations. Thus when the story opens, he has alienated his wife and children, driven his mistress to drink and compromised his integrity as a scholar, sufficient cause for him to describe himself as "a sensualist who has never had the courage of his desires, a sixty-year-old failure and that of the most boring kind, a failure with a conscience."

Mr. Wilson's plots are often reminiscent of Ibsen's plays, of the unearthing of long-buried domestic skeletons, and the opening chapters of *Anglo-Saxon Attitudes* seem to promise an Ibsenesque novel, which will culminate in some scarifying family "truth-game." But the exposition is carried out through a long series of flash-backs to the 1920's and 1930's which demonstrate the author's remarkable gift for capturing the feel of a period, but also occupy a great deal of space. By the time the cast of forty-odd characters has been introduced, the interest in the hero's dilemma has been dissipated and is never effectually recovered. He merely upholds the narrative, rather in the manner of the centre-piece of an acrobatic troupe, while the action is carried on in a series of isolated episodes at the periphery. The novel's appeal thus comes to depend on its large and this time extremely varied gallery of portraits. As in *Hemlock And After* the styles of portraiture are decidedly mixed, but here their incongruity is less disturbing. There is, first of all, the academic tribe of historians, archaeologists and museum officials, who are professionally involved in the great hoax. Here the author, who spent much of his early career as an official at the British Museum, is on familiar territory. The figures he creates out of this apparently unpromising material provide some superb comedy so long as they are regarded as individuals; but the picture he presents of the academic world as a whole cannot seriously claim to resemble any that has ever existed. There is also the by now familiar group of budding spivs, pansies and layabouts, who in their different ways make themselves indispensable to the middle-class world. But the most impressive achievements in the book are its women characters, who include Middleton's whimsical Danish wife, his avaricious French bourgeoise daughter-in-law, his Dickensian charwoman, and most memorable of all his son's young secretary, a belligerent, derisive Bohemian Britannia, the hammer of culture snobs, the most vital and unmanageable creation Mr. Wilson has yet produced. *Anglo-Saxon Attitudes* is clearly designed as a panoramic novel of contemporary society. The plan does not quite succeed because of the inadequacy of the central theme to support so ambitious a structure. It remains, however, a book that is exceptionally rich in comedy and full of brilliant digressions and it represents a further and impressive extension of the author's range.

Nothing that Mr. Wilson had written before could have prepared the reader for his latest book. In *The Middle Age of Mrs. Eliot* he has shed those elements of the short-story technique which were writ large upon his earlier novels, in particular the speed of narration and the habit of presenting a series of situations rather than developing them. He has also discarded some of the more superficially attractive characteristics of his writing, the topicality, the lethal cut and thrust of the dialogue, the deliberate overstatement, the impression of a non-stop "performance" to entertain the reader. He has chosen a more universal subject and given it a correspondingly more leisurely, muted treatment.

The book is a study of suffering, of the desolation caused by the death of those closest to us, and once again Mr. Wilson is at his task of dispelling illusions, in this case the illusions produced by material well-being and untried friendships. When we first meet Meg Eliot, she is a woman in her early forties, attractive, intelligent, childless but happily married, with a life agreeably balanced between leisure and congenial activities such as charitable committees and china-collecting. Her husband, a successful barrister, is killed in an attempted political assassination at an Asiatic airport, and Mrs. Eliot is abruptly plunged not merely into widowhood, but into comparative poverty. She possesses wit, charm and adaptability — the plot manifestly demands that she should be allowed enough weapons to put up a fight with her destiny, although these are qualities which Mr. Wilson experiences some difficulty in portraying with conviction. Prised without warning out of the protective shell of money and marital devotion, her problem is to create for herself a new way of life which will satisfy her emotions and intelligence in a world which has little need for a woman of her age and circumstances, and where she soon discovers that she has to fight for even a place on the raft. She tries at first to share a ménage with her closest friends, each of them impoverished women like herself. The price of their intimacy is to conform to their pattern and she rejects each in turn. She discovers also for the first time the sheer impregnability of the fortifications which the younger generation have erected against their elders: "Her generation had treated people as individuals, not bothering about age; these young people were returning to a seclusion as narrow as the secret lives of youth in Victorian times. . . ."

Her situation is paralleled by that of her brother, a retiring, self-denying pacifist, who runs a nursery garden and quietist community in Sussex, and whose closest friend and partner dies a protracted death from cancer. For a time brother and sister succeed in satisfying one another's needs, but it soon becomes clear to Meg that this relationship merely represents an escape into childhood, another evasion of her real problems, which she must force herself to break off, and the solution she finally adopts is arrived at, characteristically, only by work and self-knowledge.

Mrs. Eliot is probably more important as a work of transition than as an achievement in itself. There are undeniable longueurs in the presentation of Meg's personality and the supporting figures, harmless oddities for the most part, lack the grotesque vitality we have come to expect of Mr. Wilson's minor characters. What the book does suggest is a significant change of vision. The intellectual rigour of Mr. Wilson's standpoint remains unaltered. Neither Mrs. Eliot nor her brother can accept the consolations of religion in their suffering. The private conscience directed by self-knowledge is their only guide, and Meg in particular is prepared to follow it at any cost. The vital change is to be found in the author's attitude towards human conduct itself. The underlying pattern which his satire has followed in the past has been the exposure of characters whose pretensions far exceeded their true virtues or resources. Here for the first time he is writing of people whose trials bring out hidden reserves of understanding or self-reliance, and this more affirmative approach lends a whole new dimension to his observation.

Mr. Wilson has now been writing for ten years. His early work has not only stood the test of time, it is still from a technical point of view the best he has produced; none of the novels has quite achieved the structural excellence of the best of his stories. His descriptive style has always been the least impressive element in his writing. The pace and compression of the stories imposed on him a suitably clipped, laconic choice of words, but in the wider spaces of the novels his expression, never particularly graceful, lapses all too easily into clichés, redundant phrases and overloaded metaphors. It is a tribute to Mr. Wilson's narrative power that the eye so often passes over these defects and that he is praised for the compulsively readable quality of his prose. Certainly no contemporary novelist has shown himself more skilful at keeping the changing scene constantly within his sights — *Anglo-Saxon Attitudes* has many echoes of the Piltdown scandal, while *Hemlock And After* preceded the Wolfenden Report: in short Mr. Wilson has continued, as he began, a step or two ahead of his public. He is a writer possessed of a powerful moral sense and it is worth noticing where this has led him. If it was the classic satirical impulse — " 'Tis hard to write, but harder to forbear" — which first set him writing, there has always been a controlling sympathy behind his indignation which has steadily made its way into the foreground, and this growing human charity has deepened his perception without dulling its edge. His fiction continues to be dominated by a highly critical intellect, but he is now applying this constructively to the universal problems of human conduct. To use the Platonic imagery of *Hemlock And After* one might describe him as a "corrupter" in the beneficent Socratic sense of one who desires to free the mind only to set it off on a still more difficult quest for virtue. He is a writer who has never halted in his development, and substantial though his achievement already is, one may expect that the best of it still lies ahead.

Angus Wilson: Studies in Depression

C. B. Cox*

The fiction of Angus Wilson provides evidence for the great changes that have taken place in the thinking of liberal humanists during the last hundred years. In fact George Eliot would have found him a very odd humanist indeed. Particularly in the early short stories, his attitude towards human life appears to be one of disgust. There is a revulsion from the body in all his writing, and this saps his work of full vitality. For example, in "Union Reunion" he dwells upon the fat, bloated flesh of the whites in South Africa. The women are like "so many brightly painted barrels," and their eating dinner is "a deliberate locust-like advance that finally left the table a battlefield of picked bones, broken shells, dry skins and seeds." Minnie's once attractive small hands and feet now only look absurd on her mountainous body, and her attempts at foot-play under the table with her old admirer, Harry, make her an object of contempt. This kind of physical nausea occurs repeatedly. Trevor squeezing blackheads from his nose in "The Wrong Set," the young technician spitting fragments of potato as he talks to his girl friend in "Christmas Day in the Workhouse," or Tom Pirie spitting on Meg's arm as they chat together in *The Middle Age of Mrs. Eliot*, are all typical examples. The frequency with which such details occur suggests a squeamish refinement in Wilson. It is significant that in his stories there are many women, such as Mrs. Carrington in "Mother's Sense of Fun," who find the physical side of marriage repulsive.

This disgust is not only hardly suitable for a humanist, but also seriously affects Wilson's values. A. O. J. Cockshut has argued in a most intelligent essay that Wilson's "fiercest moral condemnations are mingled with aesthetic and intellectual distaste; we cannot tell where one begins and another ends."[1] Cockshut uses Celia Craddock in *Hemlock and After* as an

*Reprinted from *The Free Spirit*, by C. B. Cox (1963) by permission of Oxford University Press. © Oxford University Press 1963.

example, blamed in the same way for being a half-baked intellectual as she is for being selfish. And in the depiction of Minnie in "Union Reunion" the physically and the morally repellent are curiously muddled together. In his early work Wilson is fighting against an emotional conviction that human beings, with a few rare exceptions, are in every way contemptible, and moral action useless. Rage at human inadequacy pervades his early writing, and his values are confused by the passionate intensity of this feeling. At times he is very close to complete despair.

Living in the post-1945 world, Wilson has lost much of Forster's assurance, and this appears most clearly in his irony. Where Forster is evasive, Wilson is savage and uncompromising. His short stories are peopled by lonely hypocrites, who try desperately to hide from themselves their own futility. He is particularly successful in caricaturing middle-class affectation, and in his treatment of this expresses fundamental attitudes to character which are hard to square with his humanism. He repeatedly depicts personality as a mask, a cover for either deep-seated insecurity or egotism. His novels parade before us the self-righteous, the smugly conventional, the followers of cliques, in a great tableau of debased humanity.

Language itself among the middle classes has become a means of evading reality. With delightful irony, Wilson captures the exact intonations of that middle-class drawl which places other people at a distance and leaves the speaker in a superior, detached position. In "Raspberry Jam" Grace recounts the sins of the Miss Swindales, but does nothing to remove her child from their influence: "You've heard the squalid story about young Tony Calkett, haven't you? My dear, he went round there to fix the lights and apparently Dolly invited him up to her bedroom to have a cherry brandy of all things and made the *most* unfortunate proposals."[2]

This type of speech makes the experience of others a curiosity for drawing-room gossip; it is a game played by the middle classes to avoid recognition of the real pain and evil that surrounds them. And this evasive use of words is also brilliantly caught in the conversation of Dr. Early, in "Learning's Little Tribute," who speaks of his daughters as "his girlies," and "always in so arch a manner that one might have fancied him master of a seraglio."

More important, Wilson suggests that a large part of human personality is built upon this false assumption of rôles. Many of his characters are mere ragbags of pretence and affectation; they have no unique individuality but have become merely a series of poses. This frightening sense that personality is fashioned entirely by pretence is shown vividly in a story such as "What Do Hippos Eat?" Greta is a typical Wilson figure, whose real identity has become lost in a series of social gestures. Wilson describes ironically her "virtues as a real good pal; her Dead End Kid appeal that went through the heart." She has created this shadowy conventional figure in order to get on with other people. Her reward is the attention of Maurice, a broken-down gentleman who only wants her money and nearly murders her as they watch the hippos at the zoo. The scene is treated in a mood of farce, and the actions of such humans appear suited only to this medium.

Wilson's irony is at its most severe in condemning these false substitutes for real living. In "A Flat Country Christmas" Carola likes the thought that she is her husband's "funny little mouse." And at the Christmas gathering in this story, each character can be merry only when he assumes his "party" face. Eric tries to bridge the underlying conflicts by being "at the top of his Max Miller form." And this false gaiety is typical of all the ghastly parties to which Wilson's characters submit themselves. In "Saturnalia," "Christmas Day in the Workhouse," or "Totentanz," the party atmosphere shows in extreme form all that is meaningless in the day-to-day lives of the participants. The party masks and games are not the exceptions, but in their fantasies an expression of the poses typical of human relations.

Evasion is seen again among the Cockshuts in "Crazy Crowd," whose eccentric manners are a great game by which they hide from themselves their own egotism; and in "A Visit in Bad Taste" a pair of humanists, intelligent and cultured, cannot stretch their tolerance sufficiently far to accept into their home the homosexual relation just out of prison. It is interesting that the sin most talked about in these stories is self-pity. This blurs the honest acceptance of reality which is Wilson's own ideal.

This unmasking process is expressed by the prevailing ironic tone. In common with many other post-war novelists, Wilson often writes in a flat, banal manner which contrasts sharply with the forced gaiety or supposedly deep emotions of the characters being described. A good example is the account of the New Year's dance in "Saturnalia": "The pretty waitress Gloria had gone very gay. 'Take it away' she cried to the band. Her shoulder strap was slipping and a bit of hair kept flopping in her eyes. It was difficult to snap your fingers when your head was going round. She and young Tom the porter were dancing real *palais de danse* and 'Send me, darling, send me' she cried."[3] Here the simple sentences act as a means of deflation. This is a style deliberately made bare of all emotional overtones. Its casual ordinariness works in opposition to the jargon of Gloria, forcing home the triviality of her feelings. There is no emphasis, for nothing is worthy of emphasis here. This passage makes an interesting comparison with E. M. Forster's portrayal of Kingcroft in *Where Angels Fear to Tread.* Forster still delights in the absurdity of his comic creations; he is still in sympathy with the English comic tradition which can laugh at fools because they are the exception from the norm, and he is not altogether aware of the new notes of uncertainty that are creeping into his style. Angus Wilson does not suffer his fools gladly. He is depressed by their futility and feels only the pathos of their condition.

In the short stories in *The Wrong Set* (1949) the deliberately unpretentious style often debases all action to a meaningless animal-like series of gestures: "Then he sat in his pants, suspenders, and socks squeezing blackheads from his nose in front of a mirror. All this time they kept on rowing. At last

Vi cried out 'All right, all right, Trevor Cawston, but I'm *still* going.' 'O.K.' said Trevor, 'how's about a nice little loving?' So then they broke into the old routine."[4] And "Significant Experience" is a sort of parable to illustrate what so-called "significant" experiences are made up of in reality. The pompous Loveridge talks romantically about the value for a young man of an affair with a mature woman. Jeremy remembers the actuality of his summer affair with Prue — her neuroses, her temper, her sexual promiscuity, his own inadequacy. And Wilson's style deflates the oldest source of romantic joy. Even when Jeremy and Prue are happy together, the style makes their love appear a pretence: "Their fingers entwined more closely. It was such a *happy* evening." There are times when for Wilson all happiness is illusion; depression is the natural state for the humanist of our times.

It would be wrong to say that Wilson's attitude is wholly contemptuous, for there is compassion in his treatment of these lost people. Also, he feels that loneliness, and its compensatory illusions, are in part a necessary result of modern conditions. His people are always a prey to anxiety, psychological breakdown, even lunacy. The reasons for this are often obvious. In the aftermath of war his stories are full of girls and widows whose men have been killed, of refugees and people who can never completely suppress their fear of a nuclear cataclysm. In *Hemlock and After* the disastrous opening of Vardon Hall is in part due to the nervous strain of another world crisis: "It was unfortunate, of course, that the morning papers should have carried news of one of those periodic worsenings of the world situation, which, however familiar, necessarily crack the uneasy paste of hope and optimism of which so much confidence is compounded, and destroy the overglaze of social manner."[5]

For Wilson, pessimism is realistic and self-confidence a delusion. The power of evil now invades every corner of the humanist world, and Wilson's imagination is obsessed by breakdown and violence. The burden of modern conditions makes his characters easily irritated and a prey to moods. Their feelings shift rapidly from anger to affection, as with people who live under stress. The violence that threatens in the outside world is reflected in the characters themselves. There are constant outbreaks — the drunken scene at the end of "Fresh Air Fiend," for example, or Kennie striking the mad Colonel Lambourn in "A Bit Off the Map." Much of the writing conveys a feeling that civilized conduct is an uneasy pose above a threatening abyss. In "What Do Hippos Eat?" the animals are part of the destructive element that human beings try to forget. The hippopotamus pool is slimy and smells abominably: "Every now and again the huge black forms would roll over, displacing ripples of brown, foam-flecked water, and malevolent eyes on the end of stalks would appear above the surface for a moment." This horror is ever present in the stories, a vision of meaningless evil that haunts the imagination of the sensitive characters and at times imposes itself as the only possible view of reality on this planet.

In the short story, "The Wrong Set," and in *Anglo-Saxon Attitudes*, there are hints that an honest vitality still exists among the working classes, but no effort is made to study such people in detail. Wilson's imagination is taken up by the dead lives of the middle classes. On the one hand there are characters such as Vi in "The Wrong Set" who, amidst night-club squalor, still believes she is carrying on a genteel tradition; on the other, there are characters in "A Flat Country Christmas" who have deliberately emanci- pated themselves from their conventional backgrounds. Carola, Ray, and Sheila have left behind them various set types of upbringing—in a Baptist family, the working classes, and rich Guildford business society respec- tively; but they are left without any way of life at all in the wilderness of a new housing estate. The liberal ideal of freedom, examined so relentlessly by Henry James, brings these characters to complete emptiness. On their way to the party Carola and Ray can see the by-pass, "its white concrete line of shops shining in the dying light—the snack bar, the Barclay's bank, the utility furniture shop, Madame Yvonne's beauty parlour"; the bareness of this scene is a comment on their romantic illusions. Similarly in "Higher Standards," Elsie, the school-teacher, has been educated out of her class. She is unmarried, longing for the days before her scholarship to the "County" cut her off from the village community. Her escape from the dull village routine has brought her only isolation and neurosis. Wilson is more conscious of the psychological problems arising out of the education of the working classes than of the benefits in a widening of cultural horizons. Pro- gress through education, the ideal held so fervently by many Victorian hu- manists, for Wilson has problems of its own and offers no final solutions.

These violent changes in class structure, the breakdown of traditional beliefs, and the threat of war have brought other writers to complete aban- donment of humanist beliefs. Wilson courageously fights against his own despair and tries to rebuild the broken fragments of optimistic humanism. As he develops, he becomes more compassionate towards his misfits and failures. But he insists that humanists must take into account the facts of modern life, the suffering, the power of evil, and the failure of most human aspirations. He tries to be completely honest and he rejects the illusions which seduced Forster. He believes that human beings must accept their essential loneliness. No personal relationship, not even marriage, can over- come separateness. The whole of middle-class convention is a structure built to avoid these facts; and for Wilson Christian idealism is a form of sentimental evasion.

In many stories Wilson insists that human life does not permit any per- fect solutions, and he often satirizes misguided enthusiasts who try to sort out a tangled human situation. In "Fresh Air Fiend" Miss Eccles visits the Searles in the hope of straightening out their broken marriage and of infus- ing Professor Searle with the energy needed to start his long-delayed study of Mary Shelley. She believes in absolute sincerity, and by honest outspoken- ness hopes to let fresh air into the poisoned atmosphere. But the result is a complete breakdown in Professor Searle. We must live with the muddle of our private miseries and accept inadequacy as the common lot. This explains an apparent ambiguity in Wilson's treatment of the possessive mother. He often writes of lonely children, dominated by a mother, as with the Middletons in *Anglo-Saxon Attitudes*; but in "Mother's Sense of Fun" and "A Sad Fall" he brings out the irony of the situation. To love is to make demands on another person, to possess, and often it is better to accept such servitude than to be free. So after the death of his mother, which he welcomes with relief, Donald in "Mother's Sense of Fun" is suddenly overwhelmed by loneliness. And in "A Sad Fall" Mrs. Tanner wants to love without "holding," but knows this is almost impossible. Freedom, travelling light, is no easy solution for Wilson as it is for Forster.

These ironies and ambiguities are most clearly seen in the controversial story "Raspberry Jam." The two old women, Dolly and Marian, are the only ones who care for the boy, Johnnie, entering into his fantasy world and trying to give him the affection denied to him by his parents. Also they are repeatedly concerning themselves with lost causes, defending the broken and the worn-out with true kindness. But both are mad, Dolly obsessed by sex and Marian by the reputation of her father. The implication, repeated in so many stories, is that to *live*, to feel deeply and realistically about the human condition, is to face the danger of breakdown and perhaps lunacy. And so the two old ladies have taken to drink, and Wilson makes no concessions to sentimentality. They have invited Johnnie to tea but have been drunk for so many days that the raspberries have been eaten by the birds: "The awful malignity of this chance event took some time to pierce through the fuddled brains of the two ladies, as they stood there grotesque and obscene in their staring pink and clashing red, with their heavy pouchy faces and bloodshot eyes showing up in the hard, clear light of the sun."[6] With insane delight in revenge, they let Johnnie watch them as they put out the eyes of a bird. This ending is not just a sensational trick. The most sympathetic of the adults in this story have been driven by their neuroses into the most horrible act of cruelty. Wilson deliberately shocks the reader to force home the danger of the sentimental, idealistic view of human goodness. The humanist must act in this type of muddled situation, and he can never escape into a world of clear-cut decisions and moral absolutes.

Although Wilson uses all his intelligence to find new ways of satisfying conduct for the humanist, he often suggests that true humanism is dying, its representatives growing old and being replaced by a younger generation whose values he deplores. In "Realpolitik" Sir Harold, the "last of the humanists," has been replaced at the Art Gallery by John Hobday, the ruthless careerist; and a comparable change is the theme of one of the most successful satires, "Such Darling Dodos." Priscilla and Robin are typical left-wing intellectuals who have been involved in all the political campaigns of the 'thirties. Wilson laughs at their naïve idealism, at the ugly fashions of Priscilla, and their curiously typical behaviour; but these two did care for people, and their pathetic idealism contrasts with the dead conservatism of the modern generation. Michael, the undergraduate, does not find chapel a bore; Harriet believes responsibility is what matters in India, not freedom, and that the abolition of the death penalty is an easy luxury in the face of social duty. Priscilla's cousin Tony, who is conservative, Roman Catholic, and reactionary, feels for the first time very much at home with young people. This arraignment of the new post-war generation is repeated in the portrayal of Miss Eccles in "Fresh Air Fiend," of Maurice in "After the Show," and of John Appleby in "A Sad Fall." Appleby takes a statistical view of people; for him it does not matter if Roger dies after his fall from the roof, for there are millions more like him. Wilson still cares above all for the individual case, and in "Ten Minutes to Twelve" he sums up this feeling that a new authoritarianism is perverting modern youth. The old man, Lord Peacehaven, has lived in the Victorian tradition of individual enterprise, a great man whose energetic self-confidence hid an essential fear and anxiety and whose career ended in madness: ". . . their certainty was so limited. . . . There was only a bottomless pit beneath their strength of will." But the young man, Geoff, is like his grandfather. "Why shouldn't people be ordered about . . . , " he says, "if they get in the way and don't pull their weight. What's the good of being in charge if you don't give orders." With a few exceptions, the younger generation are like James and Sonia in *Hemlock and After,* with no sense of the danger of their own assertive wills. The humanists in the novels — Bernard Sands, Gerald Middleton, Meg Eliot, and David Parker — are all older people, fighting to keep alive their values in a society increasingly unsympathetic. Whether Wilson is right to think that humanist values are in decline in England can only be a matter for conjecture and the comparison of personal impressions; but it is worthy of note that his depression appears to be characteristic of those artists whose early manhood was spent in the atmosphere of the last war. Such writers usually find difficulty in understanding those whose memories are not crammed with scenes of violence and killing.

2

Wilson's first novel, *Hemlock and After* (1952), is a serious, intelligent attempt to sort out these various attitudes towards modern humanism, and to express them in a dramatic clash of personalities. Both *Hemlock and After* and the later *The Middle Age of Mrs. Eliot* (1958) contain elements reminiscent of James's "The Great Good Place." Vardon Hall, the home for artists sponsored by Bernard Sands, and Andredaswood, the idyllic, quietist community created by Gordon and David, are retreats from modern industrial society. Vardon Hall is to provide complete freedom for writers; it is to be a secure refuge and an example of liberal idealism in a world increasingly prone to authoritarianism. The desire for such a resting-place is a sign of a fundamental dissatisfaction with the usual conditions in which human life must operate, and this type of utopia could never exist. Vardon Hall is an impractical dream. One has only to envisage a group of modern poets trying to live together in a community to realize how much tension would have resulted, yet it is implicit in *Hemlock and After* that if Bernard had lived to guide its early years, the Hall would have been a success. Like Forster, Wilson here introduces an idyll into his usually realistic analysis of society. The results in actuality would surely have been disastrous.

But this matters little in the novel, for Bernard dies and is never able to put his ideals to the proof. The novel itself is a most realistic portrayal of the problems of a sincere humanist. Wilson addresses himself to a fundamental ambiguity in his thinking. Belief in the natural goodness of man should be basic to his humanism, but how can this faith be squared with his despairing portrayal of egotism and hypocrisy? In his novels he examines the attempts of certain exceptional individuals to adapt their humanism to their strong awareness of the power of evil.

As in "Raspberry Jam," there are times when it seems that psychological breakdown is the only possible result of a true appraisal of the human condition. In *Hemlock and After* Bernard's wife, Ella, is using all her intellect and will to escape from the conclusion that life is absurd. The strain has cut her off from her family, and for many years left her a broken neurotic. She is a Virginia Woolf type of character, and her breakdown is comparable in some respects to that of Rhoda in *The Waves*. She never doubts her basic sanity but knows that her condition cannot be cured by ordinary psychiatric techniques, not by "Sunday school ethics of discipline and control." In her mind she is trying to impose order on the chaotic, violent impressions given to her by experience. She has become so obsessed by this need that she does not realize that her illness has cut her off from other people and that she is partially responsible for the failures in her daughter's personality. Like the characters in *Between the Acts*, she has become so excessively conscious of her own mind that there are days when other people hardly seem to exist. She shuts out the outside world, for it is full of uncertainty, and she must create in her own mind some coherence. She cannot accept the confused, muddled world in which her husband lives, for she will not renounce her faith that by her will she can impose order on life. Her derangement is a natural development of the Jamesian frame of mind, the longing for moral consistency, which led to the writing of *The Golden Bowl*. Just as James created a fantasy in which Maggie succeeded in imposing a just moral order on the group of people with whom she lives, so Ella, having renounced the outside world because she is sensible enough to know no order there exists, tries to impose order on the nightmare images which invade her consciousness: "Her pale blue eyes gazed washily away over thousands of miles of ice. She tried to imagine the blocks of ice as equal squares, each floating away across the grey water, each the same in size and colour."[7] For her this activity is the only way by which she can redeem the world:

> What she could never communicate to the others was the greater reality
> of her fight against the perils and the fears that beset her. The symbols by

which they came to her — the tunnels, the caves, the icebound oceans — were, after all, incidental. The dangers were real not only for her, but for all around her. They preferred to call them threats of war, of annihilation, of death, and so, by putting them outside their control, they believed they could avoid them. Yet, by the ingenious, endless campaign she devised, she alone was coping with them. She sometimes thought that it was her selfishness that had made her cloak evil in these concrete forms of rock and ice and unfathomable water for, at least, she could face and deal with their constant changes; while to be like the others — Bernard and Sonia and Elizabeth and even Mr. Clark — was to be aware of peril, sudden and totally engulfing peril, always present a little beyond the perimeter of the world which their timidity preferred to choose as the real one, and then to build their sandcastles of creation, career, and love-affairs with the cliff-top cracking and trembling above them.[8]

For her the normal security of a healthy mind is an illusion, withdrawn from the peril of the waves. She cannot accept the island mentality of Forster's characters, for she knows that their safety is only temporary. Yet to control evil, to order the disparate elements of life, is not possible. The Jamesian ideal becomes in Ella a fantasy unconnected to the real problems of moral choice. She has withdrawn into her own imaginative world, and so killed her creative contacts with people.

As in *A Passage to India*, faith in an all-embracing order is shown to be a delusion, but for the characters in Wilson's novels this does not always lead to the cultivation of small areas of security. The problem, as Wilson sees it, is often expressed by use of the garden as a symbol. In "Fresh Air Fiend" Mrs. Searle feels that gardening puts one in a "godlike position of judgment, deciding upon what should live and what should be cast into outer darkness, delivering moral judgment and analogies. It was only by a careful compensation, an act of retribution, such as preserving the poppies she had condemned, that she could avoid too great an arrogance." This gives some help in interpreting the important symbolic discussion of gardening between Bernard and Ella:

> "I shall go and cope with that damned clematis Mrs. Rankine gave us," she said. "The thing was almost certainly diseased when she sent it."
>
> "I'm not really surprised," said Bernard, "but is it worth saving?"
>
> "Once the wretched thing's here, one's rather committed," replied Ella.
>
> "I see," said Bernard; "you don't feel like giving it a further push on its way to the rubbish heap?"
>
> To his pleasure, his wife considered for a moment before she answered. She found such an idea difficult to fit into her daily existence of ordering and constructing.
>
> "No," she answered at last, "I don't think so, Bernard. Gardening always seems to mean keeping things alive and getting them to grow. Perhaps I'm not ruthless enough."

"With weeds?" he asked in his old Socratic quizzical manner.

"Well, only because they stop the right things from growing."

"You're very sure about the right things," he commented.

Ella laughed. "Well, yes," she answered, "I suppose I am. But I don't follow *quite* blindly, you know. Some flowers are absolutely foul. Double begonias, for instance, or prize dahlias. Any of those fat, waxy things. But then I never have them in the garden." She paused for a moment. "Of course, it's quite true that I did all I could to keep that wretched euphorbia going," she added, "but I was really awfully pleased when it died."

Bernard made a decision. "Don't you ever get a kick when you forget to water those precious gentians of yours and *they* die?" he asked.

Ella looked surprised. "I never *do* forget," she said. "It's far too difficult to get them to grow at all in this wretched garden."

Bernard sighed. "Yes," he said, "yours may not be the conventional approach, but it is, after all, the proper exercise of authority." Behind his open book he shrank into his chair, as though determined to emphasize his remoteness from her.[9]

Like the gift of life, Mrs. Rankine's clematis is diseased when it arrives, and can only flourish by careful tending. The garden is an extension of Ella's fantasies, where she can impose the order she does not find in the outside world and satisfy her ideals by assisting life to flourish. Bernard tries to introduce two objections into this ordered philosophy. Perhaps it may be better not to preserve life, but instead to give it a further push on its way to the rubbish heap? And, more seriously, what about the weeds? In life, a moral choice demands commitment to one line of conduct and the exclusion of others. No absolute ideal can be put into practice and, as James saw, moral decisions are based upon a delicate balancing of conflicting duties. But how does one decide what are the right things we should help to grow? James never properly explains from what source his free spirit's ideal of balance derives. But Ella cannot live with illogicalities; she accepts the traditional groupings of sheep and goats, flowers and weeds, and adapts them slightly according to her own taste. This, as Bernard says, is "the proper exercise of authority," the proper carrying out of moral responsibility, but for him its clear-cut simplicity ignores the confused nature of life. He cannot be so sure of right and wrong, and it is in this muddled area of moral choice that he attempts to carry out his own humanist beliefs.

Ella fears to surrender her will, to renounce her faith that she has power to control the world, and in pursuit of this desire she almost loses herself among her obsessive images of crevasses and icy torrents. But she is restored to comparative health by concern for Bernard. As his depression increases, she achieves a "stronger, more total realization of the objective world than she had known for years." When she becomes active again, she achieves no Maggie-like golden bowl of harmony, but, involved with people, she begins to act again creatively. The results may be muddled, but at least she is alive.

The problem of the proper use of power and responsibility is crucial in the novel. Like Forster, Wilson expresses an almost instinctive dislike of administrators, but *Hemlock and After* contains a much more intelligent evaluation of their problems than is to be found in *A Passage to India*. Mr. Copperwheat's official jargon, his failure to create an individual personality, is satirized in the usual Wilson manner, but the treatment of Charles Murley, who has a high position at the Treasury, is more sympathetic. Like so many characters in the novel, Charles is given arguments which contain serious criticisms of Bernard's humanism. He points out that people who have to look after large sums of public money or college funds are rightly cautious when presented with a scheme such as the Vardon Hall enterprise. They cannot respond simply to the needs of one person, but must balance and weigh varying demands on their resources. And so he gets angry when Bernard lays claim to a superior honesty: "what you seem to get so excited about appears to me the simple and proper use of authority . . . you people want the pleasures of authority without any of its penalties." But Bernard shies away from this conclusion. He still wants to exercise power, to help society, and at the same time to do complete justice to the needs of every individual case. At this point the scales are suddenly weighted most heavily against Charles, as Bernard considers the effects of Charles's embittered acceptance of his official station in life: "He realized that, for Charles, Mrs. Curry and her little world of evil, Sherman's malice, Celia Craddock's prison-house of discontent, Louie Randall's pathological politics would be without interest; Charles had accepted the world of real power with its wider implications good and bad, and such second-rate failures were beneath his notice."[10] Need an administrator like Charles lack interest in the second-rate failures that his decisions affect? Bernard's view is not countered in the novel, and there is an evasiveness here which deprives *Hemlock and After* of dramatic force. Charles is surely right when he writes to Ella, urging her to persuade Bernard to act: "Do urge him, my dear, to step out of his mood of exaggerated conscience. If he doesn't use the authority that becomes him, all the little jacks-in-office and the ignorant *arrivistes* will sin."[11] But Bernard does not find it so easy to commit himself to moral action. He has always thought of himself as an "anarchic humanist," and his attitude is made clear in his discussions with Isobel, his sister, and Louie, the young, left-wing intellectual.

Isobel dislikes Bernard's views, for she believes that ideals of Liberty and Freedom can courageously be put into practice. Her opinions make clear how closely Bernard's career is modelled on that of Wilson himself:

> She did not care for her brother's works, the earlier satirical ones seeming hard and frivolous — she felt that they did not do justice to the depth and courage of his humanity — the later ones faintly imbued with quietism; not alas! the admirable bustling quietism of so many Quakers with whom she had worked, but an almost unreal religious quality, which she had to admit seemed more and more to colour his personality.[12]

In the 1930s Bernard and Isobel had worked together over the Spanish Civil War, but now Bernard has no desire to take up a new crusade. His views are closely akin to those that dissuade David, in *The Middle Age of Mrs. Eliot,* from joining actively in the Campaign for Nuclear Disarmament:

> "I don't think making stands is quite so easy as you think, Isobel," Bernard said. "You'll think I'm against you, darling, but I'm not. In a sort of way I'm even pleased that you're still so sure of what you think. But I don't think it's as easy as all that. And not being easy, I don't think amateurs should meddle, especially writers and professional people. Oh! and again, I don't think exactly that. But, for the moment, at any rate, I've got to work on quite little things which are basic — myself, for example."[13]

This is a curious view of the amateur, and Bernard admits that at this stage he is not sure of his own position. Wilson again weakens the case against Bernard by making Louie a hard fanatic, whose sexual coldness is made almost as distasteful as her opinions. Her talk is a string of clichés: "You prefer to wait until the atom bombs drop . . . and they certainly will, you know, on this tight little right little aircraft carrier," Although he is sure of his ideals — "peace, social justice, freedom to create, full use of material benefits in safe surroundings" — Bernard has lost all confidence that he understands the *means* whereby these ideals are to be achieved. His feeling has much in common with that of Lionel Trilling, who, in his essay "Manners, Morals, and the Novel," writes that some paradox of our natures leads us, when once we have made our fellow men the objects of our enlightened interest, to go on to make them the objects of our pity, then of our wisdom, ultimately of our coercion." Louie is prepared to kill, if necessary, but Bernard will have no truck with such naïve, left-wing thinking about the use of power.

Bernard's ability to act is also limited because his moral decisions try to take into account the results of his actions. He tries to solve the problems of consequential morality with which George Eliot grappled. When his daughter, Elizabeth, accuses him of being a homosexual and of not considering her brother James and herself, Bernard replies:

> "As to you and James, I'm afraid I must say that I did consider the effect my life might have, and I chose to accept its possible harm to you. Harm to others is after all implicit in most decisions we take, and has to be weighed up when taking them. In this case, I thought that apart from prejudice, and that I'd already decided not to consider, the dangers to my family were not as great as the importance of my new life to me. A selfish, but to me necessary, decision."[14]

But how is the balance to be struck? Bernard is not sure, and his uncertainty gradually paralyses his will. Also, as he thinks about this problem, he is impelled to investigate his own motives. And here uncertainty is again dominant. Elizabeth sees him enjoying his benevolence, being "the great understander," and so forcing the people with whom he deals into an inferior position. This Socratic attitude has left both his children embittered. James hates "all this universal understanding, this Dostoyevskyan emotional brotherhood," and thinks that at bottom Bernard "had nothing but utter contempt for nine-tenths of humanity." Bernard himself feels the force of this argument, and he is determined to be honest with himself about his motives. Self-knowledge is his ideal. And so when he argues with Louie at Vardon Hall, he insists that actions cannot be judged in isolation:

> "I judge trees by their fruit," she said.
> Bernard narrowed his eyes as he addressed her. "And I by their shape," he said.
> "Oh Lord! Art for art's sake. Thank God! you *aren't* going to speak at the Peace Meeting, with your personal messages and your personal morals."[15]

Art for art's sake does not do justice to Bernard's scruples. For him action is good only when rightly motivated. He does not believe that you can do the right thing for the wrong reason. And so the moment in Leicester Square when he feels a sadistic thrill of pleasure at the hunting down of a homosexual brings about a complete collapse of his will. It is almost as if a humanist had suddenly been converted to the doctrine of original sin, though Wilson does not see it in this way. This moment forces Bernard to doubt whether he can ever properly understand his motives: "Truly, he thought, he was not at one with those who exercised proper authority. A humanist, it would seem, was more at home with the wielders of the knout and the rubber truncheon."[16] In his speech at Vardon Hall he cannot stop himself from talking about this problem: "Motives were so difficult, so double, so much hypocrisy might spring from guilt, so much benevolence from fear to use power, so much kindness overlay cruelty, so much that was done didn't matter. If the scheme failed, if the young writers ceased to write, it was of small account in time; better failure than deception, better defeat than a victory where motive was wrong."[17] He perceives that self-sacrifice may be a disguise for cruelty, and this knowledge forces him to withdraw from life. He tells Eric, the young homosexual whom he wanted to help, that he can assist him no more: "I thought that my motives too were "moral," now I have no such faith. Yours is a difficult enough life without the added danger of my motives. . . ." And later he says: "How do I know where that action may lead or who it may hurt beyond my control?" He dare not oppose Eric's mother, for his motives may be worse than hers. For Bernard, those who interfere to help others can never be sure how far they are succumbing to a sadistic enjoyment of power. In his essay, "The Novelist's Responsibility," L. P. Hartley argues that "different as they are, the doctrines of Marx and Freud have combined to undermine the individual's sense of personal responsibility."[18] For Marx, action is conditioned by the class of society to which we belong, and for Freud, by pre-natal or juvenile influences over which we have no control. Aware of these forces, Bernard becomes afraid of the use of the will.

This is a logical conclusion of the humanist explorations of motive and of consequences carried out by George Eliot, James, and Forster. If a man dares to act only when intention and result are clearly seen, then action itself becomes impossible. This fear of action is an important trait of post-1945 humanism, in poetry as well as prose. Typical of the writers of the 'fifties is a distrust of that bold application of ideals which has caused so much misery in this century, and also a lack of self-assurance which finds lucid, beautiful expression in the poetry of Philip Larkin. Wilson does not need to be told the dangers of this passivity. In his first three novels he considers ways in which humanists might influence the outside world.

As in the short stories, a proper recognition of the power of evil is the first necessary step in the rebirth of humanist activity. The obscene Vera Curry — "a sprawling waste of energy in malice for its own sake" — forces upon Bernard "a growing apprehension of evil that had begun, this summer, to disrupt his comprehension of the world." Her philosophy of love, dedicated to the satisfaction of the perverse sexual lusts of all her clientele, is an extreme parody of Bernard's own desire to satisfy the needs of all the people he meets. Her party is a gathering of vampires, feasting on innocence, and like the parties in the short stories, a series of gestures created to hide a basic egotism.

This element of parody is of extreme importance in the total construction of the novel. Many of the unsympathetic characters represent some quality of Bernard carried to an extreme. Celia Craddock's possessive love for Eric, for example, caricatures Bernard's own desire to control Eric's destiny. This explains the treatment of homosexuality. In his article, Cockshut asks why Bernard should be excused, when the other homosexuals are disgusting. At the opening of Vardon Hall they "scampered about the corridors and empty bedrooms like so many mating mice." And why should Bernard not be blamed for his interference in the life of Eric, when Hubert Rose is condemned for his attempted seduction of a young girl? The answer is to be found in Wilson's conception of action. Bernard himself eventually perceives that everything he does must partake in some measure of evil. Like Vera Curry, he too cannot help enjoying his attitude of all-embracing love; like Mrs. Craddock, he wants to possess Eric, and like Hubert he satisfies his own sensual needs by interfering in a young life. It is recognition of this involvement in evil which so shocks Bernard after the arrest in Leicester Square. But for Wilson Bernard is justified by his attempts to limit the effects of his own egotism, and to avoid the excesses of the other characters.

But this knowledge drives Bernard himself to despair. At the opening of Vardon Hall disorder is everywhere triumphant, and it is again this type of scene by which Wilson's imagination is stimulated. The heat brings outbursts of temper; the arrangements for the refreshments and for the loudspeakers break down. From the microphones come strange, subhuman explosions, and the words of the poet are completely incomprehensible. We are almost in the world of Beckett and Pinter, where each man must accept his own isolation and his inability to communicate with others. It is in this chaos that Bernard makes his despairing speech, renouncing the simple humanist faith in natural goodness, and accepting with horror his own guilt. Afterwards he becomes for a time completely apathetic. When he is urged to go on writing, he replies that "one writes what one has to say. At the moment, I see Nothing behind nothing." And so he deliberately cultivates a policy of non-interference: "Once, in defiance of his body's long-learnt urge to save the weak, he forced himself to stand by while a weasel sucked the brain from a quivering rabbit. What was one more rabbit compared to the satisfaction of the snakelike creature's tensed lust?"[19]

The breakdown of Ella and Bernard represents the vision of despair that haunts the modern humanist. Life becomes a trap, incapable of being transformed into beauty and order:

> Ella had retreated far into her world of shapes and figures, and lay for hours in bed, weeping as the threatening darkness seemed once more to close in upon her, swallowing up her personality in a sea of unrelated fears. They might have been two different species, brooding, prowling in the narrow limits of their private hells, each as little concerned with the other's trapped existence as a restless, pacing leopard with a she-bear sunk in torpor in a nearby cage.[20]

As a writer Bernard feels that the use of the novel to solve conflicts, to show the development of individuals towards a better life, is an illusion: "Conflicts, so carefully brought out, so lovingly delineated in his novels, where they so inevitably and easily led to the climaxes and resolutions that released him from the strain of creation, now seemed an enveloping mesh of personal memories and guilts that offered no conceivable solution that could ease his soul."

Yet this is not the conclusion to which Wilson comes as a result of his story. Like Socrates, Bernard renounces life, but his influence remains behind him. Before his death he had not put his new-found apathy into practice with any consistency. He had inevitably been drawn once more into positive action. Here the parody of his apathy is seen in his brother-in-law, Bill Pendlebury, who is determined "to travel light" through life. Not liking to see other people hurt, he hurries on before they can make claims on him. His favourite phrase is the one used by Fielding in *A Passage to India*, and the novel here clearly shows that to travel light is not to live. Bill tells Bernard the sordid story of Mrs. Curry's efforts to procure a young girl for Hubert Rose, and says: "I suppose any decent man would have taken action about it. But I travel light, you know." At first Bernard does not want to take up this cause, for he feels too guilty himself to have the right to bring justice on others. "I, too, have to travel light," he says. But gradually he refuses to accept the logic of this decision. Although he is too uncertain about his motives to go on interfering in the life of Eric, he recognizes in Hubert's sin a clear case for moral action: "Horror at his inertia before Eric's distant drowning, however, made him resolute now to save that other unknown victim from the waves."

Hubert Rose's philosophy is an extreme parody of Bernard's individualistic anarchy. Hubert cannot face the adult world, and longs to return to the innocence of childhood; his perversion is a "frenzied search to regain those wondrous secret childhood games beside which all the pleasures of the adult world were dust and ashes in his mouth." His studio symbolizes the despair which for him is the only logical and realistic attitude. Everything is bare and cold, dehumanized "as though the owner's fear of being charged with any positive assertion either of taste or personality had forbidden him the use of all covering which, by design or ornament, might be used as evidence against him." Human life has no meaning, and only "the desolate moonlit horror of a single Samuel Palmer summed up in coherent statement the world of its owner—the empty hopelessness of a desert universe which had almost wound down to its end." Here Bernard talks to him about moral values, and their argument reveals the difference in their types of despair. Hubert believes he has the right to live below all standards of good and evil, to live directly out of his own desires; and he uses children to satisfy his sensual needs. But Bernard's despair is that of the humanist; it teaches him compassion, and to limit the field of devastation caused by the egotism of Hubert. He holds on to his humanism none the less violently because he has had to doubt whether it is a totally adequate answer to the problems of living.

Ella takes up this cause after Bernard is dead, and her action leads to the suicide of Hubert. But Bernard's action, to limit the field of devastation, is one solution to the problems of the modern humanist, and Wilson has others to offer at the end of the novel. Ella tries to comfort Bernard, to urge him that a good man, like himself, must take action. She justifies this belief by discussing their failure in the bringing up of their children. They gave them freedom and good sense, but, says Ella, "we feared responsibility." They left their children free to develop naturally for the wrong reason, because they were afraid to interfere. And so their children "wanted love, not good sense. They were and still are lonely." Ella preaches a form of commitment which offers some solution to Bernard's passivity. After Hubert's suicide, she says: "Such a lot of wicked things get mixed up with any good one does. Bernard understood that so well; but then he didn't only act in particulars, he maintained what's important in his life itself." When Elizabeth says that it's strange that Bernard's books will have so much influence in the future, although he himself did so little, Ella replies: "My dear . . . doing doesn't last, even if one knows what one's doing, which one usually doesn't. But Bernard *was* something to people—lots of people—me, for example—and that has its effect in the end, I think." And so in the epilogue we see Bernard's influence on Isobel and Eric, both of whom remember his humanity, and cannot remain unaffected by his goodness. The title — *Hemlock and After* — is justified.

Ella's last speech is confusing, for it is not clear how we can separate what Bernard *was* from what he *did*. Does Ella mean that his motives were right, even if we cannot tell the exact effect of his actions? But this idea undermines the most important dramatic scene in the novel, the arrest of the homosexual in Leicester Square. Was Bernard quite wrong to suspect his own motives? The sympathetic portrait of Bernard suggests that he was, and so there is a conflict in the novel between its emotional effect and its intellectual implications. Intellectually the development of Bernard towards self-knowledge ends in his realization that he too is an egotist; the only way he can act morally is by limiting the field of his own and other people's destructiveness. But emotionally the novel ends with the thoughts of Ella, who is convinced that Bernard was innately a man of good will. And so the total effect of *Hemlock and After* is ambiguous. It is a brilliant, experimental novel in which Wilson himself is trying to clarify his own conception of humanism.

Notes

1. A. O. J. Cockshut, "Favoured Sons. The Moral World of Angus Wilson," *Essays in Criticism*, Vol. IX, 1959.

2. *The Wrong Set and Other Stories* (1949), Penguin Books, 1959, p. 129.

3. Ibid., p. 49.

4. Ibid., p. 91.

5. *Hemlock and After* (1952), bk. ii, ch. iii. Penguin Books, 1957, pp. 146–7.

6. *The Wrong Set and Other Stories*, p. 142.

7. Op. cit., bk. ii, ch. iii. p. 163.

8. Ibid., bk. i, ch. iii. pp. 48–9.

9. Ibid., bk. ii, ch. i. pp. 125–6.

10. Ibid., bk. i, ch. v. pp. 107–8.

11. Ibid., bk. iii, ch. i. p. 213.

12. Ibid., bk. i, ch. iv. p. 72.

13. Ibid., p. 73.

14. Ibid., bk. i, ch. iii. p. 58.

15. Ibid., bk. ii, ch. iii. p. 173.

16. Ibid., bk. i, ch. v. p. 109.

17. Ibid., bk. ii, ch. iii, p. 153.

18. *English*, Vol. XIII, no. 77, 1961, p. 175.

19. Ibid., bk. iii, ch. i. p. 190.

20. Ibid., p. 187.

The Middle Age of Mrs. Eliot and Late Call: Angus Wilson's Traditionalism

Valerie A. Shaw*

In a brief review in the *New Yorker*, April 15, 1950, Edmund Wilson wrote, "After Evelyn Waugh, what? For anyone who has asked this question, the answer is Angus Wilson." Two decades later it remains striking that a major literary critic whose close interest in the symbolist movement in literature had already helped bring about a virtual revolution in criticism, and particularly in the reinstatement as critically respectable of late Victorian fiction, should have recognized in *The Wrong Set and Other Stories* not merely a talent of formidable promise but a writer with a very real claim to a prominent place in the history of English fiction. That this claim has long since been justified goes without saying, but this is not to admit that Angus Wilson's career since 1949 has confirmed Edmund Wilson's view of him as inheriting the cloak of satirical gaiety which Waugh had certainly seemed to drop from his shoulders in his writing of the forties. The *New Yorker* review itself points to important differences between the economic areas of society, and consequently the moral attitudes, to which these two writers address attention. Waugh and Wilson write of two different Englands, and the cloak is a bad fit after all:

> In the England of Evelyn Waugh, everybody had plenty of money or managed to get the benefit of other people's having money; one was free to be as dizzy as one pleased, and the incidental brutality and swindling were hardly noticed in the general hilarity. In the England of Angus Wilson, the money has been giving out, and the clever upper-middle-class people are struggling, with a somewhat damaged dignity, to get hold of or to hang on to whatever income or position is attainable. In this struggle, though they keep up certain forms, they are always jeering and jabbing; they do not flinch from frank hatchet work. They all dislike one another, and the author dislikes the lot. It is hard to agree with the writer of the blurb on the jacket of this book that "beneath the surface brilliance of these stories there shines Wilson's deep compassion for humanity."[1]

It is precisely with the development of a type of fiction to which Wilson's deep compassion for humanity is central and inescapable that I am concerned here. The overpersistent view that Wilson's early work is almost malevolent in its insistent satirical exposure of ugliness and humiliation is both incomplete and reductive in its failure to accommodate the element of moral concern, if not idealism, which invariably informs and impels the most biting satirist's work, no matter how detached and morally neutral he may render his fictional mask. But it is a view which can perhaps most honestly and justly be modified by considering Wilson's work as a progressive and continuing search for appropriate subjects and literary forms — appro-

*Reprinted with permission of the author from *Critical Quarterly*, 12, No. 1 (1970), 9–27.

priate in that the technical demands of realism and the moral demands of Wilson's creed of liberal humanism can be met equally without total reliance on an ironic method in which moral positives only shine through chinks in the dark realistic surface contrastively, flickeringly and precariously. We may agree with Edmund Wilson that the virtual absence of any "noble value" from Wilson's early work is damaging to its moral status in comparison with, say, the more biting side of Chekhov who also "plays the clinician for a failing organism": but who has "some sense of a human dignity that he hopes will emerge from the mess," but such agreement in no way precludes fruitful relation of Angus Wilson's work to a tradition in the English novel which is undeniably concerned with the affirmation of human dignity both in the individual and in the individual's social context.

"Tradition" would seem to be a key term here. As Rubin Rabinowitz has suggested in his recent book, *The Reaction Against Experiment in the English Novel, 1950–1960* (New York, 1967), Wilson's alignment in the context of the post-war English novel appears to be with such reactionaries as William Cooper and Snow who saw in experimentalism a pernicious distrust of the intellect itself. In their elimination of the venerable elements of character and plot, in the sheer difficulty of their novels, the experimentalists were seen as leading a subversive attack on the intellect from the inside, and insofar as the novels of Faulkner, Joyce and Woolf do command the reader's individual imagination rather than his reason and social vocabulary for an understanding and appreciation of them, Cooper's account of experimentalism as concerned with Man-alone, not Man-in-Society, may be allowed to stand as description, even though as prescription it is wildly over-stated. For all their legislative rhetoric, the pronouncements of Cooper and company in no way represent anything as systematic or coherent as the manifesto of a self-conscious literary movement, but are rather discursive justifications of the kind of fiction they themselves were writing. It is certainly true that while the *nouveau roman* was emerging in France many English writers were returning to traditional forms, even though they consistently went to contemporary society for their subject matter. In one of its strands at least — that to which Angus Wilson most clearly belongs — this trend towards traditionalism manifested itself in a revival of enthusiasm and respect for nineteenth-century art. The years since 1949 have seen a strengthening of the interest in all things Victorian, as the continued boom in Victorian studies in universities on both sides of the Atlantic alone suggests. Angus Wilson's own role in the revaluation of nineteenth-century fiction is by no means a minor one, and it is of interest and importance not only because it informs his own roles as novelist, journalist and teacher, but because it throws reflecting light on his changing attitudes towards twentieth-century fiction. In its early stages, Wilson's traditionalist elevation of the Victorians went along with, or even depended on, a devaluation of experimental writing. In the early fifties his antipathy towards Virginia Woolf's novels was unequivocally stated in criticisms which for some readers of Wilson's early work may seem to protest too much. The Wilson enthusiast may well feel some embarrassment if asked to defend, say, *Hemlock and After* from the charges of restricted class sympathies, ironic treatment of the socially ambitious and self-educated, and failure to resolve the problem of evil, which Wilson's 1950 essay on Woolf's fiction levelled. Although he has radically modified these early views, and now names Woolf as a profound influence on his own writing, Wilson's criticisms are relevant both historically as part of the reaction against experimentalism and, even more interestingly, as a basis for an appreciation of his own developing fictional preoccupations and methods. I hope to show later that Wilson's writing since 1958 has shown a gradual but marked movement towards a kind of amalgam of traditionalism and experimentalism — a blend which offers more than a ray of hope to counteract certain modern critics' sense that the contemporary novelist has "sold out" to the world of literary sameness.

By 1954 the cold war against the excess of sensibility which the traditionalists found to mar the novels of the early decades of the century seemed to have been won, and Wilson welcomed the loss of prestige of interior monologue and artistic sensitivity in favour of a return to "external observation, social setting, character set firmly in narrative and scene."[2] Out of this return were written *Hemlock and After* (1952) and *Anglo-Saxon Attitudes* (1956), both formally conventional in their dual commitment to the presentation of character and to the attempt to see society as a whole. By 1958, however, while affiliating himself with the reaction against experiments in technique and against exploration of personal sensitivity, and reiterating his traditionalist concern for the social responsibility of the novel, Wilson was warning against the hardening of the creative arteries which would result from any suggestion that there is an orthodoxy in which the traditional novel is the *ne plus ultra* of fiction and experimentalism a dangerous heresy. Wilson has been similarly quick to discern the limitations of "Great Tradition" critical dogma and to point to the stultifying effect on the artist himself of a literary climate in which approval shines only on those works whose traditionalist features win them a place in the first division of the literary league-table. His connection between creation and criticism is an Arnoldian one: "If 'literary opinion' or influential critics or even the educated reader impose upon the novelist the measure of some social myth, some dogmatic view of moral health, then eventually we may be sure that this supposedly life-enhancing myth will destroy the true life in the work of art. And the professional life-loving critic will then have satisfactorily rendered useless the only real gift that the novelist can make to the world."[3] This quotation alone would illustrate even to someone unfamiliar with Wilson's novels the anti-prescriptive, anti-doctrinaire tenor of his thought, and it is these qualities which so clearly associate him with the speculative tradition in English humanist writing. It is this tradition of tolerance and debate that Wilson himself admires when he praises the "adult" moral seriousness and concern for humanity in Austen, Thackeray, George Eliot and Trollope. Thus, in stressing that his own preoccupation is strongly a social and moral one, Wilson is in no way mitigating his distrust of abstract philosophy — the distrust which possibly accounts for his preference of the title "comedian of manners" to "satirist." The aims of Wilson's writing are superficially modest ones, as emerges clearly from the 1957 *Paris Review* interview where Wilson firmly denied that the novelist should give answers or benefit society directly. "[The novelist is] only concerned with exposing the human situation, and if his books do good incidentally that's all well and good . . . as a novelist I'm concerned solely with what I've discovered about human emotions. I attack not specific things, but only people who are set in one way of thinking. The people in my books who come out well may be more foolish, but they have retained an immediacy toward life, not a set of rules applied to life in advance."[4] Of course the perils in the path of the writer who aims, as Wilson says he does, to "touch the heart" are very real — too great a reliance on a knowledge, in himself and in his reader, of "human emotions" can all too easily produce a species of sentimentalism or nostalgic pessimism against which only romantic voluntarism can be opposed. Wilson is keenly aware of the destructive power of self-pity in art, and his rejection of his Marxist views of the thirties reveals a profound distaste for ideologies in general, and romanticism in particular, as setting too high a premium on individual over social values. More than the man who refuses to lay claim to any higher feelings than those he is quite certain of having, Wilson values the man who faces the ambiguities of his feelings and motives but yet still tries to reconcile these with a humanistic way of living and loving.

Most of his irony then, is reserved for those who deny the immediacy of life by accepting a pattern of behaviour and morality instead of self-awareness, and whose confusion of social forms with moral convictions calls in severe question the integrity of both. The main difficulty of finding a suitable form for the expression of his liberal humanism becomes, as C. B. Cox has emphasized in *The Free Spirit* (London, 1963), one version of the perennial humanist dilemma — in a world where the line between moral commitment and social posturing is often thin and difficult to discern, is there any "way of living" to which one can give clear assent? Wilson's answer is again a muted one — like Forster before him he insists that in life and art alike we must temper passion with intelligence and imagination with honest self-scrutiny. And in his fictional presentation of this insistence Wilson is, again like Forster, and like, at one farther remove, Trollope, anti-dogmatic, tolerant, and highly critical of the notion of heroism as it has been promulgated through the strain of moral absolutism in English romantic fiction. In the absence of religious sanctions "the most people can do is sometimes not to be as weak as they've been at other times" (*Paris Review*). While extending full sympathy to the weak and uncertain, however, Wilson demands a high level of self-consciousness in the characters who win his approval, and his concept of heroism emerges as a gentle but exacting one:

There's heroism in going on at all while knowing how we are made. Simple, naive people I'm impatient of, because they haven't faced up to the main responsibility of civilized man — that of facing up to what he is and to the Freudian motivations of his actions. Most of my characters have a Calvinist conscience, and this is something which in itself makes action difficult. The heroism of my people, again, is in their success in making a relationship with other human beings, in a humanistic way, and their willingness to accept some sort of pleasure principle in life as against the gnawings of a Calvinist conscience and the awareness of Freudian motivations (*Paris Review*).

Thus before the question "What ought I to do?" can be answered, a decision on the matter "What sort of person, friend, lover, father . . . am I?" must be reached. The possible conflict between the two answers naturally raises a third, "What *can* I do?" and it is in this area that Wilson's humanism meets its severest tests. As has frequently been pointed out in Wilson criticism the introspective and analytical self-awareness of his heroes, though seen as a virtue in itself, often leads to a paralysis of the will when the moment arrives for a moral decision to be enacted. Bernard Sands' realization that the humanist's celebration of moral and intellectual ambiguities may be a weakness and not a strength leads, in *Hemlock*, to a complete collapse of his confidence in the moral structure of his "way of living." Although Bernard's Forsterian vision of "Nothing behind nothing" does give way to a fresh gesture of commitment to "stand with the unfortunate," his sudden if contented death precludes the conversion of gesture into action, and the final impression left by the novel is that the humanist probes beneath the surface of his man-made creed at his own risk — at the risk of discovering that humanism offers no ultimate sanctions to life in a world which includes the irrational in such generous measure. That Bernard is himself a writer is of course of central importance in the novel, and one might argue that the unsatisfactoriness of the novel's resolution of his problems is a token of Wilson's own sense of the limitations of the fictive act as itself an enactment of humanistic beliefs.

Thematically, the irrational is analysed in *Hemlock* within the context of sexuality, and it is technically significant that sexuality in its ugliest form of commercial procuring should be represented by the novel's grotesque, Mrs. Curry. Wilson's creation of a flat embodiment of pure evil acts as a brake on his realism — it pulls the novel back from the realm of social observation into a realm which is more patently an imagined one. The aim here is to attain the type of complete unity of personal fantasy and social observation that Wilson detected as the mark of greatness in Zola's work. To stress the role of fantasy and literary device in Wilson's work is a necessary pre-requisite to an appreciation of his particular brand of realism — what ought to matter to the critic of Wilson, as to the critic of Dickens, Zola, or Balzac, is more the nature of the man's imagination than the facts that stimulate it. And Wilson has made the nature of his imagination progressively more accessible to his reader in his later and more recent work. While remaining true to his traditionalist thematic predilections — the interdependence of lives, the relation of self to society, the area between motive and act — he has experimented with modified forms of realism in order to explore more and more deeply the relation of private selves to public acts, and, more particularly, the role of the imagination in discerning and living out this relation.

The Old Men at the Zoo (1961) is generally thought of as marking a new departure into the genre of mythic fable for Wilson, but when one looks at the novels since 1958 canonically one can recognise a process of development to which *Old Men*, sandwiched between two apparently traditionalist novels, *The Middle Age of Mrs. Eliot* (1958) and *Late Call* (1964) is far from incongruous. About *Old Men* I want to say little more than to agree with Edmund Wilson that it is a C. P. Snow novel written by someone with more talent for fiction, and to note that technically the projection of the action into a mythical future, though not the greatest strength of the work, does evidence Wilson's awareness of the need for fresh fictional forms. This need can be seen as one for which space was made by the fulfilling of "the need to regroup the events of my childhood and adolescence" of which Wilson speaks in *The Wild Garden* (1963). He himself locates the climax of his working out of the "themes of my nervous crisis — the unthroning of man's innocence, man's two hells" in *The Middle Age of Mrs. Eliot*, and it is to that novel's treatment of the theme of imagination and reality that I wish to direct attention.

Like all Wilson's central characters, Meg Eliot is highly self-aware in her actions and relationships. Early in the novel her histrionic capacity for self-dramatization is firmly established — in, for example, the opening scene and the scene of the eve-of-departure party where Meg takes stock of her life to date and measures the distance she has travelled from the insecurities of an unstable childhood to star billing in the role of London hostess. What is striking here is the literary quality of Meg's response to her consciousness of role:

> It was a part she has always so wished to play. She had hated the muddled, shabby gentility of the occasional parties her mother had given in the intervals of a plucky inefficient struggle to live. She had always made excuses, had been late at the secretarial college, or had hidden upstairs in her bedroom with a book — a book probably in which the part her mother muffed was played so splendidly by Glencora Palliser or Oriane de Guermantes or Clarissa Dalloway. (Penguin edition, 1969, p. 44)

The security of Meg's sense of self as the happy wife of an eminent lawyer, a pragmatic realist whose life is led — and ended — under the motto "We'll keep going," is constantly saved from hardening into priggish self-congratulation by her application of the "salt of irony," and it is acceptable that amusement, not self-censure, should be the tone of her literary self-awareness. But perhaps Meg's lack of academic training tells against her here — a sharper literary eye might detect deeper and more sobering levels of irony in her subjective identification with these particular heroines, and in her tendency to use fiction to redeem unhappy memories. Be that as it may, in more obviously serious moments it is to novels in which the openness to life of idealistic girls is put to severer tests than, say, the gracious reception of the Duke of Omnium's guests at Gatherum Castle, that Meg turns. When the imminence of a journey beyond the known confines of Europe recalls Meg to her childhood fear of the uncertain, "The Horror in Between," she escapes from the painful consequences of thinking too precisely on the event into the familiar and well-charted worlds of Jane Austen, George Eliot, Trollope and James. There is even precision in the prescribed dosage: "She went to the bookcase and took down *Daisy Miller*, an old standby, familiar enough to take quick effect, short enough to anaesthetize only for the ugly hour or so until Bill's return, easily shaken off, leaving no after effects" (p. 35). That sedation by masterpiece is nonetheless inadequate is brought out clearly by Wilson in his forceful presentation of Meg's horrified confrontation of isolation and meaninglessness during the night-flight over the desert. Against the frightening sadness of dead anonymous nature neither the 'human interest' chatter of the old lady in the next seat, nor Meg's own novelistic attempts to fictionalize her observations — her "placing" of the stewardess — nor the reading of a great novel itself is potent. There is magic in neither the comedy nor the tragedy of *The Mill on the Floss*: "But Maggie herself, Maggie (Meg), the girl with spirit enough to follow her thoughts and dreams out of the narrow defeated home she had been born in; surely Maggie's tragedy would work its old spell upon her . . . It was no good; farmhouses, lawyers' parlours, fields, woods and fatal river — Warwickshire seemed lost forever" (p. 67). Meg is left with a tragic sense of emptiness from which Bill's faith in technological progress, his ability to grind "the whole desert down into facts and figures as dry and dead as itself" (p. 68) only affords comic relief — the incongruity of his rationalism to her predicament releases her back into a world of laughter and intimacy, but her regained calm is shattered by the irruption of the violent outer world in the meaningless death of Bill at Srem Panh. That a vision of the difficulty of keeping going in a complex world is given to Meg before Wilson turns the plot with the sudden loss of Bill is functional in extending the reference of the novel far beyond an analysis of personal grief. One of the central themes of the book is the relationship between sensitive observation and judgement, between what Meg's brother David calls "the immediate and supreme demands of moral activity" and the need for speculative detachment and isolation — and if the relationship is a problematic one for the middle-aged widow whose life-lines are suddenly cut, then it is also an artistic problem for the humanist writer. At what point does inner conviction that one's way of living is of value become egotistical dogma, an assertive rationalization of what one feels on the pulses? And conversely, at what point does ironic detachment and refusal to judge others in the interests of a celebration of felt life become pious sentimentalism or, even worse, a sign of indifference?

My suggestion here is that attitudes towards fiction can be seen, in *Mrs. Eliot,* not only "traditionally" as metaphors in characterization, but as indications of an element of greater artistic self-reflectiveness than is evident in Wilson's previous fiction. Meg's progress can be charted as parallel to that of an artist gaining control of his material. Despite her initial ability to see the events at Srem Panh as melodrama, Meg rejects all attempts to convert melodrama into patterned tragedy with Bill as romantic hero, and the moments where self-irony fails her and she lapses into self-pitying fantasies do not blind her to a realization that arbitrariness and chaos lie at the end of all introspection, and that one must continually short-circuit the painful process of self-examination by forming relationships — and furthermore relationships in which the critical sense is not suspended: "She tried to rest content with this 'live and let live' view, but it was no good. Puritan or not, she was made differently — made to judge; and at this critical juncture she must make judgements or cease to exist" (p. 222). Indeed Meg's commitment to judgement is even more exacting than the novelist's — at one point she reflects: "All the same, Proust could afford to find human relationships insufficient — or at any rate he could make Marcel do so — because he knew that he was to find an answer in his writing. I've got to find some meaning in life itself" (pp. 226–7). Within the scope of the novel itself, Meg comes closest to finding such meaning in the reconstruction of her relationship with her brother David, whom she joins in his pastoral retreat Andredaswood after a frightening vision of her ageing futility in a fantasy of endless mirrors of awareness. David, like Meg, has looked to the authority of art for a way out of the humanist dilemma, but in facing the prospect of a comparable bereavement he has gone farther towards acceptance of loneliness — and therefore a measure of selfishness — as a necessary condition of civilized man. He meets the contradiction between the sweetness of the voices in the howling wilderness and the "selfishness, self-assertion, ideals, dreams and so on" which lie behind those voices by measuring their magnitude; "Beethoven, Shakespeare, Flaubert, Mozart . . . were the only ones that could defy the discipline of living" (pp. 165–6). So David too has a kind of private "great tradition." But in his love for Gordon he is ruthless in the avoidance of sentimentalism; when Gordon's courage momentarily fails, David wishes "that he were able to say, I observe, I don't judge. But this sentimentalism, that passed as a wide and deep love of humanity, as the gentle wisdom taught by the years, was surely the negation of real respect for men. It would never do, least of all where respect and love were involved. Where you respected and loved, you esteemed, you judged" (p. 167). Yet this reconciliation of opposites is a shield of self-control through which the irrational can still thrust; witnessing Gordon's physical suffering David writes to Meg "an incoherent letter of anger that zigzagged across the

writing paper like random flashes of lightning. He accused his own carefully built up detachment of being only a self-induced blindness to the Evil
that governed the Universe. He railed against the childish conceit that had
let him suppose his own will and reason to be meaningful in the logic of
nightmare. 'God forgive me for prating about humanism, pretending that
pain and evil could be reduced to a pigmy human stature!' " (p. 196).
The letter brings Meg to a new sense of the limitations of sincerity if
it becomes a barrier to active love; "Do I *mean* it? Do they need it was a
better question. At least let me seek for the words, she decided, and with
them I may discover my emotions" (p. 197). Shortly after this the novel's
chief subtlety emerges as the treatment of the interaction of the lives of Meg
and David, representative as they are — though this is to crudify — of ques-
tive adherents to principles of active and passive humanism.

Early in the relationship David is firm in his insistence on the distinction between withdrawal and acceptance, the former being the necessary
"simmering down of human personality, of human achievement too . . . in
order that we can start up again" of which he speaks to Gordon's mother in
Book II (p. 237). As Book III progresses, however, we feel his grip on the
distinction weaken as he and Meg retire into "easeful communion" in which
"books and the past — their own recreation of a dead world, the creations of
other worlds by men now dead" mingle together (p. 279). This is art, not
life — as is their revival of the games of their adolescence; the parodying of
stock type novels, the game of Observations in which judgements are not
allowed, and , climactically, the attempt to build up "a little island culture
of work and pleasure deliberately kept simple, and of loneliness accepted"
(pp. 333–4) by resuming together the literary research which David had
abandoned for the vitality of nursery gardening. The dangers of the academic version of the game of Observations are exposed in David's attempt
"to fight back to the limit of its critical usefulness his natural rage for irony
that, playing around these simple, defenceless ideas, might destroy the
truth that he surely believed to be within them" (p. 334). To fight irony back
too far is to risk falling into the trap of literary sentimentalism — to wish that
Godwin's St. Leon had been allowed a life of uninterrupted tranquillity,
and to ignore the springs of Calvinist conscience which can in fact transcend necessitarianism by nourishing the ethic of work through which
David's philosophy of withdrawal was earlier enlivened and justified. His
appreciation of Meg's "vitality and surprisingness" on their last evening together is, paradoxically, a quietist acceptance of "sentimental, cosy futility"
and a denial of the separateness of the individual's unique truth. The ending
of the novel may appear pessimistic in its uncompromising refusal to build a
habitable bridge between David's loneliness and self-denial and Meg's passionate curiosity in, and involvement with, people — in this it is reminiscent
of *A Passage to India* — but it is indirectly affirmative of the priority of the
ragged edges of life over the self-contained work of imaginative art. Over
the doctoral dissertation too: that a coffee-table book on the garden flowers

of Africa may be a more valid expression of vitality than either the objectivity at which David's research aims or Meg's earlier subjective confusion of the traditional novel with life, is surely not the least telling point made in the closing pages of *Mrs. Eliot.*

Late Call is generally considered as a return from the use of moral fable in *Old Men* to the simpler style of social realism; and as a presentation of lower-middle-class life in a New Town at the beginning of the sixties, the novel may seem to be Wilson's most traditional to date. But it is wrong to see it as simply his "Scenes from Provincial Life." The novel reveals a considerable tempering of the satiric sense and proliferation of sub-plots which typify Wilson's earlier work, and in this, and in the furthering of his interest in the penetration and understanding of the feminine mind, the novel represents a furthering of the thematic and formal interests released in the writing of *Mrs. Eliot.* The ageing central character, Sylvia Calvert, confronts not only the difficulties of retirement from an active career as hotel manageress — a less genteel version of Meg's Aid for the Elderly — but also those of adjusting to life with her widowed son Harold and his family in Carshall New Town where the primacy is on youth and the aged are anomalous. Much of the novel is presented inwardly from Sylvia's point of view, and since she is, unlike Meg Eliot, and rather like Dickens' Esther Summerson, not a conventionally "clever" person, it may seem impertinent to suggest that she is an authorial *alter ego.* Yet insofar as Wilson uses her narrative as a vehicle for the exploration of the proper role of art in life, this is exactly what I take her to be. The value of myth in helping one to cope with the muddle of living is a central topic of the novel.

Sylvia's need for sustaining myths arises in part from the sense of worthlessness which the events of the Prologue have, quite literally, beaten into her as a child. In the Prologue, Mrs. Longmore, a fake liberal placed with marvellous economy in the world of cosy sentiment and genteel mannerism by Wilson's power of mimicry, has encouraged in Sylvia a sense of specialness which leads the child to break out from the duty-bound restrictiveness of her Calvinist home for an afternoon of spontaneous joy. The Knapps Meadow incident is a liberated expression of immediacy toward life — it is as though Caddy Jellyby had taken Leonard Bast's adventurous walk under the stars. But Mrs. Longmore's prurient and punitive reaction to the child's enactment of her teachings reveals the woman's belief in imagination and a "sense of wonder" as a layer of whimsy which ices over "sophisticated, sinister fears" of physicality. Can we expect more of someone whose powers of verbal imagination are at full stretch in her simile of "miniature mountain climbers" for the heels of her "sensible white shoes" which topple ludicrously over the muddy ridges of the farmyard? The disillusionment caused by Mrs. Longmore's rejection of Sylvia's imagination is carried into adult life as an intense dislike of histrionics and false sentiment — "It's only the fakes that carry on in public" (p. 33), "But that was it, people were so insincere, they exaggerated everything" (p. 35)[5] — and as a channelling of her own imaginative powers into passive acceptance of modern "folk myths." She sees life largely through pop-culture — Denise Robbins's advice columns, romantic fiction, and the T.V. serial "Down Our Way" of which the most profound philosophy is contained in Mrs. Harker's "I don't know, I really don't know." To Syliva there is consolation in mimetic acceptance of muddle as the essence of life; "It was sad in a way how little you *could* know in a busy life, but repeating the tag in Mrs. Harker's comic voice somehow made it seem all right, something everyone felt. You could stretch your legs, scratch where it itched, and go to sleep" (p. 45). It must be stressed here that Wilson's purpose in the presentation of the comfort Sylvia derives from fictions is not to *épater le bourgeois* by sneering at the myths promulgated by mass media. Indeed one of his aims in this novel is, I think, to show that vitality and vulgarity are not as mutually exclusive as the modern tendency to think of "Civilization" as lying among the ruins of time would suggest. Certainly Sylvia's authentication of her own humour and practical tenderness from Mrs. Harker's home-spun philosophy is presented as perfectly allowable. Away from a "busy life," however, in the automated, temperature-controlled, gardenless world of the 'The Sycamores' where rose-bushes are of nuisance-value and house-keeping is done by roster, Sylvia's capacity to "express her own nature, one at once practical and tender" (p. 16) in acts of kindness and love is superannuated. As her sense of uselessness increases she becomes less and less capable of recognizing that "books and life [are] not the same" (p. 50). The latest "Miss Clitheroe" book, for instance, comes too close to Sylvia's own sense of tragic reality to be borne, and fiction becomes progressively less proof against the chilling sense of vastness which Sylvia experiences when she looks out into the "awful Midlands" for the first of many times in Chapter 1 (p. 69). The challenge of the Midlands is akin to that of the desert in *Mrs. Eliot*, and Sylvia's gradual mastery of it, like Meg's, is a progress which parallels the loosening of the grip of obsessive images on her mind. So it is only after she emerges from self-identification with Wardress Webb, Mary Queen of Scots, the elderly victim of Sidney Fox and other figures of oppressed womanhood that she begins to defeat the vision of futility which attends her at Harold's production of *Look Back in Anger*. To Harold, Osborne's play is of value only as it enhances his progressivist belief in the organic unity of New Town life: "I think Osborne's hit off exactly the sort of old-fashioned, unneighbourly jungle-world Midland town that the New Towns are going to replace. The very sordidness of it all may make Carshallites count their blessings a bit" (p. 125). To him the Midlands are plain "awful" in the slang sense. But in Sylvia the mixture of tenderness and brutality in Jimmie Porter's character touches off deeper and more primitive responses. Intellectually baffled by the play, she feels blackness closing in on her: "She tried to attend carefully to the rest of the scene, but across her vision there ran and stumbled and fell a line of fat naked old women — some haggard and ancient as witches, others with rouge and peroxide hair and earrings — and in their eyes the uncomprehending terror of cows going to the knacker's yard" (p. 155). The prospect of Carshall spreading its tentacles further into "that vast stretch of country that she looked out upon from her window each night" fills Sylvia with a similar feeling of panic and emptiness from which the physical symptoms of her high blood-pressure actually give relief; "As she visualized the scene her pulse beat more quickly, and giddiness or shortness of breath intervened to save her from contemplating the struggle . . . Black desolate thoughts would creep in at such times that only made her more hungry for the penned-up safety of 'The Sycamores' " (p. 172).

Out of this containing safety Sylvia constantly looks away from the darkness to the outer world in the hope of some consoling message. She writes to Miss Priest — the old woman whose niece's murder is, to those who subscribe to the adulation of Youth, an outrage of natural order — in the hope that she may benefit from the good sense and courage that she remembers in the independent spinster. But when it comes, Miss Priest's reply is without "healing magic" (p. 203). More consoling is the old Scot's Easter Sunday sermon which Sylvia attends shortly after the witch-like hump-backed old Pole has glided into her consciousness, and the social worker Sally Bulmer has brutally reproached her for retreating from realities into the "rubbishy pretence" of historical romance and tele (p. 180). The sermon strikes a direct blow at the doctrine of good works as so vigorously preached by Harold, Sally and — from the grave — Harold's wife Beth; it is a serious, if somewhat burlesqued, affirmation of the essential loneliness of man and the mystery of human life. More than this, it affirms the possibility of something new, though not unprepared-for, in the world of Wilson's novels — the possibility of Grace as an answer to determinism:

> "Is there nothing we can do to help us to God's Grace? Indeed there is. The Lord forbid that I should preach to you folks any strait-jacketed Calvinistic doctrine. There's a good deal you can do. You can be toward. You can go out to meet God's Grace. Go out to mind who you are. Go out, not into the busy clamour of getting and spending, nor even into the soothing clamour of good works. No, go out into the dreadful silence, into the dark nothingness. Maybe ye are no but a wisp of straw, but if you go out to face the fire, out through the desert and the night, then indeed may the Lord send the light of his face to shine upon you then indeed may you be visited by that Grace which will save your soul alive" (p. 186).

Perhaps Wilson's talent for pastiche tells against the emphasis of this episode, which he uses to score satirically against the intolerance and pomposity of Harold's agnosticism. And he *is* having fun with the fire and brimstone of Scots pulpit rhetoric — but the weight of Sylvia's quiet "I found some of what he said rather helpful" is devoid of local irony. The Lord forbid that Angus Wilson should preach to us a doctrine of divine grace — and he does not — but shortly after the sermon, when Sylvia's morbid fancies have reached a phantasmagoric climax in her imaginative recreation of

Haigh's murder of Mrs. Durand-Deacon, in the mirror of whose "unanswered love" and "unappeased loneliness" she sees her own, Sylvia does begin to face her lonely fears in fact, not fictionalized versions of fact.

Sylvia's gradual movement out into the dark nothingness coincides with an attempt to find a way back to the true countryside, and thus to her own childhood. The task is hard when all paths lead back to Town Centre, and first Gorman's Wood, then Sugley Park fail to offer more than tangled squalor or a "strange gale" of imprecise memories (p. 197). When Sylvia does finally manage to break out of the controlled Carshall rural environment, the episode is deliberately kept in low key: "She had sought it so long that she half expected some miraculous change in her feelings to come about from the discovery, to walk straight into some enchanted land of good or evil, but all that came from that first two hours walk along the fields was a laddered stocking and very tired feet" (p. 199). But Wilson renders the dream-like nature of Sylvia's search in language which is at once evocative of the imminence of absolutes, and yet still entirely true to the unanalytical cast of the woman's mind. The images in the extended paragraph where Sylvia grapples with a "vague idea of return" are so much the product of her individual imagination that even the echoes of *Hamlet* seem convincingly hers as much as the author's:

> She had never analysed what revelation of horror or hope her superstitious awe of the surrounding country expected; or even perhaps thought quite consciously whether she expected any revelation at all. She sensed only that the long familiar sketchy outlines of her grey life had now suddenly so blurred and dissolved that she had altogether lost herself. If she could have hidden herself in the tightest nutshell so that from its very pressure, from its very narrowness, she could find some shape in life however small, she would have sought such a cramped cell immediately. But "The Sycamores," she now knew, was not that prison of peace. As for escape, it too had failed — neither Mrs. Harker nor Queen Anne nor Lady Violet nor Wardress Webb could swallow up what remained of Sylvia Calvert; on the contrary, the great comforting engulfing whale of fiction seemed now to have died on her, so that she looked out through its ribs to nothingness; and even that skeleton was decaying into dust from which nothing more came to her than the sweetly sick smell of romantic falsity. (pp. 199–200)

And lest this seem prose of sophistication far beyond Sylvia's reach, Wilson concludes her thought-sequence with the homely image of a child's hopelessly knitted jumper; "It seemed clear to Sylvia that she was that jumper" (p. 200). The strength of the writing in this passage is in the firmness with which it is woven into the narrative pattern of Sylvia's quest. She has constantly thought in terms of animal imagery — recall the way she sees Harold's kitchen equipment as alarming "white monsters" (p. 81) — and if this paragraph does not leap off the page as might have happened in a work employing overtly symbolist technique, it is because of the controlled way

in which Wilson sustains Sylvia's idiom.[6] Narratively too, he sustains Sylvia's muddled approach toward a sense of worth for some considerable time
after these first gropings for an idea which still seems "more something she
had been told than any personal conviction" (p. 200). There are no Mara-
bar Caves in the Midlands. We have the recurrence of obsessive, though
diminishingly potent, images of "some old woman pulped into nullity" (p.
201); the temporary release from numbed anxiety into practical tenderness
in the merciful killing of the wounded rabbit; the revulsion from pity which
this act and its association with Miss Priest causes, and the total failure of
personal communication on the evening of the Ten Pin Bowling match, as
farther dramatizations of the cruelty of Sylvia's April. All these incidents
are suggestive beyond themselves, but never does Wilson allow them to lose
touch with the ground of surface realism and to sail off into the aether of
pure symbolism.

What then is one to make of the interpolated "Old Woman's Story," so
conscious an artifice that it might seem like its eighteenth-century precedents, to have relevance only to some abstract level of meaning? My suggestion is that the tale is a concentrated presentation of an inadequate
imagination which, in contrast to Sylvia's, lacks the power to transform
perceptions and experiences and to cope with their sadness. The encounter
between the two old women has a hallucinatory quality, largely produced
by the frequent earlier appearances of the humpbacked Pole on the fringes
of Sylvia's awareness. Previously little more than a portentous extension of
the image of age and suffering associated with Miss Hutton's hump in
Chapter I, the old woman now emerges from the twilight of superstition
into reality. Although she has been through experiences which are factually
grimmer than anything Sylvia has had to bear, her story is a self-pitying,
humourless and totally unreliable slab of folk whimsy. It is also a kind of
reductio ad absurdum of the cultural and intellectual pretentiousness
which we meet in Harold's colour-supplement Film Society name-drop-
ping — the old woman's citation of authorities for her aphoristic pessimism
is dazzling and quite outrageous. Here are a couple: "And the child makes
the woman, as you will read in Grillparzer"; "As the great Count Tolstoy
says — this is my homeland" — and how many of our literature students
could provide footnotes for Lermontov's thought-provoking reference to
"capricious woman," or — even more exciting to research this one — for "the
situation of Schnitzler's comedy"? The bogus references seem to have pulled
wool over more eyes than the naive Sylvia Calvert's — critics have not been
overquick to pick up the clues to the old woman's pseudo-eclectic familiarity with "World Literature." Nevertheless, the story does act not only as an
alienating effect which deflects the reader's attention out with the confines
of Sylvia's mind, and thus prepares for the full impact of the thunderstorm
scene, but also as an ironic reaffirmation of Sylvia's qualities of humour and
compassion — the qualities which make for Grace in the secular world of
this novel. Sylvia misses the irony and allows the old woman, like Harold, to

patronize her "ignorance," but if we fail to see that she herself embodies a living alternative to the woman's generalized acceptance of darkness, then we will necessarily find the thunderstorm and Sylvia's act of heroism a contrived, obtrusively "traditionalist" device to get the author out of a tight narrative corner. Of course the storm *is* a transformation scene out of fairytale, but more importantly it is a dramatisation of Sylvia's confrontation of the darkness with that very combination of good sense and courage which the old Polish woman lacked utterly and which Sylvia recognized in Miss Priest, but not in herself. That we have seen this combination in action throughout the novel in Sylvia's dealings with her family, and particularly in her tolerant care of her impossible husband Arthur, makes sense of our calling this a "Self-Recognition Scene." In this scene, the heaviness in Sylvia's body, in her thoughts, and in the very air conveys a sense of oppressiveness in which inner and outer meet. When the deluge crashes into this stillness, Sylvia is left face to face with the fears which have pursued her throughout the novel. Her earlier images of predatory forces crystallize in a moment of sheer terror: "All the pressed in, tight packed nervous terrors of the past months burst out with the storm's explosion; yet at the same time all wandering fragments of nightmare came together in one overwhelming flash and roar. Whatever it was had found her, driven her from cover, and now would strike her down" (pp. 222–3). But Sylvia "is toward" and is rewarded for "Going out to mind who she is" — she is conveyed into the pastoral New World of liberal child-care, grass-roots anti-whimsy and kisses on the mouth. That Sylvia is saved by saving the life of the Egan child is not, however, the emblematic sentimentalism it would have been had Wilson ended on that idyllic note of Victorianism. For it is precisely within the security of Egan affection that Sylvia fights for, and gains, true salvation. The temptation is similar to that of Andredaswood — to pacify an unhappy past by transforming its memories into romantic fiction. The ghost of Mrs. Longmore is laid only when Sylvia admits the selectivity of the reminiscences with which she has entertained — and dissatisfied — the child Mandy. The decisive moment when Shirley asks "Weren't you ever happy as a kid?" is quietly touching in its simple exposure of the difficulties of being honest about past sorrows: "Oh, it wasn't as bad as all that. Yes, it *was* pretty bad sometimes. I don't think I really knew how bad" (p. 242). Here, she arrives at where she started from and knows the place for the first time, and her reward is to be freed from "the guilt of her own unhappiness" (p. 244).

Furthermore, her emancipation from the past makes a new future possible. Sylvia's energies can now be released into the business of living in Carshall — she refuses to make concessions to Harold's notions of culture and propriety, notably in her clear-sighted rejection of the false chic of the Chinese restaurant in the marvellous scene where she stands by all the vulgarity of her relationship with Arthur; she feels a new sense of pride in Carshall Community Centre; most movingly, she rebels against Harold's self-centred emotional myopia and extends full imaginative sympathy to his homosexual son, Ray. Harold is deaf to her advice that, once in the darkness, "You have to go on through it" (p. 282) and renounces Ray completely when the boy asserts his sense of self and refuses his father's compromise offer of reconciliation. Sylvia's response is that of the active humanist. Even if her comprehension and articulation are incomplete, she has her own eloquence: "You can't wash your hands of someone you love" . . . "But I'll tell you this, if nobody else goes to stay with Ray, I shall. He's been a lovely boy to me" (pp. 297, 8).

That most readers have preferred the articulate self-awareness of Meg Eliot to Sylvia's capacity to see herself in the milder ironic light of the ridiculous may say as much about our cultural snobbery as about Angus Wilson's relative success in the creation of these heroines. It could, of course, be argued that the impatience with "the simple and naive" mentioned in the 1957 *Paris Review* interview survived into the sixties and made it difficult for Wilson to elevate the stature of Sylvia sufficiently to make her capacity to endure the emotional privation of life in Carshall while yet retaining her vitality and openness to life, as convincing and forceful as his sympathy with her requires. Certainly the book is short of irony, if by that we mean the sharp comic detachment of which Meg Eliot and Simon Carter are capable, and which is shown in almost all Wilson's novels to be a saving attitude to life. But if the sympathetic presentation of the simple and naive is notoriously difficult — we have only to think of Fanny Price — it is by no means exclusive of irony, as again *Mansfield Park* illustrates. In *Late Call* Wilson not only uses irony in Sylvia's self-characterization, in the characterization of minor figures, but in his use of literary stereotypes — the Prologue, the introduction of Harold by letter, the sermon, the interpolated tale, the thunderstorm combine to add an extra dimension to his treatment of the relationship between private fantasy and public myth. Insofar as they are reminders that we are reading a novel, and not eating a slice of life, these alienating features are potentially satirical of the reader who, like Meg and Sylvia in their worst moments, make a private orgy out of their reading.

Novels are about reality, they are not reality itself — an obvious enough platitude, but one which is perhaps forgotten by readers who stress Wilson's realism. The man who makes imaginative creations is himself part of the reality he writes about, and the traditionalist writer who enmeshes in his art a sense of its very difficulties is not, as one sometimes suspects people think, changing his spots by putting on some sort of "experimentalist" disguise. He is simply increasing the range of experience with which his fiction deals, and if the relations between art and reality enter the narrative stream they do not thereby sacrifice their thematic status to considerations of pure form. For these reasons, I would wish to modify the view that finds in *No Laughing Matter* (1967) evidence that Wilson's creative powers have become inhibited by the traditional form, and that in using literary pastiche to explore the interrelations of art and reality, literature and life, he is discernibly changing gear. Certainly this novel does bring to the surface much that was previously included in the original *donné* of Wilson's creative act — it is self-reflexive in the use of irony as the instrument of ruthless examination of the ironic approach, to life *and* to literature; and in the breadth of its historical scope it may be seen as an encylopaedic personal and artistic stock-taking. But this is nothing new in Wilson's fiction — it is evidence of growth and development, and if Wilson is asking more of his reader in the way of literary acumen, then he is also asking more of his own powers of analysis. Labels simply don't stick to him.

What then of the Waugh tradition? One constant feature of Wilson's work which represents the continuation of Waugh wit in all its strengths and without many of its weaknesses is his scrupulous avoidance of sentimental nostalgia. The endings of *Brideshead Revisited* and *Late Call* are not dissimilar — both books are concerned with the faculty of imaginative memory in their protagonists and, to an extent, as Wilson's punning title suggests, with vocation. But Wilson's concentration on the present and its new social types has, although consistently related to the solidities of a world of order, involved no self-indulgent nostalgia for the twenties or the old institutions of Church and State. His pastoralism is rooted in the present, and within that present we may find the constancy of his belief in the gentle but challenging arts of friendship, compassion and self-awareness as relevant as his satirical exposure of their distortion. For one reader at least, his fiction goes far towards meeting Wallace Stevens' requirement of art — that it should help people lead their lives.

In 1956 Edmund Wilson asked, somewhat previously, after Angus Wilson, what? and suggested that the answer was Kingsley Amis. But although Amis' novels are in the same general comic tradition as those of Waugh and Wilson, they do take us one step farther into flux and chaos, and show us a world in which luck is more potent than self-knowledge. Sylvia Calvert may well expect to be taken at face value when she tells Harold that finding a way out of darkness is simply "a bit of luck," but the force of the novel suggests that grace does operate in and for the courageous and the compassionate. Besides, a much more intriguing question is "After *No Laughing Matter*, what?"

Notes

1. "Emergence of Angus Wilson," reprinted in *The Bit Between My Teeth* (London, 1965), 270–273.

2. "Arnold Bennett's Novels," *London Magazine*, I, 60 (October 1954).

3. "If It's New and Modish, Is it Good?," *New York Times Book Review*, July 2, 1961, p. 12.

4. "Angus Wilson (The Art of Fiction XX)," *Paris Review*, No. 17 (Autumn-Winter 1957), p. 89.

5. Penguin edition (London, 1968).

6. Cf. Rabinowitz (op cit.), p. 95; "Another fault which is connected with Wilson's traditionalism is his weakness in using symbolism." That Wilson's style is inimical to symbolism is not necessarily a defect; although Rabinowitz is right in naming *Old Men* as Wilson's most symbolic work, he confuses descriptive differences of degree with qualitative differences of kind when he talks of *Late Call* as "a reversion of his usual less symbolic style."

Metaphors of Enclosure: Angus Wilson's *The Old Men at the Zoo*   Irving Malin*

The Old Men at the Zoo begins brilliantly: "I opened the large central window of my office room to its full on that fine May morning. Then I stood for a few moments breathing in the soft warm air that was charged with the scent of white lilacs below. The graceful flamingos, shaded from flushed white to a robust tinned salmon, humped and coiled on their long stilts; a Florida pelican picked and nuzzled comically with its orange pouched bill among its drab brownish wing feathers; the herring gulls surprised me, as they did every day by their size and their viciously hooked beaks." The narrator, we can see, is enclosed; he wants to breathe freely. There is an opposition between the room (business, restriction) and the natural scene. But this opposition is subtly developed — it is not black and white — and it continually offers the element of *surprise*. The narrator is a keen observer, noting subtle tints (shades) and refusing to let go completely. He is an ironist. He recognizes the comedy of the pelican — and of his situation in the middle of things.

Simon Carter, the narrator, is an administrator — as we would judge from his carefully ordered, qualified rhythms — but he is also a "naturalist." He yearns for "order" *and* "disorder." Thus when he finds that a giraffe in the Zoo (where he works) has killed a young guard, he is greatly disturbed. What went wrong? Did the giraffe have too much freedom? Was the guard careless? Simon's questions are related to the personal definitions (and problems) he has never mastered. At thirty-five he is still *unformed*. Perhaps these reasons explain why he feels "furious with the shapeless, purposeless emotions that so meaningless an accident could bring." He recognizes that he is desperately involved — in order to banish morbid thoughts, to be "trapped," he thinks of his wife's thighs: "living bodies to banish the dead. . . ." He is unsuccessful.

Simon is, perhaps, more upset than the other administrators, Dr. Leacock, Lord Godmanchester, and Sir Robert Falcon, who can simply call the accident "unfortunate" and let it disappear (or use it for their different political ends). He is less political than they — this characteristic almost kills him later — and he refuses to accept all things as *means*. He is an idealist; he

*Reprinted with permission from *Old Lines, New Forces: Essays on the Contemporary British Novel, 1960–1970*, ed. Robert K. Morris (Rutherford, N.J.: Fairleigh Dickinson University Press), pp. 1–11.

worries about law and order. He feels enclosed by abstractions and by personal needs (which have not been thoroughly explored). When he thinks of going to the window again, he recognizes that he cannot view the natural scene in the same way as he did once. He knows more than the animals; he cannot be a free, unthinking beast: "I went to the window but the long legged grace of the flamingos seemed grace no longer, only stilted absurdity; and the pelicans' comicality, mere swollen folly."

Simon discusses the accident with Leacock and Falcon. Both men use it as a convenient excuse. (Simon also does, but his ultimate goal is self-knowledge.) Leacock insists that the "antiquated enclosures mean danger to life." He wants "limited liberty" — a reserve in which animals can roam within larger limits than a Zoo — and he maintains that the giraffe acted out of fear of — or anger at — imprisonment. Falcon, on the other hand, believes in the old ways. He accepts the enclosures as "natural," helpful and necessary. There are several ironies that shade the matter. Leacock, as we shall learn, pursues the idea of "limited liberty," but he has never defined *correct* limits. His daughter, Harriet, is a violent, nymphomaniacal believer in complete freedom — perhaps as a result of his obsessive views of liberty. Leacock cannot administer; he has not ordered himself (or his daughter) in any meaningful pattern. Falcon goes against his own "understated" beliefs. He constantly goes on expeditions, choosing openness rather than enclosure. He is a dandy. He is arrogant. One description captures his willful freedom: "The exhibitionist quality of his defiantly asserted archaism was thrown into highlight as he stood near the exit. His small, curly brimmed bowler hat, his broadly checked tweeds, his umbrella, gloves and vivid chestnut suede shoes seemed such a ridiculous challenge to the open necked shirts and billowing trousers of the ordinary summer visitors around him."

Simon is an alien, a strange "animal," in this setting of political deceit and corruption. He tries to follow his ideals, but he cannot get through the masks of Falcon and Leacock. He is prone to anxiety. It is, in fact, exaggerated when he confronts "old men" — self-deluded opportunists — and war: "Then the print swam in front of me, the letters diving and blurring and fading only to shape themselves into the one word — War. The stab of terror was sharp. It was also familiar. It carried memories of similar apprehensions right back into my childhood." He recognizes that somehow the accident, the muddled feelings he has, and the threatening war (which will be fought about ideas of restriction — should England remain independent or join Uni-Europe?) are bound together in one "tall story."

Simon continues to feel hostile toward the "old men." When he enters the Lion House, he believes that he "is a prisoner of the caged beasts." No longer can he delight in their sensual freedom: "I was in the wrong place. . . ." And he sees in the various Declarations of Political Powers — at one point America and Russia warn England and Uni-Europe to refrain from war — more symbols of his self-imprisonment. He even fades away from Martha, who does not share his ironic, occasionally priggish views of life.

"Wars, Domestic and Foreign" — a chapter title — begin to accelerate. Rumors move rapidly; sides are defined and redefined. I stress the shifting alliances because their erratic movements are constantly contrasted to metaphors of enclosure. The metaphors, indeed, *battle* each other. Simon, for example, hopes to "find the end to the bifurcation of his life" in the "deciduous woods." He yearns for natural freedom, unlimited liberty — he embraces the open air of the first chapter — but he cannot surrender completely to the "chance flow" of things. He must make patterns and shape movements. In the most powerful scene so far Simon searches for badgers in their natural setting — the Zoo has been given some of Lord Godmanchester's land as a reserve — and he hopes to capture their innocent beauty. Thus the details function metaphorically when he tells us: "A light breeze blew dead against me. The bracken's scent brought serial memories stretching far back into my childhood. . . . The situation was ideal." He is "free" at last; he has recovered the pleasures of childhood; he has found some fresh air. But even here Simon must make order — he waits for the proper light to study the badgers; he notes carefully shades and angles. The important thing is that he is not tortured by details (as he is at the Zoo), that he is not enclosed by duties of administration.

There are several ironies. Simon discovers in the midst of "anticipated glory" that he is exactly where he told Harriet, Leacock's daughter, he would be. By chance he has situated himself in a *fixed* position. (Wilson is shrewd here in suggesting the tangle of chance, fate, and free will in human experience). Therefore he is not so liberated as he imagined. Suddenly Harriet approaches and touches him. He finds that he is as trapped by her advances as by designs of mad "old men." Although no sexual event of great importance occurs, Simon admits that he cannot be a naturalist: "The setts by the sandy bank would yield nothing again for some nights."

He continues to be an administrator: "I got through my work, got through it competently but it was only with the surface of my mind, my body and my spirit were smothered in a fog of unhappiness. . . ." He is caged; he dislikes the "muddling, maddening, blundering" others who come near him. Because of his rigidity — he is more "limited" as a result of his sexual frustration since Martha has left him — he cannot function freely *even as administrator.* He does not know how to define substantial duties and limits. It is appropriate that he identifies with a lynx that is shot. The lynx has asserted its freedom in the reserve by threatening someone. It has overstepped the bounds — even in the open air! — and it is a shadow of himself: "It seemed so little ferocious, more like a poor house cat dazed from a glancing blow of a bicycle wheel."

More animals rebel and are punished. Often the punishment (as in the case of the lynx) is unjust. But Simon is unable to fight the growing madness of Leacock; he is on the edge himself. When Harriet is found dead — she has been attacked by her pet (her sexual object) — he almost goes over the edge. It is ironic that the incident occurs near Simon's favorite badger setts. The incident is an extreme one; it not only calls into question Leacock's judgment — he suddenly gives up his Directorship — it forces Simon to decide about his future plans, and to take a step.

Simon acts after his wife returns from America. (The war scare has lifted for the time being; she feels that she can safely live in England once more, although she does leave their children with her sister in California.) He gains new faith in the ability to balance things; he believes his hope "of blending town and country, the Zoo's office life of human contact and the Reserve's peace of heightened sight and sound was not an absurdity." He appreciates "secret unity." He need not be torn apart by "pleasure and duty." (*Tearing* is an interesting choice of word; it links the destructive accident involving the giraffe, the attack of Harriet's dog, and his own inner tensions.)

Martha functions here as support. Her approval of his decision to remain at the Zoo is crucial. She becomes a foil, as it were, to the "old men" because she is able to express things clearly. She is honest, intelligent, and forthright. This is not to say that she is a believable creation; she is too shadowy to compel our belief in the midst of administrative battles.

The British Day approaches. Falcon wants it to be a celebration of old virtues. The "quaintness" of Victorian Zoos will be shown to the public; the "antiquated enclosures," now slightly open, will be made attractive. But Simon realizes that the exotic past is not enough; odd displays and "manic-depressive" preparations by Falcon are as imprisoning to the spirit as unlimited liberty. The Zoo becomes a variety show, trapping people into comic roles and not allowing them to breathe freely. Simon tells us that Falcon "enrolled them somehow in his happy absurd antics and mixed them in with the staff and the contractors' extinction." Unlike Falcon he holds on to his sanity, as shaky as it may be. He does not let go, perverting his senses. His irony remains. The metaphors of enclosure and freedom are used again. Simon informs us that "many people at that time ran away from London, but only the foolish thought that there was anywhere to run to." He goes about his business; he stays in one place (even though it is stifling.) *He battles triviality and apocalypse.*

It is characteristic of Simon to think of the animals' survival. Despite all the talk of war and the accompanying frenzy of "old men," he believes that he must take measures in case *the world does not end*. When he proposes "safety measures" for the public and for "the animals in our care" — a sacred duty — he is attacked by Falcon: "He gave a roar like a lion and came for me. Youth tells and I had sprung aside before he reached me." Simon sees the arrival of the "age of violence," the age in which "old men" become wild beasts. He looks at Falcon on the ground and feels a "strange and unfriendly sense of power." But he will not exert unlimited liberty; instead of shooting him (even if it would help the public), he places a cushion under his head and locks him in the room. (Falcon must be "caged" for public safety.)

The Day arrives. The Zoo is brightly illuminated; the "whole Gardens seemed to be flooded with light of every colour — blue, rose, green, amber, purple" — and this lighting is in marked contrast to the natural shades Simon saw in the first chapter. Everything is garish, undisciplined, and dangerous. The "pantomime transformation" demonstrates the reckless and unthinking Falcon. Although Simon would like to submit to the "prettiness" and die, he cannot waver in his duty. (Wilson shows us how that duty increases as others pursue unlimited liberty.)

There is a joke. Just as the ceremony is about to reach a climax (there is a sexual aura about the festivity) the sirens wail: "And then came the crackling, whistling thudding sound of the universe." Simon describes chaos in a precise, thoughtful way and his comments, although superficially calm, ironically oppose the effect of the explosion. The technique is powerful. We do not know how to respond. Should we yield to apocalypse and consider only the bombs? Should we hopefully note Simon's administrative power? I believe that Wilson wants us to be caught in the middle and, finally, to admire his hero's real sense of duty.

In the next few hours Simon (and the others) work "like beavers to repair our dam against a tide that any minute would engulf us and all our works forever." The animal simile is important — men have been likened to animals throughout the novel (more in "wildness" than in work) — but the dam is even more so. Simon recognizes the need for *shelter*, shelter that does not inhibit freedom but, on the contrary, contributes to it, and this shelter is in marked contrast to the claustrophobic office setting in which we initially met him. The dam reminds us of his beloved badgers' habitat. Occasionally there are natural, comforting enclosures!

It is, of course, comic to see Falcon hanging "over the bronze lion." He has become the wild animal; his instincts have exploded, and his movements are in ironic opposition to Simon's work. He must be hosed by the firemen.

In the next chapter, "Massacre of the Innocents," the violent movements grow until they dominate the rest of the novel. (Thus we have moved from *threat* to *actuality*; the pace has accelerated.) Patterns are broken; old ways are outmoded. Simon informs us that we "lived an impoverished, all-hands-on-deck, air raid shelter, darts and sandwiches sort of life. . . ." Public disorders abound. And as the wilderness increases, it influences private arrangements. Simon and Martha battle about safety and fidelity — she relates her past feelings toward Falcon as possible lover — and their quarrels add to the general confusion.

It is during such confusion that Simon finds greater happiness in his work. He likes to repair things; he loses his identity in group tasks: "The closer the threat of general devastation, the harder we worked to preserve. Against a background of ruins and stench we banded together to save the

collections. . . ." He resembles a beaver once more. But even now his pleasures are interrupted by "old men" who insist that their priorities come first.
Thus Beard commands him to save the anatomical specimens and place
them in cold storage. The refrigeration plant, which is in the country, functions as the most claustrophobic enclosure we have yet encountered. (I have
not mentioned Beard's family life — he comes from "a family of lunatics,
cardiacs, spastics and hysterics" — but it distinguishes his mad activities at
this point. The family is, indeed, a "refrigeration plant" in his case, causing
him to function coldly.)

Before the expedition to the plant (notice how carefully Wilson uses
expeditions throughout the novel; most end in disaster!) there is another
crisis at the Zoo. Simon is at work sorting out minutes that are "essential for
future historians. After all history had as high a claim as anatomy." He
rushes to the window — as he did in the first chapter — when he hears explo-
sive noises outside. He sees a wild crowd intent upon capturing and devour-
ing the animals. The slogans reverberate: "Men not Beasts." Simon notes the
"ugly sound" because he refuses to separate men and beasts (except within
disciplined limits). By not accepting the natural innocence of beasts, men
become bestial. *They break the bonds of living creatures.*

Simon runs down into the crowd, but he is too late to save Matthew
Price. With the "holocaust of witches" at hand, he longs to return home — to
Martha; nevertheless, he stands firm: "to give up now would be to make
nonsense of all proper order, of anything I believed in. . . ." He yields to
Beard's request to save specimens.

The expedition begins. Simon wants desperately to talk to Beard, but
he realizes that the other man is so enclosed in his private nightmare that
communication is impossible — they do not share the same ideas of "all
proper order." When he begins to have stomach pains, Beard insists upon
the priority of saving his specimens. There is a blur of violent pain — wild,
starving people attack them — and then Simon finds himself near "long used
entrances to badger setts." Shelter at last! Wilson does not spare the irony.
Soon Simon is so weak that he — as do the other townspeople — kills and eats
his beloved animals: "Nausea fought with hunger in me." His ambivalence
is so great that he passes out and his last words in this "massacre of innocents" are "The room span round. My head fell back on the cushions and
everything became dark, became nothing."

The next chapter opens with sharp contrasts. Time has passed; the political order has changed; "nothing" has become "everything." Simon and
Martha sit and enjoy a rich meal at the Englanders (who, ironically, are
loyal Uni-Europeans). But he feels guilty; he is aware that this comfortable
room is even more enclosed than his former office. And his guilt increases
when he agrees to work at the "new" Zoo, which will now be made up totally of European collections.

There will be a new ceremony to celebrate the reopening of the Zoo.
Although Simon seems not to remember (or at least mention) the previous

celebrations, especially the Great Day, we grow fearful. (Ceremonies are for Wilson necessary but wild; they subvert "all proper order" if not "enclosed" properly.) He brings together fauna "of every kind, grouped geographically, upon migration, breeding, general demography, adaptation to human environments, relation to human economy." But as he begins to note, he is so enclosed by his work that he does not see "the changing world outside." He is in a "cocoon of busyness." He is not ready for the final ceremony.

The weather is beautiful — there are "soft" breezes; lilacs fill the air with perfume. The crowds are controlled. Everything is peaceful (in marked opposition to the preceding chapters). A verse is recited to honor the occasion: "Peace shall come to this house/When the hoopoe lies down with the grouse." Simon is at ease in the "house."

We expect the change. Suddenly crowds march in — they are made of "all who [are] too obstinately individual to fit in, yet too weakly individual to make their mark" — and they clash with the fashionable observers. The old political battles of England and Uni-Europe resume; it is the Uni-Europeans who have the day. Blanchard-White, an enemy of England and Simon's temporary superior, reveals a display: "There in a pit dug seven or eight feet below ground level was an old mangy brown Siberian bear." The bear is treated as a political symbol: "The Russian Bear in Difficulties." (We remember how at the beginning the giraffe was used by Leacock and Falcon for symbolic, political reasons.) Simon laughs at the idiocy, thinking "things would soon come right," But his laughter is hollow; he is again in an "untenable position" because his sense of proper order has been violated. He cannot lie down (or work) with his enemies.

It is fitting that the final chapter (and the shortest) is entitled "Down and Up Again." Throughout the novel Simon has fallen and risen (as have the political alignments). Now we understand the metaphorical implications of this "tall story": *there are no set arrangements in human affairs — men are enclosed in never-ending cycles.* When they fail to move within the flow of things (either by attempted, obsessive "freedom" or willing imprisonment), they lose whatever capacities for creative expression they possess.

In this chapter Simon is seen drinking, then raping Martha (who has lost all respect for him), and breaking down. He is thoroughly down and out. (Work is pictured as a liberating force; Simon is at his best when he finds satisfaction in administrative order.) Time, however, moves rapidly. He finds himself (after his actual imprisonment in Enfield Camp) as Acting Director of the Zoo. The Uni-Europeans have been defeated; England is independent once again: "Stability of a kind had come to us. The last three years had given me a wealth of ideas for the Zoo's future and a corresponding wealth of caution and moderation in my belief in their possible application." There is the chance that he will be made permanent Director.

There can not be a happy ending. Simon remains unsure; he does not know (does anyone?) whether he is up or down in this "tall story." As soon as he learns of his future position, he returns home. He is "determined" (a play on determinism) to repair his relationship with Martha; he finds, however, that she treats him as a child and says: "If you get to be a nuisance, Mummy will send you away." When his children (who have finally returned to England from America), ask about the "strongest" animal — is it a giraffe? — he replies that he doesn't think a giraffe can kill people. Thus we are back at the beginning. At the end of all the changes that have occurred, Simon has learned true wisdom: there is no *complete freedom or enclosure*; all that he can know finally is that "I'm not sure yet."

Angus Wilson: Between Nostalgia and Nightmare
Bernard Bergonzi*

. . . Of the novelists who have emerged since 1945, Angus Wilson particularly embodies this English cultural preoccupation, while, at the same time, infusing it with his own highly personal predilections or even obsessions. He is both a writer of middle-brow appeal and true literary seriousness, a fact which enables him to elude confident critical placing. Without doubt Wilson is a writer of unusually fine intelligence, wide reading and great sensitivity. Yet for him, as for many of his contemporaries, writing is just a question of writing, of saying what one wants to say, without theoretical worrying. He has been applauded for his pragmatic approach by John Bayley: "The common reader probably clings to novelists who appear unaware that a loss of confidence in their old-fashioned power of creation has taken place— in England, Anthony Powell or Angus Wilson" (*Essays in Criticism*, April 1968). (It is, of course, in England that such unawareness is easiest to sustain.) I do not, in fact, think that John Bayley's point is true of Anthony Powell, since, in my reading, many of the stylistic strategems of *The Music of Time* are precisely attempts to cope with such a loss of confidence; but in respect of Angus Wilson his point is well taken. A similar observation has been made, though from an opposed critical stance, by a novelist of experimental inclinations, B.S. Johnson:

> It's silly to pretend that one can solve the problems of writing in the middle twentieth century with the methods of Henry James, and even less with the methods of Dickens. One thinks of a very good writer like Angus Wilson who, I think, is a marvellous observer of twentieth century *mores*, and I'm sure social historians in the future will look to Angus Wilson and say, "Yes, that's what it must have been like to live then." But the actual methods he uses are those of Dickens, which seem to me to

*Reprinted with permission of the author from *The Situation of the Novel* (London: Macmillan, 1970), pp. 151–61.

conflict with what he's writing about, a conflict, in fact, between form and content. (BBC recording, 1967: "Novelists of the Sixties")

Broadly speaking, Wilson's attitude to his craft is similar to Snow's, although he does not share Snow's ideological opposition to the achievements of the Modern Movement. At least, if Wilson once disapproved of Virginia Woolf, he now admires her very much (Rabinovitz, *Reaction*, p. 67). His first three novels, *Hemlock and After*, *Anglo-Saxon Attitudes* and *The Middle Age of Mrs. Eliot* — published between 1952 and 1958 — are very English in their nonchalance about form, in their precise social mimicry, and in the nature of their moral preoccupations. Despite a sense of what James called "felt life" and, in the first two, a Dickensian range of characters, the thematic elements in these novels are obtrusive. One is constantly invited to ponder questions of responsibility and guilt, the familiar Wilcox-Schlegel opposition between the public life of busy achievement and the private life of spiritual cultivation, and the dilemmas inherent in truly understanding the motives for one's actions. Whereas for Baudelaire true progress lay in diminishing the traces of original sin, for many English novelists it lies in diminishing the traces of self-deception, in steadfastly eradicating the original Emma Woodhouse from one's soul. Wilson is a distinguished practitioner in this tradition, whose brightest luminary is George Eliot: the novel is seen as the vehicle for a particular liberal ideology, where characters are secure in their freedom to refine on their motives, truly to understand each other, and, above all, themselves. *Nosce teipsum* is the beginning of all true wisdom, and one wholeheartedly admires the achievements of a tradition so splendidly dedicated to the cause of moral clarity. Yet with a mid-twentieth-century representative of this tradition such as Wilson, one's admiration is tempered with a sense that the questions so searchingly gone into for the nth time in this or that novel are beginning to look trivial, both intrinsically and in the larger context of the history of our times. It is in the centripetal nature of its preoccupations that English culture can look parochial and irrelevant to outsiders. For writers who have known, and often still live in, a world where torture and deportation, the arbitrary exercise of unlimited power and the familiarity of casual violence are a part of daily experience, the dilemmas of the English liberal are likely to seem a little fine drawn. The experiences that have gone into the fiction of Camus or Pasternak or Günter Grass are of such a different order to those reflected by someone like Angus Wilson that a critical comparison is difficult. Wilson is aware of these disparities, and in *The Middle Age of Mrs. Eliot* he makes an interesting effort to cope with them: Meg Eliot, the archetypal liberal heroine, whose forebears can be found in Forster and George Eliot and Jane Austen, is good-looking, sensitive, intelligent without being clever, and modestly complacent. Yet she loses her handsome, devoted, successful husband in a bit of casual political violence at the airport of an Asian country they are visiting, and the rest of the novel shows her valiant attempt to make something of her life in widowhood and poverty.

Certainly, within clearly defined limits, *The Middle Age of Mrs. Eliot* is an admirable novel, which shows, among other things, that Wilson is better at creating memorable female characters than male ones. I am much less convinced of the enduring qualities of his first two novels; their plots seem creakingly contrived, and I cannot work up anything like the degree of interest in the dilemmas of the self-flagellating Bernard Sands or the spiritually sluggish Gerald Middleton that Wilson so urgently invites. Nevertheless *Anglo-Saxon Attitudes* does offer the relaxed interest provided by a busily crowded fictional canvas — with part of his mind it seems that Wilson has always wanted to *dépasser The Forsyte Saga* — and it shows his fascination with the years just before 1914. The whole elaborate plot of his novel depends on an event in the year 1912 when a pagan fertility idol is introduced into the tomb of an Anglo-Saxon bishop. The hoax, which reverberates through the novel (and is clearly a fictional version of the Piltdown Man scandal), was perpetrated by a friend of the young Gerald Middleton called Gilbert Stokesay. Although he was killed in the First World War, Stokesay persists in Gerald's memories as one of the central characters of the story: a reactionary poet and essayist of the cast of T. E. Hulme and Wyndham Lewis, a disciple of Nietzsche and a sadist. Although, as a good liberal, Wilson deplores such types, he is evidently interested in them; one finds them again in *The Old Men at the Zoo* and a short story called "More Friend Than Lodger." There had been one or two Edwardian echoes of a sinister kind in *Hemlock and After*: the corrupter of children, Hubert Rose, affects Edwardian speech and appearance, and Sherman Winter and his degenerate friends misbehave in the bedrooms of Varden Hall because "it was somehow, they felt, Edwardian." In both novels, and again in *The Middle Age of Mrs. Eliot*, there is plenty of evidence that Wilson's liberal imagination is deeply affected by recurring images of violence and cruelty, in ways that both point to deep-seated private obsessions and reflect the public violence of our times. C. B. Cox has accurately remarked of Wilson's first three novels: "There is an ambiguous relationship between the vivid dramatic action and the intellectual analysis, almost as if Wilson feels that nightmare is truth, and the reconstructions of his art, like social poses, are only coverings for a reality which is inescapably horrible" (*The Free Spirit*, 1963: p. 152). The sense of nightmare, apparent in the first three books in isolated incidents and recurring images, provided the central material of Wilson's fourth novel, *The Old Men at the Zoo*, a venture into prophetic fantasy. After rereading it, I feel that I dismissed it in much too summary a fashion when discussing Wilson's work a few years ago.[1] It undoubtedly has major faults. The first part of the book, which deals with the petty intrigues of the directors of the London Zoo, reads rather like a wooden and slow-moving imitation of Snow; the prevalent animal symbolism makes its point, but is too heavily handled.

In later chapters, however, the book becomes imaginatively alive. In the situation that Wilson describes the England of 1970 is militarily threat-

ened by an alliance of European powers; the impending war lends an apocalyptic note to the story, but the atmosphere is hardly suggestive of the
outbreak of the Third World War as usually imagined in such fantasies, or
even of the advent of the Second World War; rather it seems to recall the
summer of 1914, and in the idea of an alliance of European powers threatening Britain it looks back to the alarmist stories of imaginary wars and
invasions of Britain that appeared in abundance between 1870 and 1914,
and which have been discussed in detail in I. F. Clarke's *Voices Prophesying
War*. How far the distaste for a unified Europe presented in his story is part
of Wilson's own view of life is not clear: as a proponent of the English ideology he has gone on record as objecting to anything that smacks of continental metaphysics. John Holloway has quoted Wilson's remark at the
International Writers' Conference at Leningrad in 1963: "Until yesterday I
think that most of the English delegates listened with surprise to the unfamiliar, and for us sterile, disputations expressed in a distorted metaphysical
jargon. However, yesterday we heard addresses which were expressed in
the simple, direct tone which we are used to" (*Listener*, 19 January 1967).
In *The Old Men at the Zoo* the only committed pro-European is a vulgar
fascist demagogue called Blanshard-White who talks of "throwing off the
puritan legacy" and getting closer "to the rich vein of Mediterranean brutality on which our European legacy so much depends"; he plans to revive
the gladiatorial shows of Ancient Rome by putting on public combats between political prisoners and the animals of the Zoo. Blanshard-White
offers a simplified version of the attitudes of Montherlant or Maurras, or
rather of the kind of deracinated Englishman who might be expected to
admire them. Blanshard-White is only a minor character and a sketchily
rendered one at that, yet he does seem to embody some puzzling phobia in
Wilson's imagination, where repulsion is mingled with a degree of secret
fascination. In this aspect *The Old Men at the Zoo* echoes, in a more sinister
way, the gallophobia of Kingsley Amis's *I Like It Here*. In so far as its infra-
plot touches on recent history, one notes that *The Old Men at the Zoo* was
published in 1961, the year when Britain first applied to join the Common
Market (an attempt which was to be twice rejected by the French).

In this novel Wilson tries to show his narrator, Simon Carter, struggling with larger moral dilemmas than have previously concerned the characters of Wilson's novels. That is to say, politics impinges on private life in a
somewhat un-English way. Carter, the secretary of the Zoo, who is both an
animal-lover and an efficient administrator tries to carry on with his work
as best he can after England has been defeated by the Europeans. In doing
so he embodies the classical dilemma of the public servant in a period of
defeat and oppression: should one try to keep society going and risk being
labelled a collaborator, or should one keep up a possibly vain and even disastrous resistance? By temperament Carter inclines towards the first
course, but finally the excesses of pro-Europeans like Blanshard-White are
too much for him and he tries to escape from London, only to be thrown

into a concentration camp, from which he is rescued, at the end of the novel, by an incredible, fairy-tale "Liberation."

Where *The Old Men at the Zoo* seems to me to achieve its maximum imaginative intensity is in the remarkable chapter called "A Good Old, Rare Old, Armageddon." Here the new director of the Zoo, Sir Bobby Falcon, a rakish old gentleman, who looks like a figure in a whiskey advertisement, and who has a passionate love of everything Victorian, is putting on a special exhibition called a British Day; at the same time the outbreak of war is imminent, and the Zoo is bombed (with small, old-fashioned bombs) before the exhibition can be officially opened. In this chapter Wilson achieves a striking juxtaposition of insular nostalgia and apocalyptic nightmare. The British Day, as Falcon conceives it, looks back to the Festival of Britain in 1951, but it also anticipates the camp patriotism of the Sunday colour-supplements:

> On that clear, moonlit night, the extraordinary theatricality of the Zoo's new decor merged happily into the starry background. We wandered round looking happily at the great massed beds of auriculas and tulips and wallflowers that spelt "God Save the Queen," and "Norman, and Saxon and Dane are We," and the fountains playing in coloured jets. Here at the entrance to what was being shown as the Old Victorian Zoo were to be the recitations and the tableaux and later a show of fireworks with two set pieces — a British lion and an Indian elephant. The Old Zoo looked particularly charming with all the Decimus Burton Houses picked out with very subtle lighting (Jane's work), with a chalet for the old woman who was to sell fresh cows' milk and bags of buns, and booths for the peanut man and coconut shies, with goat chaises, and a wondrous bear pit. Beyond the Old Zoo, the Lemur House, its modern lines disguised with ferns and hot-house plants, had been converted into a *chef d'oeuvre* à la Paxton; and in this great glass palace, to Matthew's delight, were to be housed birds from every corner of the earth that was now or ever had been British. For, of course, it was only by cheating and taking in history, that a British Day could cast its net wide enough. From this show centre of the Old Zoo, the aviaries and the gardens, five separate roads led off each to a separate continent — to Stanley's Africa, to Botany Bay, to a Hudson Bay fur station, to the jungle of the British Raj, and, a little incommensurately (but by a determined whim of Bobby's) to the Apes of the Rock.

In this colourful assembly, patriotism is reduced to childlike regressiveness; but the splendours of the British Day are soon dimmed. The bombs fall, and we see our last of Falcon in a posture of calculatedly absurd symbolism: "There above us on top of the bronze lion that crowned the Lion House was Sir Robert Falcon, doubled up with pain, but still wildly shouting, blown on high by some freak of blast, whole though bruised and shaken."

The Old Men at the Zoo seems to have performed a kind of blood-letting for Wilson's imagination, as though it enabled him to face, and for the time being at least subdue, his own inner fantasies. His next novel, *Late*

Call, is, by contrast, a work of considerable serenity and relative freedom from obsessions, although the serenity is tempered by spiritual bleakness. In contrast to Wilson's earlier novels, one might call it "positive" or "affirmative," although one should, perhaps, preserve a cautionary memory of Bernard Sands, the novelist hero of *Hemlock and After*, who read with sardonic enjoyment the eager though uncomprehending reviews that described one of his books as a "refreshing, if unexpected, source of renewed hope and affirmation in living" and "a sadly needed testimony to the endurance of the human spirit." "And all this, Bernard reflected with amusement, proceeded from an irrational preoccupation with evil that was probably the result of nervous anxiety." Wilson has not lost his own sense of evil, but whereas in the earlier books it had shown itself in intense marginal fantasies, like the grotesque procuress Mrs. Curry in *Hemlock and After* or the corrupt Irish youth Larry O'Rourke in *Anglo-Saxon Attitudes*, or the innumerable scenes of brutality and mutilation in *The Old Men at the Zoo*, in *Late Call* it is integrated with Wilson's principal strength as a novelist, his infallible sense of social fact. *Late Call* explores the spiritual desolation of life in a New Town in the Midlands, where the gimmickry of affluence has become a way of life rather then an aid to living.

The heroine of *Late Call*, Sylvia Calvert, is a woman in her sixties, who has retired after a lifetime spent managing small, unfashionable hotels. Accompanied by her sponging idler of a husband—one of Wilson's most crisply drawn characters—who cares only for playing cards and reliving the days when he was a temporary officer in the First World War, she goes to live in the New Town of Carshall with her recently widowed son, Harold. He is a progressive headmaster and educational theorist, a writer of profitable books with titles such as *The Blokes at the Back of the Class* and an active citizen of Carshall and believer in the ideal of the New Town. Harold flaunts his filial feelings and warmly welcomes his parents to his handsomely equipped modern house. Why, and how, the Calverts cannot live with Harold and his three teenage children is the story that Wilson goes on to tell.

Sylvia Calvert has some affinities with Meg Eliot, but does not fit so easily into the literary archetype of the liberal heroine. Although basically shrewd, she has a limited intelligence and very little education; her sensibility is formed by popular biographies, light historical novels and sentimental television serials. In achieving so much with a character so far removed from what most novelists would consider an appropriate fictional consciousness, Wilson has done remarkably well. The essential point about Sylvia is that she represents a standard by which to judge the progressive pretensions of Harold and his children, and the ideals of the New Town generally; and, significantly, her own standards are based in the vanished pre-1914 world. *Late Call* opens with a beautifully written prologue called "The Hot Summer of 1911." which shows Sylvia as a child of ten on an East Anglian farm, bullied by her boorish parents and weighed down with the responsibility of looking after a brood of younger siblings. She is at first patronized, then victimized by some middle-class summer visitors. Taken separately, this "Prologue" reads like one of Wilson's sharpest short stories. it scarcely idealises the world in which Sylvia grows up—one is only too aware of the prevalent snobbery and insensitive treatment of children—but it shows how the values Sylvia absorbed as a child have remained with her throughout her life, and establishes the difference between her and Harold and his friends. In fact Wilson uses Sylvia's honest but often baffled consciousness to make a remarkably sharp exposure of contemporary progressive attitudes. *Late Call* is, in essence, a highly conservative book, although it puts forward no propositions, and does not seem unfairminded in its descriptions of British life in the 1960s. Wilson aims some accurate satire at what one might call the *Observer*-ethos, with its naïve love of gadgets, doctrinaire progressiveness, would-be-exotic eating habits, cultural status-seeking and neurotic concern to be with-it. There is a nice illustration when Harold explains to his mother the workings of a new electric cooker: "With this heatview you've got a double check—this marker is going up and down the whole time, it's just as if you had your beloved gas flame." It is on such things, or Harold's eagerness about them, that his relationship with his mother starts to founder.

On Easter Sunday Sylvia is taken to church—though the church is more like a meeting hall—to hear a sermon by the local vicar, who is much admired in the New Town for his up-to-date ideas: "Last Easter he gave a sermon on the eleven plus." But he is ill, and the replacement, an elderly Scot, preaches a traditional sermon, with Calvinist overtones, about Grace. Harold is deeply scandalised by such obscurantism, but Sylvia has been touched by the sermon, and addresses a word of thanks to the old man. In Wilson's earlier books religion was regarded as, at best, an evasion of human responsibility; but in *Late Call* Sylvia's response seems to suggest that it might be a touchstone for various kinds of contemporary insincerity. In so far as Sylvia is the embodiment of a set of attitudes deeply at variance with the dominant assumptions of the age, then *Late Call* can be called a nostalgic work in the positive sense described by D. W. Harding: "It can be said in general that complete absence of nostalgia in a modern writer is suspect, suggesting complacent fellowship with the main commercial group, or seclusion with an academic group, or life among the cliques, or too little questioning and testing of the tradition" (*Scrutiny*, May 1932). It is, I think, better written and less diffuse than Wilson's earlier novels; if it is, at the same time, more thematically limited, it is arguably his most achieved work of fictional art.

Several critics have, however, reserved their highest praise for Wilson's most recent novel, *No Laughing Matter*. This is his longest and most ambitious book so far, in which he returns to the crowded canvas and broad temporal sweep of *Anglo-Saxon Attitudes*, tracing the fortunes of a not very ordinary English upper-middle-class family called Matthews from

1912 to the present day. Wilson uses the Matthews family as a focus for his fictional attempt on the Condition of England question: he might have taken as his epigraph George Orwell's remark: "A family with the wrong members in control — that, perhaps, is as near as one can get to describing England in a phrase." We first encounter them — William and Clara, known to their family as Billy Pop and the Countess — together with their six vivacious and articulate children, a globe-trotting maiden aunt and a comic cockney servant when they are visiting the Wild West Exhibition at West Kensington in 1912. The handsome, bland William is a literary gent in the casual Edwardian fashion; his principal work is a study of cricket in English literature. Clara is darkly beautiful, witty, vain and consumingly egotistical. We never see the Matthews family in such an agreeable light again; the opening chapter, which describes their visit to the exhibition in fascinating and meticulously researched detail, is a brilliant performance by Wilson, showing once more the extent of his imaginative attachment to the pre-1914 world. As the children grow up we observe the decline of their seemingly radiant parents into debt, infidelity and increasing seediness, and the growth of implacable hostility between parents and children. *No Laughing Matter* is a defiantly traditional generations-novel, with a bustling variety of characters and a great deal of exuberant interplay between them. At the same time Wilson's prose is richer and more relaxed than in his early novels, and his language is able to embody a wider spectrum of feeling and to draw on a greater variety of technical devices. Indeed, several of the chapters take the form of playlets imitating the successive theatrical styles of the past fifty years; a nice example of Wilson's mimetic talents and one that, on the whole, comes off. The novel contains many brilliant episodes, yet the successes remain local and remind one that Wilson began his literary career as a short story writer, and has always had difficulty in responding adequately to the structural demands of the full-scale novel, greatly drawn to it though he is. Increasingly in *No Laughing Matter* one feels that Wilson has not been able to muster sufficient imaginative energy to animate the whole of his ample design, and there is a palpable weariness in the last part of the book, as compared with its brilliant opening.

Undoubtedly the novel represents a continuing desire on Wilson's part to take in history and the public world, as opposed to the largely private concerns of the first three books. The obsessions have largely disappeared, or at least been mastered, and replaced by an attempt at a calmly comprehensive panoramic vision. The Matthews family are more than just a collection of latter-day Forsytes; their changing situation does in some sense identify them with England, "the family with the wrong members in control," from the seemingly elegant Pop and Countess of 1912, already nurturing the seeds of dissolution, down to their great-grandchildren, students at a New University in 1967. And for all their liveliness, they cannot sustain such a representative role. There is plenty of history in *No Laughing Matter*, at least as brilliant particularised description, like the account of a fascist march in Bermondsey in the thirties, but not much sense of history. Wilson's gifts are fully in evidence in this novel, and so are his limitations. His intuitions and his power of mimicry are as keen as ever: he can instantly reveal the subtle tensions in a complex family relationship, or the unexpected contortions of a consciousness suddenly brought against a new level of reality. He is, above all, a novelist of manners and not at all of ideas, and ideas are what *No Laughing Matter* conspicuously lacks; not, of course, as conversational tags or fashionable allusions, but as a significant dimension in the narrative. Despite Wilson's admirable wish to include history in this novel, it does not transcend the personal.

Note

1. *New York Review of Books*, 23 February 1965.

The Lion and the Unicorn: Angus Wilson's Triumphant Tragedy
Jean Sudrann*

The haunting resonance of Angus Wilson's *No Laughing Matter* is difficult to account for in an English literary scene where elegiac reminiscence and angry self-castigation of national dinginess have dwindled into cliché. Yet the feelings evoked by the novel are sufficiently persistent to suggest that Mr. Wilson's acknowledgement of the emasculated British lion signifies something other than the conventional, and conventionally ambivalent, lament for lost Empire. Indeed, clues to discovery of the difference begin with the conventionality itself. In 1967, Angus Wilson seems to have written an almost aggressively conventional English family novel. Sporadic references, for example, to *The Forsyte Saga*, whatever the particular effects of irony, function to force the reader's attention on the genre. Yet coupled with this insistence on recognition of the novel's traditional form is a continuous critical commentary on the problems of the creative imagination and a continuous exemplification of the workings of that imagination from cowboy ballad to Theatre of the Absurd. While the Lion expires, the Unicorn is yet rampant.

This complicated texture of homage to the Muses creates its own formal structure, which plays against the traditional forms of the family novel to create the full statement of the work, a statement that embraces not only a history of the disintegration of a way of life but also an exploration of the beautifully various attempts of the human mind to create histories out of the succession of days.

The outward form of the family novel, carries, as the form tradition-

*Reprinted with permission from *Studies in the Novel*, 3, No. 4 (1971), 390–400.

ally does, the chief burden of the "condition of England" theme — here, an elegy for lost Empire, lost land, and lost moral identity, which is the ground melody for the whole novel. The four generations of the Matthews family who populate the novel, the chronological structural divisions from "Before the War" to "1967," the thematically insistent intermingling of public and private events, the image of the family house to define and link individual and national destiny, are all familiar devices. These are the avenues through which we have come to the Baineses, the Forsytes, the Wilcoxes, the Wilchers. Simply to note that *No Laughing Matter* begins on the Coronation Walk of the Exhibition Grounds at Earls Court in a happy daydream of Edwardian family unity — "scarcely known before"[1] and never to be known again — and ends in a small dusty North African town where the might of the heraldic British lion has been reduced to the ornamentation of a socialist perfume factory, Plantagenet Perfume Ltd. ("All those old . . . queens in wimples made such wonderful advertisements" [p. 493]), is to define the image of national collapse embodied in the novel. In the final paragraph, the terms of final collapse are prophesied as the Arab Hassan ponders his promised inheritance of the perfume business from Marcus Matthews:

> As perhaps Marcus — his good, noble, kind friend — might now see how absurd were these cooperative ideas at the factory. Perhaps he might even alter the foolish clause in his will by which the factory was to continue on these mad lines . . . It was not as if, when he [Hassan] was owner, he would pay low wages or any foolish old-fashioned thing like that, if Marcus feared it; on the contrary, Miracle Germany — Stuttgart, Düsseldorf, Frankfurt — all that he admired most in the modern world, even his favourite journal, *Time* magazine, urged high wages, but also seemly ambition, high profits, and determined management (p. 496).

Miracle Germany and *Time* magazine: these are the values that will endure, this is what is No Laughing Matter, the end of the Edwardian West Kensington daydream, and it is of a piece with those other apocalyptic visions of England's fate which pervade Angus Wilson's fictions. One remembers particularly the young grandson of the mad Lord Peacehaven in his role as the darkest man present going out to the garden on New Year's Eve to usher in a "year of adventure and action" — 1956: the year of Suez[2] and, of course, those Old Men at the Zoo who made a Victorian holiday while holocaust arrives, who send up showers of colors from "the great firework setpieces . . . God Save Our Gracious Queen, the British Lion, and the Indian Elephant"[3] to meet the bomb-burst descending from the skies.

In themselves, these scenes recall the excited tone of a young American novelist envisioning the same possibilities a century before the collapse. In 1877, Henry James confessed that "even the 'decline' of England seems to me a tremendous and even, almost, an inspiring spectacle, and if the British Empire is once more to shrink up into that plethoric little island, the process will be the greatest drama in history!"[4] Spectacle and drama, forms of fiction, shape James's prevision of social catastrophe: and by the use of forms of fiction and comment on the functions of fiction, Angus Wilson seeks to comprehend and communicate the meaning of that catastrophe.

In the first place, the novel is almost wholly peopled by artists and connoisseurs. All of the six Matthews children, who comprise the central generation of the novel, are directly concerned with the arts. Even the housewife, Sukey, runs a successful BBC series and the businesswoman, Gladys, makes her profits from the sale of antiques. Their father, William Ackerley Matthew (Billy Pop), is a failed Edwardian belle-lettrist, while the youngest son, Marcus, although he never becomes a great painter, does become a superb collector of great paintings. Quentin the journalist, Margaret the novelist, and Rupert the actor complete a family roll call that is also a listing of the makers and purveyors of art of the twentieth century. Moreover, the fabric of the sophisticated epic that is the novel itself is wrought from an immense variety of creative forms. Daydreams, plays, popular songs, newspaper accounts and television broadcasts, even a short story, complicate the family narrative, stretch and alter the traditional form of the family novel. In this way, from its opening pages, Wilson suggests that his novel is "about" art as well as life. At the novel's conclusion it is clear that some definition of the relation of art to life, of fiction to fact, is essential to its meaning, deeply related to its apocalyptic vision.

The central question is immediately posed by the opening paragraph which describes, not the moment in historical time at which the narrative begins, but rather the recording of that moment by an art form: the 1912 Earls Court Exhibition as shown on early newsreel film. The camera, the author notes, has caught much — crowds, popular amusements and popular fashions, mingling classes, Imperial vastness — yet it has not caught individual people, has failed to create a record of how it was and how it felt that summer afternoon on the Coronation Walk. If the camera eye, ultimate refinement of realistic art, fails so signally to immortalize the moment, how then is the novelist to proceed? The complicated structure of the whole novel's narration represents Angus Wilson's attempt to answer that question. In like manner, each member of the Matthews family asks what growing up is, what life means. Through the narrative of their lives, each creates his own answer. Thus the question the author poses in his opening paragraphs, like the question his characters ask, can be answered only through the art of the narrative. Indeed, he and his characters alike are asking the same question: how do we know what is real? And the novel keeps answering: man makes his reality by self-conscious creation.

The five plays within the novel provide the simplest exemplification of the process. Put on stage at specific moments in the chronicle time of the family history, each is a parody of a dramatic form popular during the years which that portion of the novel is representing. *The Family Sunday Play*, enacted in Book II: *1919*, is a Pinero well-made play in three acts in which the family crisis that threatens to disrupt the family becomes simply a strengthening force in the tie that binds; *Parents at Play* of 1925 is a Shavian social drama in which the cockney servant, Regan, predictably emerges as the sole indispensable element of society; the curtain that rises on *Pop and Motor: A Catastrophe* rises on a wonderful reprise of the life and times of the children's parents, the Countess and Billy Pop, in images of sex and violence, in a catalogue of physical facts and a climax of bomb-bursts that belongs to Beckett and the Theatre of the Absurd. Marvelously witty, these parodies, as parodies, each adds its own complicating irony to the title's dictum: no laughing matter. Yet, within the complete pattern, each makes a wholly serious contribution by suggesting the variety of ways in which contemporary art defines the contemporary scene. If the camera eye of the opening paragraph defines a crowd scene of mingled classes and varied costumes of value to the sociologist and the costume designer, the dramatic voice of the play-parodies demonstrates popular ideas shaping quotidian existence. Of course *The Family Sunday Play* ends in a tableau of a loving family happily united against the forces of wealth and self-importance; for this is 1919, and this is what a family is. Of course the Countess and Billy Pop decide against a legal separation in the comedy of *Parents at Play*, because neither can get along without a servant and only together can they keep Regan; this is 1925, and satire on materialistic values is fashionable. The parodies thus make their contribution to the *Cavalcade* aspect of the family chronicle, for the history of an era is as much the history of its ideas as of its events.

But the very wit of this means of chronicle suggests that the plays are more than costume design for historical romance. The air raid that kills the Countess and Billy Pop in their West Country hotel retreat from the London blitz is a casual Baedeker raid on a cathedral town (in itself no laughing matter, for by 1940, the Countess and Billy have certainly become Historic Monuments). Yet the Matthewses die in a full-length drama: "A Catastrophe" in the modern manner. Who, if not the dramatist, has created The Catastrophe, has turned casual extinction of life into an image of human disaster? In this way, then, these plays reach to the heart of the novel's concern; for this reason, Angus Wilson has prefaced his family novel, not with the usual family genealogy, but with "Principal Players," "Supporting Roles," and "Additional Cast."

If the epoch's dramatists fashion the age's actions into human meaning, the characters themselves must create meaning for the moment. This they do by luxuriating in daydreams of a promised end, an Eldorado to match the Apocalypse, and by making up The Game, a proto-Drama. Appropriately, the daydreams come first, come immediately with the opening of the novel as the novelist's corrective to the jumble of images caught by the camera eye, as well as his device for getting his Principal Players on stage. These are wonderful daydreams which take their impulse from the outward event of the Wild West Show of the Exhibition; they are furnished into comic verisimilitude by the everyday props of the everyday lives of the characters (Eldorado, thinks Sukey, will be like Cromer — and there will be very nice neighbors); and they are given their shape, their plot-line, by the inner pressure, the inner desires of the dreamer himself. In their common delight in the joyous, prosperous family unity which makes feasible the family journey through the dangers of the wild, wild West, makes unquestionable the passionately desired arrival at Eldorado, these dreams are the Edwardian National Dream, as illusory as it is comfortable. In their differing adventures and differing visions of Eldorado itself, they prefigure the drama about to be created from each individual life; they unroll a cast of characters in search of a life.

The eldest son's, Quentin's, imaginings are the most instructive here, for not one but three Quentins ride the prairie of the daydream. Most simply, he rides as "proud watchdog eldest son," guardian of the family. But the family which he would guard, in his birthright role as eldest son, has rejected him, sent him from home to live among the Victorian amenities of Granny M's Ladbroke Grove villa ("Oh! How the Sunday afternoons of stamp albums and stereoscope with pictures of the Russo-Japanese war killed the hungry heart" [p. 8]). Already his simultaneous resentment of the rejection and guilt at his failure to share in the family's "shabbiness and sudden violences" (p. 8) has evolved another role, the Quentin to whom unity is all, who rocks, lulled in the womb of the daydream saddle, regardless of guardianship obligations, until he is disturbed by the third Quentin, Quentin the "looker-on," the objective critic.

The three Quentins illuminate further the novel's question of apprehended reality. Formulated by a daydream, each role is tested by the chronicle events of the family home, 52 Gilbrook Street, London, S. W. 1. The "eldest watchdog son" has his chance when, after being wounded in World War I, he returns to No. 52 to lead the Nursery in revolt against the shabby disorder, the crippling irresponsibilities of the Countess and Billy Pop. The revolt fails, of course, and when the disastrous day is over, when the kittens have been drowned and the Nursery has capitulated to the Drawing Room, it is the youngest son, Marcus, who reminds us that we should have known that this Quentin could have no real existence, belongs only to the sentimental self-regarding aspect of the daydream which creates the eldest son in cliché terms: "lean, eager, simple, and straight as a die" (p. 8). That night in the Nursery, Marcus, with deadly aim, points out quietly to Quentin how enormously Quentin has enjoyed playing the role of protector, even though the protection failed.

Prophesied by the daydream where the "unity-loving" Quentin is pulled out of the illusion by the "ironic commentator" Quentin, the Quentin who longs for unity — unity of self and with others — is never realized. However much Quentin has longed to be with "the others" — in the Nursery, at Oxford, with his various women or his fellow journalists — the desire is wholly unrealizable. And in his dying moment, Quentin knows why. He cannot live; the hungry heart has indeed been killed.

Into the third role, the onlooker, Quentin casts his professional self; from it, he makes the reality of his personal narrative — the image of Q. J. Matthews, the sardonic leftist journalist and popular television personality. Yet it is Quentin of the dead heart as well as the ironic tongue who plays his role as judge to the end by calling *everything* a spade. And the unity-desiring Quentin's failure to find the brotherhood of man in socialism lends the intensity of disillusion to the commentator's early discovery of the fake unity that conceals the horror of the Stalinist purges.

From London daydream to Karachi jet-plane disaster, Quentin's life adventure is that of choosing among his roles, of learning which one he can play. Yet since no single one of the three selves first defined on the prairies of illusion emerges as "the real Quentin," the novel seems simply to be raising a further question. How can art be expected to fashion a single figure that has shape and wholeness, that can be distinguished as a single figure and one, without telling lies by making the disordered and the contradictory into a tidy pattern? In the treatment of Rupert's attempt to relate Malvolio the fool to Malvolio the desperate agonized man for his performance in *Twelfth Night* and of Margaret's attempt to relate Aunt Alice the victimizer to Aunt Alice the victimized for her novel, the question receives its most explicit formulation. That Rupert glimpses an answer while waiting his turn to speak from the Kingsway Hall platform at an anti-Fascist rally of the thirties is simply another way in which the novel insists on the radical identification of individual and national destiny as well as the radical relationship between the techniques of life and art. Out of a rare moment of compassion, of felt humanity, Rupert makes himself a better artist. Herr Birnbaum, a German refugee writer of children's stories, one of the speakers at the rally, has been pompous and rude to Rupert in the lobby before the event. Yet when Birnbaum speaks from the platform, Rupert is deeply moved.

> How could he have judged the man solely by his manner and words in a short meeting? He should have been indulgent from the start to such a . . . But "indulgence" pulled him up. What appalling patronage! No, the truth was that the great storyteller was an odious, conceited boor. But he had his vocation, his special powers, and what Hitler had done to that vocation was odious, wicked, and infinitely pitiable. To sweeten the man in order the better to resent the outrage upon him was unpardonable sentimentality. Unpardonable as his . . . yes, this was it . . . [.] He should have known. But tonight he would give some thanks to Birnbaum by repairing as far as he could his patronage of Malvolio (pp. 405–6).

And he does give a superb performance that evening — a performance so fine that Margaret, somewhat unwillingly in the audience, scribbles him a note of appreciation before she leaves the theatre. "Rupert, my dear darling, it was *so* good! Don't have any doubts. I thought from the crits that you had honeyed it all over, but you haven't — he's odious and worthy and when he's brought low it's unbearable and as soon as he's up again he's odious once more. Thank you ever so much — you've solved my problem. Mag"

(p. 408). Her problem, of course, is the problem of her novel and she hurries home "to let Aunt Alice fall apart into all the various unrelated persons that she now knew bobbed up and sank down like corks in the ocean inside that old raddled body as inside all our bodies" (p. 408).

What Rupert learns, momentarily at least, from life, and Margaret learns from Rupert's art, is a truth the novelist himself demonstrates through such devices as the three Quentins journeying to Eldorado and, in fact, also demonstrates by letting Rupert learn from life and Margaret from art: no thing is just one thing and no tool for apprehending truth is the only, or even a wholly adequate, tool.

The Game, as the Matthews children devise and play it, works as yet another of the novel's technical devices to explore this multiplicity of "various unrelated persons" which "bob like corks" inside the single self. The Dramatis Personae are the elder Matthewses, Aunt Mouse and Granny M as well as the Countess and Billy Pop, and Regan, the family slavey; the Actors are the children themselves. While the daydreams unfold the roles of the future, The Game dramatizes the imminent past, offering the reader fresh insights into both the mimickers and the mimicked. Marcus's role is foreshadowed by the scene in the hall of laughing mirrors at the Great Exhibition where he greets his reflection "all flashing eyes and beaky features" with hysterical screams, trying to "magic away" the image he sees there, which, all the others agree, *is* Her, the Countess. For The Game, he assumes her role, and as he plays it out, Angus Wilson is able to dramatize a complex variety of psychological truths: the love-hate relationship between the Countess and her unwanted baby son; the shrewdness of the Countess transformed into the shrewdness of her son; the double-twisted irony of the Countess and her entourage of lovers called up in mockery by the homosexual Marcus and his entourage of lovers. Through it all, Marcus directs the thrust of his mimicry toward the exposure of the fake gentility of the Countess. For The Game is critique as well as portraiture. Evaluating through its action, it creates an image of the future generation by the way in which it records the image of the past. Once again the novelist holds up his laughing mirror to Art so that we too may preside over the creation of Nature.

As proto-Drama, The Game defines art born out of human need. It is brought into being, Angus Wilson tells us, by the Matthews children's "need to relieve their pent-up shame, distress, and anger in histrionics, to heal their hurts with mimicry's homeopathic sting, and no doubt as well to indulge some sexual urges" (p. 131). The children instinctively seek to fictionalize life, to make drama out of raw emotion, as a way of making life bearable. And the mimicry that is art makes life bearable because it demands order, "observation," and "the distance" imposed "by the demands of technique" (p. 132). Again and again the novel's characters learn and exemplify the rich implications of this lesson. Margaret painfully erases the masterstroke of irony by which she has concluded a scene in a Carmichael story, her private fictionalizing of the life at No. 52, because she knows that the masterstroke is fake; it represents her personal victory over the fictionalized Matthewses of the story. In the midst of a Bermondsey street clash between British Fascists and cockney East Enders, Marcus is suddenly appalled by the "stinking armpits," the "greasy, scurfy hairs," the rearing horses and jeering youths: "Was this what Picasso's wonderful 'Guernica' stood for, this Roman holiday? No form, no rich colour, no pale elegance. Nothing. Nothing to satisfy in this shapeless human muddle" (pp. 350–51). Sukey, cushioning herself against the terror of war that threatens her personal creation of family order, lives out a sentimentalized version of Granny M's definition of being grown up: the recognition that "however silly you have been in the past it's all part of you, you can't refuse it. . . . But laughing too a little. . . . Remembering all the funny things that have happened in the family" (pp. 104–5). When her schoolmaster husband must shift schools so that schoolboys may be out of bombs' reach, and Sukey must disrupt the pattern of her days by welcoming ungrateful German-Jewish refugees to her home, she begins to broadcast her stories of such family adventures as "How to Climb Snowdon Without a Tin Opener" and "When Santa Left Too Many Cricket Bats" (p. 422). For twenty years, she supplies the local radio and the local newspaper with these sentimentalized fictions of life: With the Pascoes on a Nile Houseboat; the Adventures of Winnie the Wolseley. The refugees depart; the war ends; Sukey's adored youngest son, P. S., is killed in "that Palestine business." Yet Sukey goes on telling stories. The last time she appears in the novel, after the BBC and the local press have stopped carrying her material, she is seen in the Lady Chapel of the Cathedral at her prayers. She is telling God how " 'P. S. and I decided to walk to Porlock that afternoon, haven't I ever told you? Well, of all the embarrassing things, I was suddenly taken short. So there was nothing to do but ring the bell of this old dilapidated rectory — all covered in ivy, you know' " (p. 477).

We are shocked into laughter by this grotesque image of the aging Sukey telling God a story just as Marcus is shocked into fury by Margaret's Carmichael Wedding story in which his own existence is simply described as " 'so mysteriously lost for hours of the night among London's bright lights' " when all the while, Marcus rages, " 'Do you want to know what I was doing 'lost among London's bright lights?' I was flitting from one sordid old man to another trying to sell my bum' " (p. 208). Early in the novel, Regan carries on a wonderful counterpoint conversation with Sukey in the kitchen of No. 52 in which she mingles hardheaded no-nonsense comment about the behavior of "the poor" with a wholly credulous response to the murder account (" 'It was the left luggage ticket that done for im, you know. They couldn't identify on burned legs alone' ") she is reading in *The News of the World*. " 'It seems er sister ad seen it all in the cards. . . . Everythin. Right down to the boiling of the ead,' " she solemnly reports, just after she has reprimanded Sukey: " 'You don't want to believe all you're told' " (p. 80). Each of these episodes is a necessary reminder that while fictions can heal hurts and create meanings, they remain, nevertheless, fictions: tools of life, not life itself.

The final dissolution of No. 52 Gilbrook Street while it does not, significantly enough, end the novel, does appropriately call for a reprise of the novel's themes to achieve their full harmony. The Countess and Billy Pop are dead; the war is over; the children gather together, for the last time in the novel, to settle the estate, to estimate what is salvageable from the "dust and pinched memories" of No. 52 before the house is sold. Once again the children enter as a cast of unknown characters, but this time the multiple selves of the daydreams are replaced by solid physical figures posing the question of accomplishment, not potentiality. Is the "slim-figured, balding man" a window dresser? a portrait photographer? "The elegant, thin-faced, tall woman" a buyer of Paris models for a London shop? The head-mistress of a school? (pp. 435–36). As before, the camera eye gives no trustworthy clue to the identity of Marcus and Margaret. As the children range the house, they take up familiar postures before familiar pieces of furniture: Rupert at the out-of-tune grand piano; Sukey at the kitchen stove. Each assesses the extent and the manner in which he has been bred by No. 52: to what extent released; to what extent fatally crippled. And then they slide, once again and for the last time, into The Game. At first the mimicry is simply a revival of past performances. Then Quentin joins in to pronounce the final judgment, resuming his Nursery role as Mr. Justice Scales:

> ". . . let me sit on the Judgment Seat. . . . let me take the place of Jehovah himself, the Ancient of Days, with a long white beard down to my navel. William Ackerley Matthews, your sins are forgiven you. Maud Iseult Matthews, your sins are forgiven you. Clara Madeline Matthews, your sins are forgiven you. . . . Henrietta Peebles Stoker, your sins are forgiven you. Give them all harps and haloes."
>
> Sukey clicked in disapproval. Marcus quickly snatched up Sukey's fox stole that lay across the sofa back and cast it stylishly round his shoulders.
>
> "Billy," he called, "Billy, is that God prosing away there, impertinently forgiving us all? Turn Him out of the house at once. Just because He's always been out of all the fun and games is no reason why he should bring his great self-pitying clay feet in here, ruining my carpet. . . ."
>
> Quentin stood over his young brother with his fist raised as though to smash him in the face, then lowered it and went back to his seat. Marcus fussed with the fur about his neck, but he said no more.
>
> The silence was broken by Sukey the practical.
>
> "Well, the sooner we get everything sorted out the better. Supposing I do the nursery. Will you do the upstairs bedrooms, Gladys?"
>
> . . . .
>
> But even she did not find the courage to ask for her fox fur stole to be restored to her. It was better, she thought, just to get on with things (pp. 451–52).

A superb climax, the passage is a brilliantly ironic apotheosis of the life-killing vitality of the Countess, a summary judgment of the adequacy of Quentin the judge, a final comment on the relationship of Quentin and Marcus, and a pyrotechnic display of Marcus's wit and shrewdness. Most important of all, it is a fittingly complex resolution of the way in which the novel has continuously played art against life, art through life, and life through art. For through the art of The Game, truths have been told that life itself can only silently recognize, pausing for a moment before getting on "with things." The indeterminate phrase marks the limits of life and suggests yet another definition of the relationship: life will "get on with things"; art will then give those "things" their name.

Neither Play, nor Game, appears in the novel once No. 52 is dismantled. All but two of the children leave England, expatriates and wanderers. The Edwardian daydream of Eldorado has been revealed as the desert waste land of Mogador. Yet the Saga has not been without its glories, and the deliberate flatness of the concluding sections images a "get[ting] on with things" that some future art will surely name. Moreover, Marcus's knowledge, that "out of shapeless human muddle" came the splendor of Picasso's *Guernica*; and the reader's experience, that out of "the pent-up shame, distress and anger" of Britain of the sixties was evolved The Game that is this novel, testifies amply that the power of true art is indeed No Laughing Matter.

Notes

1. Angus Wilson, *No Laughing Matter* (New York: Viking Press, 1967), p. 4. All future references will be to this edition and will be cited in the text.

2. "Ten Minutes to Twelve," *A Bit Off the Map* (London: Secker & Warburg, 1957), p. 193.

3. *The Old Men at the Zoo* (London: Secker & Warburg, 1961), pp. 274–75.

4. *The Letters of Henry James*, ed. Percy Lubbock (New York: Scribner, 1920), I, 58.

The Fiction of Pastiche: The Comic Mode of Angus Wilson
Malcolm Bradbury*

There was nothing for it, Gladys thought, but to make them laugh. After all, she'd suggested the mirrors, so she couldn't let them spoil the afternoon. But when she saw herself she was too disconcerted at first to speak. "Look," Sukey cried, "Gladys is upside down." And so it proved — at the top of the glass, white boots in reverse; at the base, a plump face grown

*Reprinted with permission of the author from *Possibilities: Essays on the State of the Novel* (Oxford Univ. Press, 1973), pp. 211–30.

red with surprise. They all at last could laugh. To keep the fun going
Gladys stood on her head on the shiny, linoleum floor . . . .
                                        — Angus Wilson, *No Laughing Matter*

1

The number of postwar English writers whom we can regard as major,
as of long-term importance and representativeness, is clearly no more than
a handful; still, Angus Wilson is obviously one. To many people he stands as
the most developed and impressive novel-writer of his generation, the generation after Virginia Woolf, Evelyn Waugh, Graham Greene, Anthony
Powell: a writer who carries an enormous substance in and behind his
work, who has produced some of our bulkiest, socially most solid novels,
who has expanded extraordinarily from the witty, economical brilliance of
his malicious early stories into a fiction of extended historical and human
scope — *Anglo-Saxon Attitudes* (1956), *Late Call* (1964), *No Laughing Matter* (1967). He has brought alive the possibility of a substantial, compassionate fiction, a realistic writing of moral evolution and growth; he has
humanistically reactivated the tradition of the past, so that to read him is to
feel the force of what nineteenth-century novelists as various as Jane Austen
and Dostoevsky might pass on to a contemporary author; he has lived a
significant, central cultural life as an observer and a critic, existed seriously
for us as, in the broadest sense, a modern man of letters. That said, we must
add that his reputation, though very high in credit, is very mixed in basis;
the admiration in which he is held is based on judgements remarkably varied. Moreover, nearly every critic who has written on him seriously has felt
an ambiguity, of emphasis and perspective, in his writings. Wilson himself
has encouraged them in doing so, pointing, for instance, to the "fierce sad-
ism and a compensating gentleness" which leads to a simultaneous love and
hate in his view of his characters,[1] to his sense of the dual nature of all
action, at once rational and self-satisfying, and his awareness of the strange
autobiographical illusions and obsessions that are involved in all writing.

What is more, there is something elusive about his gifts — a way of
driving home his points unsteadily, or not sustaining the compelling substance of a theme — which seems mixed with this, *and* with the ambiguous
status he has always attached to writing as such. In his confessional book
The Wild Garden, Or Speaking of Writing (1963), he remarks on his early
discovery that one purpose of story-telling was to exert charm, and win success, often by spurious means; in his *Writers at Work* interview, he speaks of
the importance of recognizing that fiction is trickery: "All fiction for me is a
kind of magic and trickery — a confidence trick, trying to make people believe something is true that isn't. And the novelist in particular is trying to
convince the reader that he is seeing society as a whole." Knowledge of literature as counterfeit is a recurrent theme in modern writing; in Wilson's
case, the understanding cuts deep into the speech and words of his charac-

ters, giving them something of that self-mimicking quality which is a typical attribute of tenure in his universe. But it also reaches back into the writer and implicates him. It promotes the admirable pastiche qualities of *No Laughing Matter*, but also those strange positional insecurities that keep on arising as the relationship between Wilson's narrative posture and his characters keeps proving oblique and surprising. Those who have seen his work as a realistic fiction of social range and moral maturity have always this side of his work to come to terms with; it is the biggest problem his writing poses. Of course he is that sort of writer: he offers himself as a moral power; there *is* in his work a singular moral maturity and perceptiveness. But to overlook the elements of self-doubt and self-mockery would be to miss something quite as essential, and quite as creatively significant, having to do with an uncertainty towards, or a qualification of, that fiction of adult social seriousness he so much admires.

The area in which this is best elucidated is, I think, that of comedy; and Wilson's comedy is of a decidedly elusive and protean kind. *Hemlock and After*, his first novel, a brilliant work of liberal moral analysis, explores a novelist, Bernard Sands, who has developed from *enfant terrible* to moral scourge. "If he had forced from the public and the critics respect and hearing for his eternal questioning of their best-loved 'truths,' " the text tells us, "he must never allow them to feel that they were indulging the court jester. They should continue to take from him exactly the pill they did not like, and take it without any danger of whimsy." Sands has his moral energy and point. But the moral scourge is also Wilson himself, who straightway moves beyond the moral sophistication of his agent to a point outside and beyond him: "If on occasion he mistrusted his own powers, it was not a mistrust that he intended others to share." Wilson establishes, as an aspect of his narratorial power, that Bernard Sands's humanism can arise from impure motives, psychological inconsistencies. This he does by establishing a critical perspective which contains equal parts of moral wisdom and toughness — of a kind that Jane Austen or George Eliot might have approved — and something very like malice. The moral toughness is concerned with eliciting self-awareness and responsibility; the malice is concerned with exposing such competences and establishing that there is, in the end, no such thing — all motives are impure, human action is puppet-like, absurd. This is, I think, one of the reasons why Wilson's six apparently substantial and stable novels, socially panoramic and dense, do not in fact hold steady when we read them, but dissolve into a distinctive kind of grotesque. And it is also one of the reasons why the narrator himself, moving between the creation of his characters and of a design and attitude which might contain them, tends to shift and increasingly to dissolve with the books, giving the writing an increasing flavour of mimicry or pastiche. This in fact becomes more or less the complete mode of *No Laughing Matter*, and hence a very explicit formal attribute. I link the pastiche and the odd moral stance because they lend, I fancy, a very distinctive texture to the writing and form a distinctive set of perceptions about our social and human nature. Above all, I think, they point towards or attempt to cope with an emptiness at the centre of all human action, manifest as a persisting theatricality which informs it. Human life is a role or performance, society is a theatre, the masks and disguises are irrevocable and they are total. The self we live with is counterfeit, and in that situation the trickery reaches back to the narrator himself, who acts too, as creators must, but in so doing does not so much make a meaningful society and meaningful agents in it as mimic them both.

This gives a very protean kind of comedy, one that makes Wilson's novels interesting, complex, and decidedly hard to assess. The fact is that it is all too easy to find in him the figure of the novelist he might have been, had his dedication to a kind of novel that he obviously values — the novel of great social substance, in which the fictional action illuminates through dense and serious individual lives the density and texture of the society as a whole — been that bit surer, more complete. But there surely also resides in his work a decided questioning — moral, intellectual, technical — of just that sort of novel; his comedy and creative energy partly depend exactly on this. In an early essay he claimed that the feel of the solidity of society is often gained fictionally at the cost of depth, especially depth in psychological perception and awareness. If the modern novel has become engrossed by anything, it is by the events in these realms, and it is clearly a substantial part of Wilson's own proceeding that an adequate compromise must be managed by any modern writer seriously concerned with the expanding possibilities of his form; as he puts it: "We are on the threshold of a psychology for which the older novel forms do not provide."[2] Any account of his interest and value as a novelist has to include the real attentiveness he has given to the moral uncertainty of the novelist once the idea of unconscious motive and Freudian drives is accepted, when neurotic or perverse experience of any kind becomes part of the central substance of fiction.

The difficulty in talking about Wilson's work, indeed, is that we can see very different species of novelistic activity and ambition proceeding at the same time. It is not surprising that various critics have sought to explain and explore his writings by stressing one or another. Some have recognized him as a direct inheritor of a central tradition in English fiction — the socio-moral tradition, concerned with the moral analysis of life in society; seen in this light, he carries on the habitual concerns of story-tellers from Jane Austen to Forster, and especially that vein of humanist concern with the moral conduct of persons, into the context of postwar uncertainty.[3] Of this tradition, a predominantly liberal and realist tradition, Wilson has written appreciatively; similarly he has praised the attempt of a number of postwar English novelists to restore "the social framework in which human hopes and despairs must be viewed if duty and responsibility or defiance of duty and responsibility are to have full meaning."[4] Wilson always creates his people, whatever his psychological concerns, as members of society; he creates society as a dense, historically specific web in which we are all involved; he expands his work contingently through social time and space. It is a selective society, characteristically upper- or middle-middle class (as is the community in which most English fictional characters live, though not most English people), vaguely intellectual, decidedly stylish — as is clear from the lists of dramatic *personae* that Wilson usually gives us; *No Laughing Matter* has an "additional cast" of "Husbands, wives, lovers of various kinds, university teachers, and undergraduates, Russians, members of Society, politicians, journalists, members of Lloyds' and of the Bloomsbury Group, Cockneys, German refugees, staffs of preparatory schools, English residents abroad, Egyptians, actors and actresses, Moroccans, financiers, Scandinavians, and representatives of the Younger Generation." The camp and comic edge, as well as the metaphorical theatricality, of the list are all to the point; still, it *is* an extended world, and to see what a good reach it is we have to think back to the great Victorian novels, with their grasp of social and historical span. We also have to recall another feature of the liberal-realist novel, its controlling moral concern. Wilson is unmistakable in his tough-minded interest in moral responsibility, and the milieu of extreme strain and tension in which moral acts are conducted; at times he is unsparing in his capacity for satirical exposure. Even as he relishes his world for its style, its social flamboyance, he measures and judges according to a comic and ironic mode. And one of the functions of irony and comedy in his work is to be directed, as it is in Forster's novels, towards a centre, showing up moral and emotional atrophy, self-deceit and unrecognized failure in the realm of the personal. If, as Ian Scott-Kilvert tells us, the basic action of Wilson's work is satiric and its prime object of attack "the façade of middle-class values and manners, the hollowness of the respectability, the decorum and the apparently 'progressive' virtues which can mask hypocrisy, meanness, immaturity exhibited to a pathological degree, and above all cruelty,"[5] then that concern suggests a place in a liberal-radical line of writing that has spoken to the good for tolerance, personal sanity, and individual decency, a line of decided force and worth sustaining at a high level of credit. And any practised reader of Wilson's novels will indeed find his own instances of the way that delicate acerbity, that critical intelligence, that sane moral appreciation, has been exercised.

This is *one* of the ways in which the satirical thrust of Wilson's work has been employed; but it is not the only or the final way. There is something else, and again a tradition for it, reaching back to the Victorian period; what it is Wilson, in various essays and in *The World of Charles Dickens* (1970), has himself made very explicit. "The intense haunting of my imagination by scenes and characters from Dickens's novels has continued and developed into my middle age," he has told us; and gone on to say that he is aware not so much of the wholeness of Dickens's novels as of parts of them, of an "atmosphere and scene which are always determinedly fragmentary."[6] Dickens's vision of society is of course decidedly different from that of the novelists of more composed manners; society does different things to his characters and gives them different natures. Raymond Williams has helped to define this; as he puts it, Dickens's characters "speak at or past each other, each intent above all on defining through his words his own identity and reality; in fixed self-descriptions, in voices raised emphatically to be heard through and past other similar voices."[7] It might be added that the expressing of identity is often a kind of flattening, a self-dramatization which is also a psychological simplification; and that we have the novelist there in his comic guise to encourage the process and elicit the individual nature as an aspect of social grotesquerie. This kind of comedy gives us a world both familiar and alien, lifelike and distorted, containing evil and nightmare as well as beneficence and community, a world where identity is easily lost, where the psychological and social interact strangely, that interaction being expressed by grotesquerie and surreality, by curious mimings and exaggerations which evoke stress and tension. Wilson has seen this in Dickens, noting his total "unspoken atmosphere" made up of themes of wandering and imprisonment and flight, modes of make-believe and false seeming. This is social and panoramic, but not in George Eliot's or Tolstoy's way; the world is a strange and unreal city, the consequences of living in which are tension, psychological distortion, stress. And this atomization, this sense of personal fragility, awareness of society not as a solid substance but as a seeming, is in Wilson's writing too, and, as in Dickens, it poses strange problems of control. For the point of the writing is to release energy and invention, to generate fable, to draw deeply on autobiographical feeling and awareness, afterward shaping and designing what comes forth. The result is a novelist who is less a controlling artist capable of moral poise than one acting vigorously as an inventor and putting himself at risk by indulging the power of his own imaginings and obsession.

To get at Wilson's work, one must note how strangely the two debts coexist. The dimensions of the analytic moralist are there: so is the writer of running inventiveness, the mimer and the player, the maker of grotesque. In places the rigour of moral analysis we know from Jane Austen is very evident, and ultimately, in *Hemlock and After* and *The Middle Age of Mrs. Eliot*, dominant. Even there it is strangely placed against the material, for the world on which Wilson works is not neat or contained, the characters judged and measured are tinctured with unreality, touched with absurdity, and so elusive. Often we are asked to apply the test of a moral realism to personages whose moral substance the method of creation throws into doubt. We think we discern a compelling flaw of character, the features of a social snobbery or exploitation or cruelty, which the writer excoriates, for these are the telling crimes of his universe; but the moral point here does not transcend the situation, for the creator depends too much on hypocrisies of this sort for his total vision of man. We see the bondage of the family, the harsh subtext of exploitation underlying conventional relationships, the endless war of parents and children, husbands and wives; the crimes are classic liberal violations, but then they become the very stuff of existence itself, for is not all love exploitation and are not all morals self-rationalizations of need? The same problem arises with social and political judgements. Wilson's politics are ostensibly liberal and progressive, and he seems to condemn false social institutions and values; there are hints of political exposé, and of higher historical promises, of better worlds that might be, greater equality, increased tolerance. His bourgeoisie is insecure and in some way sunk in an illusion which the novelist exposes. But history, though an active force in all his writing, hardly looks, on closer inspection, regenerative. The world of the welfare state, of which he has offered many apt portraits — including the brilliant one of the new town in *Late Call* — does not transcend evil, but simply provides a new frame for its continuance; the revolutionary promise is never made real, but is another falsification or illusion. The point is that Wilson acts as if historical redemption might come; he writes the liberal-humanistic, or the radical, novel but qualifies it, taking its world often for his essential world but then touching in many insecurities.

These insecurities reach back into the narrator himself, as I have said. Wilson once commented that he had drawn from nineteenth-century fiction the form of omniscient telling he uses and needs: "In *Hemlock and After* and *Anglo-Saxon Attitudes* I chose quite naturally the 'God's eye view' in frequent use among the nineteenth-century novelists I admire. I was surprised to find how unfamiliar this had now become; indeed, in the United States it had to be explained as a revival (I am glad to say successful) of an archaic form."[8] It is in fact a commonplace form of the times, and we find it in much modern realism, satire, and comedy. But the point about Wilson's way with it is that he uses it very freely and unpuristically, as a story-teller above all interested in his story might, moving in and out of his characters as the need arises, presenting his material through many eyes, committing himself to extended episodes of exposition, allowing himself to make acerbic moral points and judgements. This use is imprecise, which is to say that Wilson performs many transactions which writers for whom such things are prime ends, basic organizational instruments for eliciting the form of art, would eschew. His material has to grow of itself, by being freely mimed and acted, in a mock-theatre in which the author creates fixed terms within which the play may occur. What Wilson needs indeed is a mode of writing which allows him a high degree of social mimicry and involvement and then a means for the assertive control of it; this duplicates the narrative activity, and potently divides it. This, I think, he has seen and worried over, which is one reason why the mode has become itself a matter for study in some of his more recent books. He has spoken in a letter of his feeling "that the traditional form has inhibited me from saying all that I wanted to say. I tried to move out of it. . . ."[9] The writer of secure management, the God-like writer with free entry everywhere yet the right to pause and judge, the author making a solid substance, has never been as secure as he might have been. And by *No Laughing Matter* he is very oddly placed indeed.

2

"But then the English novel is not an aesthetic novel, it is a social novel. *The Forsyte Saga* has great importance as the mirror of the British high bourgeoisie": so Herr Birnbaum, the Jewish-German children's novelist and refugee, who has a minor part to play in *No Laughing Matter*. The observation is clearly applicable to Wilson's own *œuvre*, and especially to some parts of it; Wilson does mirror the British bourgeoisie and its liberal intellectual associates, though with the extraordinary dimensions of mimicry, in the form both of self-identification and comic mockery, that I have mentioned, and with obvious aesthetic aspirations. The aspirations themselves have not remained steady, and they have taken him in many directions, through a pattern which seems less like a direct growth than a process of dissolution and recreation, a re-assimilation in new form of energies already employed, so that they break up the old frame. As a result of this Wilson's novels have been formally very various, and given to extraordinary surprises. As for *No Laughing Matter* itself, it is indeed a social novel, not an aesthetic one, and something of a *Forsyte Saga* or mirror of the British bourgeoisie done on a larger scale than Wilson has ever before tried. We could see it as Wilson's closest approximation to the "condition of England" novel, a social and historical fiction of wide sweep and capacious ability both to reflect, and reflect on, the culture. Its time span is broad, from 1912 to 1967; there are five books, and nine distinct time-sections, each chosen to illuminate some significant moment of interaction between the characters and modern times. Two World Wars are touched on, if indirectly and lightly; the apolitical bounce of the twenties, the darkening political and increasingly ideological picture in the 1930s, with the Bolshevik dream going sour and Fascism rising, the collapse of Empire and the crisis of Suez, the bleak emptinesses of the modern economic miracle — all these things are put with force at the centre, in a stylistic spectrum itself sufficiently variable to catch at the modes of the periods covered. There is much concern with money, and its general influence and specific usefulness; there is a good deal of concern with sexuality, especially in its more exploitative forms; there is much about class relationships, and the historical shifts and changes in social structure.

On all these matters the book is very knowledgeable, detailed, and eclectic; it is a book filled with styles, with the styles of life, self-expression, popular culture, and art which are the embodied and of course shifting historical life by which we feel the clock of things, the texture of things, changing. The novel's geography is socially broad; primarily English, but it takes in European and Northern African episodes, and the presence of Europe is very much felt. It is the geography of a modern politics. Politics and history are decided forces in the book, and administer, with usual Wilsonian severity, some salutary shocks and anguishes; in different ways the characters are forced into encounter with the outrages of Hitlerism, and a long episode about anti-Semitism and the pre-war climate, including two scenes of violence and more of weighty verbal assault, are there to drive home the point. There is a very large cast-list and a very ranging one. To it Wilson establishes a very fluid centre in his Matthews family, the six children of feckless parents who move, with some typological neatness, into various fields of modern experience and whose lives, given to us through a mode of multiple narration, separately followed out but brought on occasion back into significant conjunction, are given over a long span and involve stark experiences of change and dissolution. Through their lives, we see ways of living through a time of crisis, and the book moves from the hopes of a new world in the immediately postwar period through the political realities of the 1930s, into the post-Suez world of "hire-purchased Hoovers and a sleeping-pill salvation" on which Quentin grimly comments.

We should add, though, that the historical background is presented only through these central characters, never really reported beyond them. Along with that, the family world and the historical one are held in interesting balance. So, for obviously calculated reasons, a number of significant events in modern history are dealt with very obliquely, as a glance at the basic time-slices (1912, 1919, 1925, 1935, 1937, (brief 1942), 1946, 1956, 1967) shows us. A number of significant years (for example, 1926, the General Strike) are avoided, and the two World Wars are shown only at a distance; only in the 1930s and in 1956 do we come close to compelling events and see the characters directly encountering, or evading, them. Wilson, then, does not seem interested in representing his characters facing some compelling historical event or threat head-on, learning history direct. This, you could say, has something to do with one of his recurrent concerns, which is the theme of evasion. Indeed evasion is a compelling matter for analysis. Thus Sukey's gentility, Marcus's narcissism, Rupert's and Margaret's artistry, Gladys's female evasion of full financial responsibility, and even Quentin's politics with their strange underlying sexuality, are figures for a certain sort of escape from history — which in turn *makes* a history. In this way their saga has "great importance as a mirror of the British high bourgeoisie," and you might take it as a compelling condemnation of it. The bourgeois generational novel, the dynastic novel as we have it in *Buddenbrooks* or *Der Stechlin* or *The Forsyte Saga*, is a well-established realistic form, a very substantial and material species of fiction, able to give the sense of social substance, of historical motion, of familial rise and fall, of the interlocking of a family and a culture; but the telling point in *No Laughing Matter* is the subversion of this — the family is not a communion or a coherence, its financial roots are weak, and the substantive relationship between individual and culture is itself unreal.

The family, in fact, collapses in the opening chapter, as we see the Matthews group for a moment in "a union of happy carefree intimacy that it had securely known before and was never to know again," sharing an interlocking or communal day-dream, and then walking out confidently together on the social stage with all the authority of their class until the scene collapses in squabbles, the financial dependence of the parents on their parents (and later on their own children) becomes apparent, and the farcical reverse of the images is made manifest. The Matthewses lose their identity and the familial communion as the book starts; the effort, then, of the younger generation is to try by various means to recreate and assert it again. In this they may be said to fail; they make their peace with the older generation and nearly all of them end outside England, in the Algarve or the Moroccan desert of exile and dryness: "There [Marcus] lay on his stomach in the hot sand among the broom bushes and pressed himself deeper and deeper into its dryness . . . Didn't she . . . know anything of how he had let himself be measured and dried by life until he was at peace with the hot sand?" The historical cycle moves, not with them, but *beyond* them, so that they are superseded. They are dried, too, and the novel seems to utter a moral and historical condemnation and certainly creates larger horizons than any the characters have seen — and hence a pre-eminent sense of failure. "As we get older," says Rupert, "we don't distinguish greatly between what might have been and what is"; but the novelist seems to do that, to enforce the failure, and above all to see it as a failure to connect with reality, the significance of the relationship between modern politics and the characters' own situations being evaded in narcissism and illusion. Quentin suggests as much in the Game when he reveals his Marxism:

> I thought when I retired that I should have to condemn you [the Matthews parents] as a generation, or rather as two generations, indeed as all the older generations, perhaps as the embodiment of accumulated history. You are, after all, all we know of the past. It's you who've put us in the soup and you don't seem prepared to help us out of it for fear of scalding your fingers. Not to put any pretence on it, you are a guilty lot. But as in my moments of retirement I reflected, I soon saw that this business of generations would not do. Here we have a system and a class in decay . . .

But the fact is that a directly political reading of the novel will not do. For Wilson's satirical mode reaches beyond this into a much more fluid position.

3

This largely arises because of Wilson's relationship with his central family. The Matthewses are, from the start, one of the famous appalling families of Wilson's fiction, camp, self-aware, high stylists, histrionic performers. They thus show themselves to be founded on a shaky emotional and fiscal economy; but this state of being is one which Wilson is particularly fond of entering into, and a decided element of identification occurs. Moreover the great gift of the Matthewses is for caricature, for self-caricature and the caricature of others. And they in their turn are caricatured by an author who proves, as I want to say in a moment, very active, very creative, and also decidedly protean, a figure notable for extraordinary disappearances, rhetorical disguises, mixed registers, and much pastiche and parody on his own account. The world of false-seeming is not an object for satire as such; indeed it is precisely the world which the book seeks not just to expose but also to enjoy. In this way *No Laughing Matter* is very much a laughing matter, or history as a certain kind of farce. It is shrill farce; the farce is itself conditioned, for one feels that the comedy and absurdity, the entire theatre, is a theatre derived from society. But theatre it is; the metaphor is very exact, and it is very total. The idea exists in all of Wilson's novels; in the earlier books we have the text presented as a kind of play, in which well-defined characters exist and well-defined scenes occur, the author then participating as actor and mime and standing back as dramatist to produce his distinctive scenario. But in this novel the metaphor is very obsessive and extensive.

It is, at one level, a figure for illusion, the social illusion, the false-seeming which allows the bourgeois family to feel that, whatever the facts of society and history, they stand at the centre of the stage. But to do that they cast off character and assume roles, roles with artificial social meanings; they are players in the sense of being people who take on other identities. The distinctive thing about the Matthews family, especially in the early pages of the novel, is that they are self-knowing actors, mocking as well as mocked people. They speak in an elaborate, self-parodying discourse drawn from stage, literature, music-hall, newspapers and general cliché ("His Nibs"); they play their part in life, so that they seem at once curiously over-full and over-empty, people with great self-awareness but no substance, people through whom society or cliché speaks. This is all part of a prevalent self-awareness, the knowledge each has of the self-deceptions practised by others; it has much to do with the insecure foundations in family, and money, and society, on which their lives are built. But the theatrical metaphor is also obviously a figure not alone for false illusions in society, the disjunctive images of a declining class, but for life. The novel does not simply reveal the false theatre of disconnection, which we could then measure against reality; it creates a more total theatre in which every human being is implicated, the theatre in which we are all products of many images and perspectives. It must be said that this total theatre, in which the author is highly involved, dissolves somewhat as the novel progresses; a more literal, realistic, and indeed traditional register emerges. But in the early part the theatrical metaphor takes in many modes of self-display and self-caricature, but also creativity and artistry, and it decidedly takes in the novelist himself.

It is to the point to say that we live now in a time when the analogy with theatre has itself become very compelling for us, in a time of extravagant event and extravagant self-display, coupled with an uncertainty about selfhood, in which the idea of life as a theatre has both a vigorous and a disturbing multi-significance. In sociology the "dramaturgical analogy" — to take Erving Goffman's phrase from *The Presentation of Self in Everyday Life* — has become very telling and part of the essential basis of sociological imperialism; *homo sociologicus* is the role-player, his task ascribed to him by the total and already written social theatre in which he must take up parts, his degree of individual interpretation small, his nature made manifest in interactions with others. In psychology the theatre is social and mental; it arises in the play of early relationships and is re-manifest in all later ones. The analogy has significantly penetrated recent fiction, in, for example, Muriel Spark's *The Public Image* and John Fowles's *The Magus*, two novels stylistically not remote from what Wilson is doing here. But both postulate narrative means for the control of the theatre; Muriel Spark operates at long technical distance, and John Fowles has his surrogate impresario, the Magus himself. Angus Wilson is his own impresario, is a part of the theatre he manifests. The world within the novel is a histrionic world of acting, false-seeming, game-playing; the task of the novelist, too, is that of the mime, the *pasticheur* and parodist, for he must live inside his characters, mime the dialogue, create the scene and the style, play out the drama of inter-relationships. On this kind of activity there is considerable speculation in the text, which repeatedly realizes the metaphor in problems of appearance and reality. The characters begin by miming their parents, in order to mock them; they attempt to turn the Game into a trial, with Marxist Quentin performing the newly needed part of Mr. Justice Scales. But can a trial by mimicry be judged? On the matter the text has an answer, and it runs:

> Was the man or the woman able to be another also the most suited to defend that other's interest? Yes, for simulation, whatever its motive, demands identification. But was he or she sufficiently detached to be able to offer a defence intelligible to others as a defending counsel should, without the confusions and blurs of subjective statement? Yes, for simulation and mimicry also demand observation: in them compassion is tinged with mockery or mockery by compassion, and identification is distanced by the demands of technique. But could this simple mixture of opposites which mimicry requires, of affection with distaste, of respect with contempt, of love with hatred — be justly defined as a sort of reasoned apology? Yes, if passed through the tempering fire of the scrutiny of Mr. Justice Scales. The rules established, the Game could now proceed.

As for the novel itself, it proceeds according to the answer, and is indeed very game-like, especially in the earlier part. Here society is a very unsubstantial theatre; it gets more solid and severe, in the form of a basis for conflict between individual lives and onerous changes and threats from outside, as the book goes on. Some critics have found the opening parts the more brilliant; they constitute some of Wilson's freest invention yet and some of his cleverest, offering a world curiously rich and curiously unsubstanial, a very rococo and elaborate world of images and perspectives with very curious narratorial logics and very great delights: much parody, much comedy, much high style and camp, much drawing on the collage of popular culture and theatre, much allusion. It is also true that the theatre in question is very openly conceived, so that we have parodic devices used for an enormous variety of divergent intents: for the establishing of a histrionic extravagance common to all of the characters, for the presentation of subconscious fantasy, for the establishing of social style and texture, for the ironic observation of one character by another, for narrative presentation, and finally for authorial ironies.

This enables an enormous amount of perspectivization to take place in the text; the opening pages are, for this reason, extremely difficult to read. For the book opens on a plethora of images: first the screened images, Gaumont Graphic or Pathé Pictorial, of the Wild West Exhibition at Kensington, itself a mishmash of borrowed cultural artefacts, and then to a close-up of the Exhibition itself and the Matthews family, who "as they came that hot July afternoon through the crowds . . . might so easily have been frozen and stored away in the files of the National Film Institute," there to catch the eye of "the costume designer, the lover of moments of good cinema, or the searcher for social types"—in short, other image-collectors. But Wilson dismisses his camera to try to define their happiness: "no recording machine yet invented" could have preserved their happy carefree intimacy, he says. The content of that is more images, communally passing from head to head and taking the form of fantasies about life derived from the Exhibition. These are presented as "free" or "unconscious" but at the same time strangely interfused, so that our perspective on them is unclear and the positional source of the discourse perplexing. But from what Wilson calls the "parapsychological" stage we pass back to the social one; the shared communion links the family's social being, their *public* image; we stand with the crowd and watch them walk singing through the Exhibition. "Many in the large crowd turned with amusement or surprise to see these posh youngsters singing so loudly in public. Mr. Matthews, by now conscious of the public gaze, smiled and swung his walking stick a little at the attention of the passers-by; his wife smiled, too, to see him smiling. 'Billy loves public notice, don't you, darling?' . . ." In that he differs not at all from the rest of the family who, as the communion dissolves and the ongoing family quarrel reveals psychic and financial stress, retire on to their own stages. They act themselves and, in a sense, they act what others expect them to be. They are the central point of multiple perceptions, collations of images and products of long angles and distances; and throughout the novel they appear in counterpoint on stages, or alternatively through images themselves very plural and flamboyant. As Margaret reflects, returning to her novel: " . . . she had to hurry home to let Aunt Alice fall apart into all the various unrelated persons that she now knew bobbed up and sank down like corks in the ocean inside that old raddled body as inside all our bodies."

The cultural and psychic confusion in question is itself the result of social being, social languages and styles. The characters project roles on each other, and the world too—thus Stoker, the comic cockney servant, and her "Wild West" fantasy:

> Needed indeed now and again by Miss Stoker who, a good-natured, true serving cockney, will do anything, does do anything, for her charges. Yet in Miss Stoker's mind is the clear realization that faced by buffalo, grisly or Indians it is she, the "down at the Old Bull and Bush I shall shortly own er, walks among the cabbages and leaks" Hetty Stoker who (in her masters' version), for all her galley roaring, heart-as-big-as-the-Elephant-and-Castle loyalty, will panic, take fright, pee her knickers or otherwise betray her lowly origins instead, as the legend should be, of dying by sucking the poisoned wound of her youngest charge (Master Marcus) when the Indian arrows are flying fast and furious. Sensing their hidden view of herself indeed, Miss Stoker needs all the force of Miss Rickard's (Sourpuss to her) communicated grim irony to restrain her wish to spit in their bloody faces. But as it is, and so fortified, her version takes in theirs and, Comic Western to the life, she falls over the prickly pear, mistakes the porcupine for a camp stool . . .

The language here is so difficult because it comes from everywhere. As discourse it arises from many corners of society and literature, from popular song and children's dirty joke, cockney and mock-cockney, story and stereotype. As a set of perspectives it arises from many of the characters, from Billy Pop to Miss Rickard's, a set of overlapping, played-off versions of self. As narrative rhetoric it arises from Stoker's own inner consciousness, the consciousness of those who see her as servant or protector or comic clown, and from the novelist's own pleasurable extravagances and repetitions. It is this gives all the characters the flexibility to appear in the various modes and manners of narration; but it also allows each of them to be at once very self-aware and very unreal, and be so because he or she exists in a play in some sense predetermined by others. All are types, and play themselves at the rococo edge of things where it verges on camp or self-parody; each takes the self-mimicry of others as real or valid, but then further mimics it to show its falsity. They guy their own parts dreadfully, as fat Gladys does, or camp them to stylistic excess, as Marcus does, or turn them into forms of art, as Rupert and Margaret do; society becomes social farce—"Giggling and imitating, it was some time before they fell asleep." The Matthewses' capacity "to be another" is part of their psychic salvation too; the theatricality used for moral blackmail is used for moral recovery and finally moral judgement, through the Game, itself "born of their need to relieve their pent-up shame, distress and anger in histrionics, to heal their hurts with mimicry's homeopathic sting, and no doubt as well to indulge some sexual urges."

The mode *starts* in the characters; it extends to the author. It gives us a very protean mode of narration, marked by enormous variety of means and point of view. There is straight narrative, sketches, interspersed playlets, extended mock-plays. At all levels, there is much direct pastiche, which is to say the use of borrowed stylistic modes and manners, rhetorical mimicry; and much outright parody of particular authors — the text contains an Ibsen parody, a Shaw parody, a Chekhov parody, a Beckett parody, and, in the episode in which the kittens are killed, some pastiche *Macbeth*. Elsewhere in other ways the register is playful and in that way less than authoritative. Much literary allusion occurs; a number of stories — Margaret's Carmichael stories — are included. Much of this is very funny, in the spirit of revue. But it is also functional, another logical aspect of the multi-functional perspectives in which all life on this human stage takes place. Similarly, there is a striking element of double presentation of characters, so that structures associated with them are subverted, as in the laughing mirrors at the Kensington Exhibition; Sukey is made "soppy," Margaret "sour," Quentin "sneery," Rupert "wobbly," Marcus "beaky," and Gladys, upside-down, is ridiculous. These modes of ambiguity and distortion, and parody and pastiche, make it hard to discover the authentic register of the novel; there is a decided stabilization of the text in the latter half, but it is an evolution itself somewhat disturbing, since it involves a reduction of rhetorical energy. On these matters, too, there is speculation, especially through the character of Margaret, who has her problems in making words authentic. Her writing itself is a fearful activity, constantly at risk — "these imposed patterns falsify" — and also a psychic necessity, so that through it she evades relationships and quells anxiety, relaxing by means of "the familiar stringing together of words." Margaret advances far into irony and becomes something of a writer's writer; the danger is that of the human figures "being petrified into figures and lettered proportions," the dangers of escaping life.

To Margaret's risk Angus Wilson himself offers an implicit compensation; she is ironic and anti-Dickensian, but he has a sense of thriving life as well as an asperity. At the same time, though, there is a great literariness, a great caricaturing, an indwelling problem about the depth of individual being and the degree to which we feel what we are reading is life known and understood. Indeed the novel is in some sense about the interplay: "Never," says one critic, "except perhaps in James Joyce's work, has the pull between the two opposing tendencies of the novel, between its desire for an accurate 'realistic' rendering of life and its desire for an autonomous creation, been so clearly demonstrated as in this novel."[10] The demonstration is clear: there are questions about the outcome, for the result can hardly be said to be a balance, a synthesis. This, it seems, is because Wilson would like to have the ebullient creative energy that makes parody and the mimetic sympathy that makes the sense of life on the same side. And this they cannot quite be. These produce an equivocal form. Thus Wilson raises large questions about the density of social substance, and its absence, about the wholeness of a person, and his emptiness; but he does not find the form for an answer, in part because the questions themselves are simultaneously "real" and highly fictional. My own sense of the novel — and it is a novel that delights me — is that the balance is not exact and cannot be, that the rich and rococo display of the early pages and the sense of emotional desert that haunts the last pages cannot be brought together.

As for Mr. Justice Scales, the final judge on the world at once there and mimicked, his judgements are themselves at risk. "Let me convey your verdicts . . . ," says Quentin at the end of the novel.

> Sukey clicked in disapproval. Marcus quickly snatched up Sukey's fox stole that lay across the sofa back and cast it stylishly round his shoulders.
>
> "Billy," he called, "Billy, is that God prosing away there, impertinently forgiving us all? Turn Him out of the house at once. Just because He's always been out of all the fun and games is no reason why he should bring his great self-pitying feet in here, ruining my carpet. . . ."

As Quentin's world and Marcus's angrily co-exist, so do the two elements of the textural management of this realistic *and* game-like novel. It is a book which has great rigours of judgement, but they can apply only if we take the characters as having lived out a real life; it has great freedom of literary invention, but that exempts the characters from seriously living in that life. What comes out of the book is the problem of its formal wholeness, the problem of significantly interpreting the historical sequence of events, which is a problem in judging the degree of their substance, the intensity of their reality. We have had this imbalance locally in Wilson's earlier novels, but it has never come through at this level of risk. Of course there is something here that is very much of a piece with other current speculation about fiction, and about the illusion of reality, and the significant breaking-up of or intrusion into the substantive reality of a fiction. One could deduce that something that is happening to realism is happening in Wilson's fiction too. This, I think, would be true, especially if we discern in a number of contemporary writers not the attempt to transcend realism by fiction but the attempt to make realism and fictiveness co-exist. In this case neither the form nor the narrator balances things, except in the way that all great fictions are finally balanced. For *No Laughing Matter* takes its chance as a great release of creativity; a remarkable, buoyant, comic creation, loose, contingent, rich, playful, and as humanely and intelligently done as it can be.

Notes

1. Angus Wilson, "The Novelist and the Narrator," *English Studies Today* (Second Series) (Bern, Switzerland, 1961), 43–50.

2. Angus Wilson, "Diversity and Depth," *Times Literary Supplement*, LVII (15 August 1958), viii.

3. For this view of him, see especially C. B. Cox, *The Free Spirit: A Study of Liberal Humanism in the Novels of George Eliot, Henry James, E. M. Forster, Virginia Woolf, Angus*

Wilson (London 1963). Also see the important stress of Valerie Shaw, *"The Middle Age of Mrs. Eliot* and *Late Call:* Angus Wilson's Traditionalism," *Critical Quarterly,* XII, No. 1 (Spring 1970), 9–27, which offers a valuable counterweight to the emphasis of my discussion.

4. Wilson, "Diversity and Depth," cited above.

5. Ian Scott-Kilvert, "Angus Wilson," *Review of English Literature,* 1, No. 2 (April 1960), 42–53.

6. Angus Wilson, "Charles Dickens: A Haunting," in *Dickens: Modern Judgements,* ed. A. E. Dyson (London, 1968), 30–9.

7. Raymond Williams, *The English Novel from Dickens to Lawrence* (London, 1970), 32.

8. Wilson, "The Novelist and the Narrator," cited above.

9. Quoted by Rubin Rabinovitz, *The Reaction Against Experiment in the English Novel* (New York and London, 1967).

10. Herman Servotte, "A Note on the Formal Characteristics of Angus Wilson's *No Laughing Matter,"English Studies* (Amsterdam), 1, No. 1 (January 1969), 58–64.

[Angus Wilson and the Novel of Compassion]

James Gindin*

During the late 1940's and early 1950's, Angus Wilson acquired a reputation as a writer of sharp, astringent short stories in which the pretense or hollowness of characters' poses were torn apart by people or events. Carefully analytic, the early short stories, collected in *The Wrong Set* (1949) and *Such Darling Dodos* (1950), give some support to Wilson's reputation as a satirist, but even in those, and more certainly in the novels that follow, the reputation is both oversimplified and inaccurate. In an interview published in *The Paris Review* (Autumn/Winter 1957), Wilson said that he did not regard himself as primarily a satirist, using Orwell's *Animal Farm* and Butler's *Erewhon* as examples of satire, but that he thought of himself as writing more traditional and less "abstract" fiction, with irony as a principal approach. In classifying satire as "abstract," Wilson was probably referring to the need for an assured standard, an aloof stance from which the actions and characters satirized can be seen as ridiculous, a point of view that in itself expresses an all-inclusive theme. More appropriately for Wilson's amorphous fictional world which is not amenable to a single, all-inclusive theme, irony, far from depending on a fixed standpoint, reverses or undercuts the expectations without making a judgment between the value of the expectation and the value of the reversal. Irony emphasizes man's lack of knowledge and assurance, his need to live and act in a world where he never fully knows the causes or consequences of his actions; satire, on the other hand, emphasizes man's foolishness, as if he could and should know better.

*Reprinted with permission from *Harvest of a Quiet Eye,* by James Gindin (Bloomington: Indiana Univ. Press, 1971), pp. 277–96.

In all his novels, Wilson never judges his estranged central characters from any single or assured point of view, never establishes an imperative that would have made life more rewarding or satisfactory for the central character.

In Wilson's first novel, *Hemlock and After* (1952), a consistent ironic mode, a questioning of motives and a skepticism about perceptions, protects the story, to some extent, from the potential sentimentality of the account of a central character discovering himself. Novelist, humanist, public figure, successful originator of a government scheme to provide a country house, Vardon Hall, for talented young writers, Bernard Sands is superficially at the apex of a distinguished career that is neither fraudulent nor hypocritical. He has always recognized and contended with a certain amount of ambivalence in himself: an individualist who generally ignores authority and governments, he has nevertheless been able to put through successfully his scheme to aid writers; since his wife, some years earlier, lapsed into a psychotic withdrawal, he has had two homosexual affairs. But, now, during the months in which the novel takes place, Bernard is troubled by a sense of "evil," a force in human affairs more nakedly malign than any he has noticed before. With his kind of conventional middle-class decency, he cannot handle the cruel plots of the sickly sweet procuress, Mrs. Curry, or the malice of some of the camp followers. In an episode central to the novel, Bernard also recognizes in himself an "evil" he had not hitherto known. While waiting for a friend in Leicester Square, Bernard is asked for a match by an importuning young man. He offers matches but does not respond to the advance. Then a police detective approaches, arrests the young man, and asks Bernard if he will offer evidence. Although Bernard refuses to join the aggressive belligerence of the police, he recognizes, within himself, connected with his own homosexuality, something of cruel pleasure in the harassment of another: "But it was neither compassion nor fear that had frozen Bernard. He could only remember the intense, the violent excitement that he had felt when he saw the hopeless terror in the young man's face, the tension with which he had watched for the disintegration of a once confident human being. He had been ready to join the hounds in the kill then." The insight into himself, even in these rather melodramatic terms, influences Bernard throughout the rest of the novel, causes him, for example, to make the darkly elliptical speech at the opening ceremony for Vardon Hall, a speech which helps turn the ceremony into a chaos of insults and polite destruction. Bernard can neither extenuate nor move away from the glimpse of his own basic nature, a glimpse that he connects with his failure as a husband, a friend, a father to his two children and to the younger writers dependent upon him. He dies from a heart attack, feeling that he has failed even to come close to the humane, intelligent man he tried to be.

Were this the whole novel, *Hemlock and After* would be only a sentimental and melodramatic self-discovery suffused in pity for the self-delusion of the humanist. But, ironically, Bernard's final judgment of himself turns out to be almost as inaccurate, and certainly as overstated, as his original complacent decency had been. Just before his death, his wife, Ella, emerges from the misery and isolation of her long illness, an illness in which she learned to recognize and handle "evil." She is almost miraculously restored to psychic health, a detail convincing enough in ironically reversing Bernard's expectations even if it is not clinically convincing, and she can deal with experience even after Bernard's death. His death also has a salutary effect on some of his other associates: his sister, with whom he quarreled at their last meeting, resigns from teaching, finally able to recognize that Bernard had been accurate and compassionate; the young homosexual with whom he had his more recent affair is able to leave his suffocating mother and take a flat in London on his own. Yet Wilson's sense of irony causes him also to qualify these triumphs at the very end. In the final scene, taking place months later, one of Bernard's most cherished principles about the writer's home has been overthrown. He had insisted that the writers administer it themselves, but they choose to hire a professional political administrator to save time and trouble. Bernard, Wilson makes clear at the end, never did know himself or his world very well. His triumphs and defeats qualify each other through irony, an irony which both defines precisely Bernard's limited degree of survival beyond death (a survival more dependent on personal influence than on public pose), and saves the novel from the sentimentality involved in excessively fondling his discovery of "evil."

The resolution of Wilson's next novel, *Anglo-Saxon Attitudes* (1956), is also presented through a series of ironies. The central figure, Gerald Middleton, recognizes, in his early retirement and his comfortable insulation from the banalities of his profession and family, that he has always avoided responsibility. In a large, extended world that contains many versions of "truth," the narrow scholar's petty documentation, the paranoid scholar's obsession with a fixed idea, one of Gerald's son's conventional codes of society and religion, another son's oversimplified and melodramatic public exposures of flaws in the social structure, Gerald's wife's indiscriminate and suffocating nourishment of everyone, his young grandson's assurance that patterns always fit together, Gerald manages to work out, with great difficulty, the "truth" of the past he has evaded for so long. But discovering the "truth" and acting on it in an attempt to redeem the past do not necessarily lead to triumph.

Irony qualifies and defines the motives and the impact of all Gerald's attempts to act on the basis of his newly discovered "truth." He does find out and publish the truth about an archeological fraud, which involves a number of reputations and careers he cares about, and his account of the fraud is generally heralded by the scholarly world as both an accurate solution of a discrepancy and an announcement of his return to active scholarship. But one important and pedantic new scholar accepts Gerald's new stature only because he sympathizes so strongly with the fact that one of Gerald's sons, the shabby pseudo-radical commentator, has been permanently injured in an auto accident. The narrow pedant regards the young man who invents wide and unsubstantiated public causes as a popular hero. Irony limits the utility of Gerald's actions even more strongly in his private life, for, although private and public concerns, domestic lives and careers, impinge on each other strongly, they are not necessarily resolved in the same way. Gerald acknowledges to his former mistress, whom he loved but abandoned in order to stay with his wife all the years the children were growing up, that he ought to have married her, but a realization and an acknowledgement cannot make up for thirty lost years. He also confronts his wife and daughter, in a dramatic scene, with the "truth" that the wife had, in a moment of hysteria and cruelty, deliberately pushed the daughter, when an infant, into the fire which maimed the infant's hand. But he learns that his daughter had suspected this all along and still, like her brothers, reveres her soft, wheedling, emotionally fraudulent mother more than her humane, truthful, but hitherto remote and indifferent father. These ironies suggest a constant lack of connection between cause and effect, between motive and consequence, in human behavior. The irony demonstrates how little man ever knows of what propels him to act or of what the consequences of his action will be. The final scene of *Anglo-Saxon Attitudes* adds another dimension to the irony by quickly presenting an exterior view of Gerald. After all his efforts to discover, acknowledge, and publicly affirm the "truth" of his experience, after fully abandoning his isolation, Gerald is about to leave to deliver two lectures in Mexico, a flight signifying the active resumption of his career. At the airport, he meets a prying and aggressive female novelist who, after he leaves, pronounces on the shame of men with brains, money, and good looks wasting their talents in easy, conscienceless inactivity. The irony of human misjudgment comes full circle.

Wilson's next novel, *The Middle Age of Mrs. Eliot* (1958), also depicts a character's efforts to come to terms with experience after a period of comfortable isolation. In this instance, however, the end of isolation is forced, for Meg Eliot's pleasant wrapping of social and charitable activity is ended when her husband is killed in Srem Panh by some students who intended to shoot a local government official. Left without sufficient money to continue living as she had been, finding relationships altered because her position in society is altered, Meg must emerge from isolation in order to establish a life for herself. The irony in this novel is frequently dramatic, the author's foreshadowing of events to come. Talking with her husband, the night before they are to leave on the fatal trip, Meg speaks of the horror of her mother's life with "the person you loved simply not there"; when she first sees Srem Panh, she thinks of it as only rather remotely exotic, a place where "nothing that happened . . . could ever concern her." Dramatic irony, as in classical Greek drama, informs the audience how blind man is. Blindly, Meg goes through a series of episodes with old friends in which she either manipulates or is manipulated, in which she finds no way of working out her future, until, breaking down, she retreats to her brother's large commercial nursery in the Sussex Downs. The nursery restores her to health, but, after a year or so, she must leave, for she cannot accept another form of isolation, another protective wrapping that covers her in comfortable evasions. Her brother, David, a pacifist, a quietist, a homosexual content to live for years with a faithless lover, has been and is content to swaddle himself in trivial tasks, but Meg cannot permanently accept such passivity for herself. In addition, she fears changing the direction of David's activity, pushing him to resume the scholarly career he had abandoned at least fifteen years earlier. And for Meg, dominating, always too easy, is another form of evasion, another way of avoiding meeting experience. Ironically, the environment that restored her to health must be abandoned, at the end, for the amorphous world of contemporary London that helped precipitate her collapse. Her decision marks her rediscovered capacity to meet experience, a life of "sane" involvement within the contemporary world.

Wilson has himself commented in *The Wild Garden* (1963), the published version of three lectures he gave at the University of California in Los Angeles on his own life and work, on the similar central figure apparent in each of his first three novels. He views all three as estranged, as caught between the hells of the contemporary failure to communicate despite the cocktail parties and jobs and government connections, and of the long and lonely reveries attempting to examine experience, "the opposed hell of the maze of self-pity and neurosis." Bernard, Gerald, and Meg are, at different times, caught in each hell. In *The Middle Age of Mrs. Eliot*, the progression from one hell to the other is most direct, Meg moving from the social hell of superficial activity and meaningless communication to the hell of neurotic loneliness after her husband's death. All three of the central figures, fundamentally, in Wilson's terms, decent, sensitive, and responsible, recognize their alternate hells, and Gerald and Meg go further than Bernard does in attempting to break down the estrangements, to live on the complicated earth instead of making themselves as comfortable as possible in one hell or another. And a frequent use of irony prevents these novels, particularly the latter two, from being read as the desperate struggles of noble put-upon heroes to emerge from loneliness. All the central figures are made too aware of themselves and their ambivalence, are too qualified by their own responsibility for their estrangements, to endorse such a sentimental reading.

Less fundamentally ironic than the earlier novels, *The Old Men at the Zoo* (1961), although in part a parable or fable applied to human government, also deals centrally with human isolation. The narrator of the novel, Simon Carter, the secretary of the London zoo during successive and very different administrations, is another of Wilson's detached, isolated, self-protective figures. Wilson uses some irony in having Simon discover himself through the fact that, in the midst of a war, fleeing the zoo on a mission alien to his principles, he is forced to kill and eat badgers, the animals he once protected as his primary zoological interest, in order to survive. The irony forces Simon to recognize the necessary atavism within the human creature, within himself, and this recognition chastens him, makes him less arrogant, priggish, detached, and inhumane. Yet the sense of irony that propels the change in Simon, that allows him to take principled stands in the necessarily political conflicts of a society instead of preserving his detached accommodation to whatever political or governmental mode temporarily reigns, is not made central to the novel or sufficiently complex to qualify human triumphs and defeats.

The focus on breaking down a central figure's protective evasion in order to admit a wider sense of life and the development of attitudes through irony are both dominant in Wilson's next novel, *Late Call* (1964). The central figure is Sylvia Calvert, the retired manageress of a seaside hotel who, with her husband, comes to live with her son, the headmaster of the secondary modern school in Carshall New Town. Early scenes at the seaside hotel before leaving and on the train to Carshall establish Sylvia as one who needs to minister to others, to help smooth things, to find herself through relationships with others. Accustomed to a lifetime of caring for the guests and burying herself completely in their needs and their concerns, she now, without occupation, needs to discover something more central about herself. In contrast, her husband, Arthur, is blustering, irresponsible, the old sport who uses any new acquaintance as audience for his tall stories and his aggressive geniality. As Sylvia, with genteel embarrassment, listens to Arthur rewrite the past or change his view of any friend or member of the family to suit his momentary convenience, she recognizes that relationships exist for great lengths of time which benefit neither party, and that communication is not always desirable or meaningful. After something like forty-five years of marriage, she summarizes: "Stale rows leading nowhere; intimacy that did not signify. Yet in novels you read of family feuds that went deep enough to kill young love for ever, and that the brush of a hand roused tenderness enough to mend the fiercest quarrel. But books and life were not the same; there was no sense in expecting such a thing." Sylvia of course reads only bad books. She is sound enough about her own life. Even when Arthur dies, having for months in Carshall New Town continued his career of story-telling, gambling, borrowing money from whomever he could with no intention of returning it, Sylvia's reaction is far from sentimental.

The avoidance of sentimentality in *Late Call* is important, for the story of Sylvia, the woman who develops a deep sense of the darkness at the center of human experience, who can pierce through the healthy busy-ness of New Town life to see the various darknesses that trouble each of her three grandchildren even though she misunderstands the smart, contemporary terms and references they use, is potentially sentimental. Yet Wilson's irony displays her inadequacies, her occasional denseness, her frequent self-abasement originating in misunderstanding. And Sylvia herself is not sentimental, for she clearly sees the rural slum, the poverty, the drunkenness, the parental brutality, and the rigid class system that helped to form her and prepare her for a life of service. Although she recognizes some of the pompous hollowness of the New Town, she also knows that it is generally less restrictive and less inhumane than her own background. Irony qualifies, prevents either the sentimentality of an overwhelming nostalgia for a dimly remembered past or the sentimentality of overwhelming faith in the progressive, problem-solving present.

Sylvia's own tendencies toward sentimentality are also depicted as her greatest inadequacy. In trying to discover relationships to replace those of her former occupation, Sylvia shows tremendous sympathy for victims: for benighted women in television soap operas and bad historical novels, for the lonely and helpless victims of famous murder cases, for a woman she once knew at the hotel whose niece was murdered, for her grandson's homosexual friend who gassed himself rather than face disclosure. Yet her recognition of human darkness and her sympathy for the victims are not enough to give Sylvia any sense of meaning. She identifies with her victims too closely, immersing herself in a subtle form of self-pity, falling into one of the lonely hells Wilson described for the central characters in his first three novels. To avoid isolation, Sylvia must do more than recognize and sympathize.

At first, in Carshall New Town, her efforts to help her family (her son's wife has recently died) seem futile. The organized and mechanized household runs without her; her son and her grandchildren patronize her into a remoteness from their concerns; the various trivial jobs thrust upon her, she can easily see, are meaningless and mechanical. Her only reaction is to immerse herself even further in the useless and banal sympathy for soap opera heroines and victimized old women. She needs, instead, to discover herself, the entity of individual reactions and attitudes behind the lifetime of service and sympathy, the self that can make demands on others as well as be imposed upon.

Her discovery of her past and herself emerges in ironically unlikely places. She first begins her awareness of self through the sermon of an old Scots preacher who comes to Carshall as a last-minute replacement on Easter Sunday. His homey and anachronistic sermon, asking for "God's Grace" and imploring man to face the hollowness and darkness of his own being, shocks the consciously contemporary and progressive local citizens, but reaches Sylvia. Later, on one of her walks outside Carshall, she saves a precocious American child from a bolt of lightning in a sudden storm, takes the child home, and collapses in the strange family's house. Recovering, she begins to talk to the child's parents, discusses her own childhood on the farm, her own opinions and perspectives, establishes a relationship that is not dependent on charity, condescension or service. Ironically, it is significant that the child's family is American, alien (like the Scots preacher), outside the normal range of Carshall life or of Sylvia's hotels, even includes customs and informalities hitherto strange to Sylvia. The "late call" of the title has changed from the instruction left at the hotel front desk to the self-recognition of one person's own value late in life.

Wilson himself has said that grace is the theme of the novel. But to talk of grace, or to say (as one critic has) that the novel advocates salvation by grace as opposed to salvation by works, is to falsify Wilson's position and oversimplify the novel. Wilson does not oppose the alternatives of grace and works as if he were a party in a seventeenth century theological controversy. Rather, he demonstrates that only by acquiring a personality, a force, a kind of non-theological grace, can Sylvia liberate herself sufficiently to establish any kind of constructive relationship, to have any impact on others. Good works, relationships, exterior activities, can be meaningless if they simply serve others or if a sentimental sympathy is the only motive; but good works can also be genuine and important if they originate in the response of a vital human being, if they emerge from a kind of human grace. In Wilson's agnostic theology, salvation by grace and salvation by good works are far from incompatible.

Once liberated from her own image of service, Sylvia can help her family more directly. When her son Harold suffers a minor mental collapse, breaks down in wailing that his children really hate him and that he is helpless without his wife, Sylvia, now a person instead of an object for charity, is able to understand and bury the darkness for him, return him to his safety of town planning and sociological questionnaires. The treatment of Harold introduces another kind of Wilsonian irony. Immersed in his ponderous principles, his schemes for organization, and his fascination with contemporary domestic gadgetry, Harold had, early in the novel, seemed simply an object of satire, a modern version of Dickens' Gradgrind. Yet, ironically, through the very satire, as Harold increasingly is isolated in his principles, fails to organize his family in his own terms, and fumbles ineptly with his gadgetry, the reader feels more and more sympathy for him as another human being whose schematic efforts to understand life are futile. Harold hasn't the capacity for Sylvia's grace, but he is, almost ironically, human as she is. Harold can never face the darkness as fully as Sylvia can, just as he cannot accept the fact that one of his sons is homosexual, for not all people in Wilson's fiction are equally sensitive and responsive, equally able to face the world without a protective fabrication like service or the progressive principles of New Town life. Only those of special sensitivity, like Sylvia, or Gerald Middleton or Meg Eliot, are able to accept and thrive on the breaking down of barriers, the abandonment of protective remoteness.

The preface to *Late Call* is a long chapter about a poor farm child, never named, in 1911, whose sense of joy and independence, of "beauty" and "wonder," is crushed by a combination of the exigencies of farm life, the ignorance and brutality of parents, and the ineffectuality and class snobbery of the rich family boarding with them for the summer. This preface hangs over the novel as contemporary events begin through the focus of

Sylvia's consciousness. As Sylvia releases and discovers herself toward the end of the novel through talking of her background, references clearly indicate the farm girl as Sylvia, the story as the crystallization of events and attitudes that formed her. The preface is always there, although not understood, for the cause of the phenomenon is irrelevant until the phenomenon itself is recognized. The past is simply a story, a meaningless and unconnected lump, until its force and relevance are realized in the present, as the revelation of what happened to her two dead children and the real story of her marriage are carefully controlled by the utility of the past event for the present circumstance. The development of Sylvia's consciousness — the unravelling of the protective withdrawal into service that characterized the life-long hotel manageress, and the gradual emergence of the human being — is never violated.

Wilson's most recent fiction, *No Laughing Matter* (1967), continues the emphasis on psychological causation begun in *Late Call*. In a vast novel that follows the lives of the six Matthews children and their separate careers for more than fifty years, a kind of history of middle-class England from 1914 to 1967, Wilson carefully demonstrates what has made each of the children what he is. In an early episode, just after World War I, when their parents cruelly drown a litter of motherless kittens belonging to the children, the children formalize "the Game," a ritual and ironic family drama in which each of the six enacts the role most relevant to him.

The oldest, Quentin, raised by his paternal grandmother because his financially feckless parents, constantly living beyond their inherited incomes, cannot take care of such a large family, plays Mr. Justice Scales, "the dispassionate, objective outsider," who governs the trial and arbitrates the issues and arguments that come up during "The Game." The second child, Gladys, the victim, imposed upon sexually by her father and then almost continually by a boorish lover for whom she goes to prison, fulfils a psychological role in the family in terms of class by playing Regan, the earthy Cockney cook who remains loyal in spite of not receiving her wages and not often being permitted to demonstrate her skill at French cooking. Rupert, the handsome young actor, his mother's favorite, plays his father, "Billy Pop," a dreaming writer full of financial and literary schemes that he never completes, a spineless and adoring husband who evades his wife's demanding scenes and her infidelities by spending most of his evenings with cronies at his club. Margaret, the analyst, the novelist even at an early age, portrays her great aunt, Miss Rickard, the sharp-tongued spinster who had brought up her mother, the intelligent and caustic wit who continually travels without ever finding a home of her own. Margaret's twin, Sukey, the girl who dreams of peace, order, and domesticity in an old-fashioned country house, plays her soft and conventional paternal grandmother, a survivor from an earlier age who believes in all the homilies she has never examined. The youngest child, Marcus, grandiosely effeminate, plays their mother, "the Countess," who has always hated and rejected him, who imposes on all her family to support a graciousness she has never earned and an aristocratic indolence she cannot afford, but who reserves her most bitter reproaches and denials for her youngest child.

"The Game" establishes the conditions for the novel, the deterministic framework in which each of the six develops. Products of inadequate parents and surrogates, each child mirrors the problems that ironically thwart his efforts to incorporate a wider and fuller life. Yet each child does, in his own terms, make efforts, does attempt to become something more than he is, an extensively demonstrated complexity that saves the novel from the mechanism of simplistic psychological determinism. Despite these efforts, however, all the children really work out magnifications of their childhood roles. Rupert, for example, the mimic of his father, becomes an actor regarded as brilliant in Chekhov's "Three Sisters," in which he plays Andrey, the parasite on his sisters, and makes "that fat white slug" seem "pathetic and loveable." The "fat white slug" is a repeated image for "Billy Pop." In later roles, however, in attempting more contemporary characterizations that do not mirror his father, Rupert is inadequate, shallow and imperceptive. And, like his father, Rupert is always dependent on his wife for any insight or personal definition.

The problems of remoteness and estrangement are still important to Wilson in *No Laughing Matter*. The three most intelligent and sensitive children, Quentin, Margaret, and Marcus, are frequently locked in isolation, desperately trying to establish contacts that their very intelligence inhibits. Quentin cannot trim his shrewd political judgment, although he loses jobs and is once beaten up for it, just as he cannot alter the sense of sharp pragmatic appraisal that makes him use women as only temporary bed partners. And Margaret cannot turn off the astringent perception that makes her a good novelist, cannot make her wit seem other than indifferent even though strong feelings shelter just behind the sharp tongue. Like her great aunt, she is an inconsolable traveler.

At the same time, in *No Laughing Matter,* even those with less intelligence and sensitivity are treated with compassion, for Wilson is here less limited to sympathy for a type with whom he feels some identity than he was in some of the earlier novels like *Hemlock and After* and *The Middle Age of Mrs. Eliot*. Gladys, the victim, is given an emotional honesty and a concern for others which make her entirely sympathetic. Even Sukey, despite the demonstrated falseness and insularity of her country house dream and the appalling garbage of her heartening wartime broadcast talks, is, at the end of the novel, ironically made somewhat sympathetic as an aging woman, passed by time, who has lost her favorite son in one of Britain's futile imperial gestures, and who makes pathetic attempts to extend her own sympathies beyond the limited dream she has tried to live.

Wilson's attitude, in his novels, has always been one of compassion for the estranged, particularly for the estranged trying desperately to re-establish significant communication with others and himself. In *No Laughing*

Matter, with its emphasis on all the complex forces that determine the shape of human beings, that compassion is extended, given wider meaning and reference, for the determined conditions of experience make many more of us isolated or alien, divide us from our dreams and our attempts. The focus on psychological causation widens the definition of the estranged or the remote, multiplies Wilson's central character by six, even beyond six in that "Billy Pop" and the "Countess" can also not be entirely condemned, and increases the compassion for the many who find human experience and communication so difficult. The greater the understanding of human hang-ups and their origin, the more dense and complex the explanation of human attempts to break through the protective prison of self, the greater the respect and compassion for the human being.

This focus on the individual is not, however, the only focus in Wilson's fiction. The novels also describe, characterize, and rely on a great many sociological and historical phenomena of the last fifty years. From the characterization of Bernard Sands's son as a specimen of the new post-war Tory with a taste for Anouilh's nostalgic plays, and the earnest young garage mechanics of the fifties who, in *Anglo-Saxon Attitudes*, listen to *Salome* on the gramophone in suburban semi-detached houses, to the early sixties' progressive rhetoric of the New Town in *Late Call* and the evocations of night life with the military in the West End during World War I, clammy public meetings on worthwhile causes during the thirties, and the Bermondsey riots in *No Laughing Matter*, all of Wilson's novels provide extensive chronicles of the years they describe. On the level of social chronicle, the novels describe overall attitudes as well as evocative details, carefully delineate perspectives changing through time instead of merely ticketing by the year in the fashion of the television documentary. In addition to providing the chronicle, Wilson's novels also demonstrate how constantly public, social or historical issues impinge on the private existence of the individual. The public and private are always intertwined, as in Gerald Middleton's self-protective remoteness or in the fact that Sylvia Calvert's lifetime of service is both an echo of an older England and the account of a single individual. Nevertheless, as with Gerald Middleton or Bernard Sands, the public and private are not necessarily resolved identically. Rather, in Wilson's world, the individual is always connected with, although never completely defined by, public identities like society, class and history. The public and private can, at times, be separated, but the individual who separates them as completely as possible, who lives either in a world he has made for himself, or solely in terms of a public slogan, is either disastrously isolated or stupidly self-denying. The healthy self requires connections to entities outside himself, yet also requires some independence and some capacity to impose the self on the world outside.

Wilson's constant interest in public questions is most directly manifest in his fable, *The Old Men at the Zoo*. Constantly linking man and animal imagistically, the novel describes the assumptions involved in various ways of administering the zoo as analogues for more general human questions of both public management and private morality. Wilson examines the different forms of government: the rational and liberal government, giving the creature the greatest liberty commensurate with general security, which Wilson calls "limited liberty"; a rigid kind of Victorian conservatism that tries to balance its strict confinement of the animals with brass bands, colored lights, and patriotic slogans; the totally irrational neo-Fascistic government of the Uni-Europeans. The more liberal governments are unable to handle the human creature.

After the inevitable war, the Uni-Europeans gain control and establish a zoo in which the conventional difference between man and animal is diabolically reversed. In the early 1970's, the director sets up an exhibit with a chained, shoddy Russian bear and a caged, mangy, miserable American eagle, and then invites a mob of presumed people to tear the animals apart. Up to this point in the novel, the fable works well and the parallel between the terms of the novel and their application to human government is made convincing. But Wilson was apparently unwilling to leave his futuristic society to the Uni-Europeans, just as he was unwilling to leave his statement about the nature of man inextricably locked in the center of brutal depravity. Just at the point when the Uni-Europeans seem in complete control, when even the cautious, ironic Simon Carter, who retains some amount of outmoded sensibility, has been exiled to a concentration camp, the Uni-Europeans are inexplicably overthrown and human sanity is restored to the world. Wilson gives no indication of how, in terms of either plot or concept, the bestiality is removed from control of human government; he just refers, in a single sentence, to "Liberation Day." The defeat of the Uni-Europeans is only a gesture, a cry of faith, that does not mesh with the structure of the fable. The fable traces, in careful stages, the developments that lead to the primacy of the Uni-Europeans, the gradual steps that mark the increasing central darkness of the human being. But the steps back to the light are omitted, and, since the allegory of government consists in the examination of steps and causes and processes, the omission seems a serious one.

A novel can, of course, end in a gesture of faith, but, in this instance, the terms of the novel, the fable, work against the credibility of such a gesture, and it is difficult to accept a conclusion, however heartening, plastered on without reference to the demands of the form. The statement that I assume Wilson intended, in order to provide coherence for the novel, pertained to a bestiality at the center of man that is nevertheless palliated, civilized, controlled, by a sense of human sanity and rationality, a bestiality that exists but is seldom visible at its naked worst and is, fortunately, partially squelched by its very invisibility. Yet the complexity of this possible statement is made less articulate than it might be by the rigid demands of the fabulistic form. According to the expectation of the fable, Wilson's theme should "work out" in terms not only relevant for Simon Carter as an individual (which it does) but also relevant for the general political implications of the subject. Yet the political theme is too tenuous, too complex, too much a part of its shadings and emphases, to work within the confined abstractions of the fable.

The public and political dimensions of *No Laughing Matter* are handled more successfully because less rigidly than those of *The Old Men at the Zoo*. In *No Laughing Matter*, each of the characters' private concerns invariably leads him into public attitudes. The attitudes may be convictions or poses or merely by-products of personal relationships, but they become part of the person himself, part of the human being divided between an individuality and an extension into the public domain. Political attitudes also have their personal counterparts, working through each individual in different ways. Quentin, for example, becomes an able socialist journalist, gaining a reputation in the radical press of the thirties as an authority on housing. On a visit to Russia, he is disillusioned about Communism, noticing the strange absence of various distinguished friends from previous visits. When he returns to England, none of his radical associates can credit his disillusion with the Soviet's noble experiment and he is regarded as an outcast. After speaking at a political debate, he picks up a young girl art student and takes her back to his flat for the night:

> And when she said, in a naive, schoolgirl's downright way, that, for her part, she couldn't see how it was possible to be anything but a party member, to be anything else was a failure to comprehend the logic of history, he forced her into bed again almost brutally. He thought with excitement of her reaction when she read his article the following Friday in The New Statesman, giving his analysis and his prophecies concerning hidden events in Russia.

For Quentin, politics and sex are completely mixed, even though, for Wilson, at this point in Quentin's career, his politics are admirable and his attitudes toward sex brutal and indiscriminate. Yet in both are evident the man who, thirty years later, will enthrall a wide television audience with supercilious comments like, "I have no concern for the common man except that he should not be so common."

In both *The Old Men at the Zoo* and *No Laughing Matter*, political or public evil is associated with the Nazis. Although the Uni-Europeans in the former are, in part, a brutalized version of the idea of the Third Force so popular in the early and middle fifties, they are much more significantly and consistently an echo of the Nazis with their codified bestiality, their irrational intensity, and their insistence on purity in the human product. The leader of the Uni-Europeans is named Blanchard-White. In *No Laughing Matter*, all six of the Matthews children work themselves, in one way or another, into anti-Nazi positions during the thirties. Quentin and Margaret, always consciously political, are strongly anti-Nazi throughout the decade, but their brother Rupert joins them on the platform in a meeting at Kingsway Hall to protest the German treatment of the Jews. Gladys, usually so passive, rebels at her lover's statements praising the efficiency of the Nazis and affirming the importance of preserving good business contacts no matter what the political issues. Marcus, at a snobbish party, quite heroically asserts his philo-Semitism and, when accidentally involved in the Bermondsey riots, acts with energy and force against the British Nazis. Even Sukey, insulated in her narrow public school, belatedly summons sufficient conscience to take in a German Jewish refugee. In fact the Matthews family, including "Billy Pop," although excluding the snobbish and self-indulgent "Countess," consciously defends Jews in the midst of considerable British anti-Semitism. Although "Billy Pop" writes that anti-Semitism is not a problem unique in the thirties having existed in Britain throughout his lifetime, it does become a touchstone, a measure of the individual's humanity in both personal and political terms, during the decade of the Nazi threat. All the Matthews children, whatever their other deficiencies, pass this test; they are anti-Nazi, they can laugh at the idea of racial purity and oppose inhumane dogma and brutality. In the sense that the six children represent alternatives for the reasonably responsible, humane, and literate British middle classes, their actions during the thirties reveal them at their most cohesive and admirable point. Wilson wisely never grants the British middle classes the sentimental triumph of Mrs. Miniver or "their finest hour," but he does demonstrate something of political value in a class that refuses to abandon its humanity to what seems the inevitable direction of European civilization.

But, in this novel, full of examples of both dramatic irony and the irony of self-discovery, Wilson does not allow the triumph of the middle classes to stand without qualifying it through a final comprehensive irony. Nineteen-forty inevitably shades into 1967. By 1967, when the final scenes of the novel take place, Marcus, the youngest, is over sixty. Only Rupert and Sukey, always the least humane and the most self-involved, have themselves had children, and their grandchildren, who appear in the final scene, represent something different, something graciously alien to the Matthews generation. Margaret and Quentin, caught in all their remoteness and defenses against their feelings, have never been able to love, have symbolically never earned the continuity represented by children. Gladys, willing victim until too late, never married before she was almost fifty. Marcus is homosexual, yet his final achievement, the establishment of a cooperative factory in Morocco, seems momentarily to have the best chance of preserving through time whatever worth or value the Matthews family represents. Marcus plans to leave his factory to Hassan, a young Moroccan who had, as a pretty boy, been his lover about ten years earlier. Yet Hassan, never sufficiently sensitive to learn through art as Marcus had when an older lover had first given him paintings to begin his career as an art dealer, is callow and represents no continuing tradition of knowledge, insight, or humanity. The final passage in *No Laughing Matter* is from Hassan's point of view:

And perhaps Marcus—his good, noble, kind friend—might now see how absurd were these cooperative ideas at the factory. . . . It was not as if, when he was owner, he would pay low wages or any foolish old-fashioned thing like that, if Marcus feared it; on the contrary Miracle Germany—Stuttgart, Dusseldorf, Frankfort—all that he admired most in the modern world, even his favorite journal Time Magazine urged high wages, but also seemly ambition, high profits, and determined management.

Whatever virtue and humanity, individually and politically, the Matthews family represented is more inimical to "Miracle Germany" and to Time Magazine than to almost any other forces in the world of 1967. The more than fifty years of the Matthews family, the relatively sane, responsible, and self-aware British middle classes, are over. The family, despite all its flawed achievements and tenuous survival, has been dissolved by time.

Irony, however, qualifies; it doesn't destroy. The political stand of the Matthews family is part of experience, crucial at certain moments in time, like the thirties, less central and less visible at others. The incipient anti-Nazi is a starting point, a beginning for humanity. Beyond that, difficulties, complexities, ambivalences appear, but sufficient humanity to avoid belief in the purity and brutality of Nazism is necessary for Wilson's interest. To complain, as one critic has, that Wilson never analyzes or deeply examines the fascists he depicts is to miss the point: for him, the inhumane, the man who never doubts himself, the purist, or the ideologue is a political evil, and Wilson is far more interested in how the sane man, with all his doubts and ambivalences, combats evil than in the nature of rampant political evil itself. *No Laughing Matter* is far more effective than *The Old Men at the Zoo* in conveying the human being's struggle against evil, against the hardening of social generalization into dogma, brutality, or inhumane abstraction. *The Old Men at the Zoo*, the fable, is itself too abstract, too simplistic to present convincingly all the dilemmas and humane doubts that bother the sane and sensitive. In contrast, *No Laughing Matter* moves historically and chronologically rather than fabulistically. Issues change and dissolve as time moves, characters both change and remain the same, humanity coheres at specific points only to dissolve again, politics are and then again are not central to the human being. Through the framework of history, Wilson can achieve a complexity of individual and social characterization that the philosophical simplicity and single-mindedness of the fable restricts. History, in Wilson's non-teleological world, is the final irony for man. . . .

People in Paper Houses: Attitudes to "Realism" and "Experiment" in English Postwar Fiction

A. S. Byatt*

Much of the debate about appropriate form in the English novel since the war has been concerned with the acceptance or rejection of appropriate or inappropriate models. Thus what has been called the "reaction against experiment" of the 1950s was much preoccupied with rejecting the model of James Joyce and Virginia Woolf. We had C. P. Snow's reductive description of the innovations of these two writers as "a method, the essence of which was to represent brute experience through moments of sensation";[1] we had the linked complaints of Kingsley Amis: "The idea about experiment being the life-blood of the English novel is one that dies hard. 'Experiment' in this context boils down pretty regularly to 'obtruded oddity,' whether in construction . . . or in style; it is not felt that adventurousness in subject matter or attitude or tone really counts."[2] The "avant garde" of the 1960s and 1970s have now rejected this rejection, declaring that the "nineteenth-century novel," with which many novelists of the 1950s felt a continuity, is the convention now leading novelists into bad faith, and a perverse ignorance of the revolution that was effected once and for all by Joyce, the "Einstein of the novel." Thus we have the desperately hectoring voice of B. S. Johnson, berating writers who do not realize that "literary forms do become exhausted, clapped out . . . ," and that "the nineteenth-century novel" was finished by the outbreak of the First World War: "No matter how good the writers are who now attempt it, it cannot be made to work for our time, and the writing of it is anachronistic, invalid, irrelevant and perverse." Johnson's description of the nineteenth-century novel is, in fact, quite as inadequate as was Snow's account of the modernist experiment. For him, its wrongness is that it tells a story — and "telling stories is telling lies."[3]

These irritable territorial definitions have taken place against the background of a critical discussion of contemporary fiction which has been, in this country, decidedly thin; and against a critical lore which has been — and this is important — characteristically moral and prescriptive. We have the Great Tradition. We have John Bayley's *The Characters of Love* (1960), an immediately attractive and sympathetic book — particularly, I suspect, to writers — which distinguishes the literature of Nature from the literature of the Human Condition, and advocates a realism, characteristically English, which depends on love, in author and reader, for characters as separate individuals. Related to this is Iris Murdoch's essay of 1961, "Against Dryness" — a "polemical sketch" pleading for a return to the realistic depiction of "free, separate" characters as a way out of a philosophical solipsism

*Reprinted with permission from *The Contemporary English Novel*, ed. Malcolm Bradbury and David Palmer. Stratford-upon-Avon Studies, No. 18. (London: Edward Arnold, 1979), pp. 19–24, 36–38.

and a simple welfare utilitarianism we have too easily embraced. Iris Murdoch gives clear and good historical reasons why it is not now possible simply to mimic the nineteenth-century realists, and certainly her novels do not themselves do so. Nonetheless, her prescription is roughly the same as John Bayley's. We must *learn from* tradition — from Shakespeare, and the nineteenth-century novelists, especially the Russians. Bernard Bergonzi's *The Situation of the Novel* (1970) is extremely sympathetic to Bayley's position; it does, though, share B. S. Johnson's anxious sense that modern English realism is "no longer novel," but depends on exhausted forms and concepts. The paradox is, according to Bergonzi, that the most vital contemporary literature is also totalitarian and dehumanizing, and as for his examples of that vitality they are French and American, not English: Heller, Pynchon, Burroughs, Mailer, Robbe-Grillet, Genet. There are similar anxieties in David Lodge's *The Novelist at the Crossroads* (1971); Lodge's crossroads mark the paths pointing away from realism, but nonetheless offers "a modest affirmation of faith in the future of realistic fiction" — a faith that can be reasonably born out by a look at the kinds of novels many writers today are publishing.

Behind that Great Tradition, there is, of course, the spirit of "Tradition and the Individual Talent." "But we *know* so much more than they did," protests Eliot's hypothetical artist, asked to contemplate his forebears; "Precisely," replies the voice of authority, "And they are that which we know." It was Eliot who complained that our literature was a substitute for religion, and so was our religion. Respect for the tradition of the realist novel is apparently a very rooted fact, and is inextricably involved in a very complex set of responses to the decline of religion and the substitution of a Religion of Humanity. The fictional texts of the Great Tradition are indeed the texts of the Religion of Humanity; and many novelists now seem to feel that they exist in some uneasy relation to the afterlife of these texts, as the texts themselves once coexisted with the afterlife of Genesis and the Gospels. They are the source of enlightenment, but not true. Or not true, for us.

Thus it seems that much formal innovation in recent English fiction has concerned itself, morally and aesthetically, with its forebears; and in a way for which I know no exact parallel in other literatures. This has its dangers: as Nathalie Sarraute declared, in "Rebels in a World of Platitudes," the true enemy of good art is not mass society or technology, but "the only real, the deadly danger, the great works of the past,"[4] which must be absorbed and rejected simultaneously. This is, of course, the anxiety of influence, of which Harold Bloom is the prophet.[5] This anxiety, in the English novel now, seems to operate in odd ways — with and against the moral force of the Great Tradition, which still exerts its power, to produce forms sometimes limp, sometimes innovatory, sometimes paradoxical, occasionally achieved, and sometimes simply puzzling. The state is recognizable; but traditional critical methods for the study of influence and of plagiarism are often distracting here. When Dr Leavis isolated the ways in which James's

The Portrait of a Lady is a reworking of part of Eliot's *Daniel Deronda*, he was pointing to a kind of "reader's greed" in the writer which is, in fact, perfectly characteristic of George Eliot's own work. I take it that some need both to re-read, and to better, certain stories that caught her imagination was behind her own reworking of an episode from Gottfried Keller in the climax of *The Mill on the Floss*; of the description of George Sand's Jacques as a Saint Theresa born out of his time, in *Middlemarch*; or of the animated tableaux from Goethe's *Wahlverwandtschaften* in *Daniel Deronda*. Not parody, not pastiche, not plagiarism — but a good and greedy reading, by a great writer. The phenomenon, then, is not novel. And yet it inevitably looks different in modern novels — because of the pressure of the past, because of the accumulation of literary criticism, and because of the weight of anxiety as it shows itself in modern form.

II

Perhaps a paradigmatic case is the development of the career of Angus Wilson. In an illuminating interview with Jonathan Raban, Wilson said, "I nearly always feel when I'm writing a scene that this has been written before." Raban comments, "But life itself tends constantly to the second-hand; our responses are so conditioned, our behaviour so stereotyped, that it is immensely hard for us to extricate ourselves from these literary precedents which plot the course of our own feelings and actions." Wilson's "literariness," Raban adds, is a function of his characters, who read and use literature to interpret their lives, and is not, in this, like "the formal allusiveness of most modernist writing."[6] Indeed, the hero of Angus Wilson's first novel, *Hemlock and After* (1952), is a writer, Bernard Sands. And Angus Wilson requires of his reader that he inhabit Sands's experience, including the writing, but imaginatively, in a "realist" way. The essence of this experience is a vision of aimless evil which undercuts the meliorism of Sands's traditional humanist position, and comes perilously close to undercutting the Religion of Humanity itself. Sands is, like George Eliot, like Angus Wilson, a person who controls an acid wit and a natural cruelty in the interests of justice. His opponent, fat and smiling Mrs Curry, the procuress, is a two-dimensional Dickensian vision of something irrational, predatory, and powerful. Both characters are nineteenth-century, the good one centrally "realist" in morals and presentation, the bad one (whom the reviewers found paradoxically "thin" at the same time) suggesting, with hindsight, possibilities of "experimental" fictional techniques, derived from Dickens's grotesque. (Dickens has been behind other "experimental" variants of realism, notably those of Paul Bailey.)

Meg Eliot, in *The Middle Age of Mrs. Eliot* (1958), remains, I think, Wilson's most successful attempt at the Jamesian ideal of sustained, inner imagining of a character. She, too, is literary, and has her personal collection of texts, characterized as "the escape she and David had found in the past. *Emma, The Mill on the Floss, The Small House at Allington, The Portrait of a Lady* . . . the basic necessities of the voyage." Reviewers and critics pounce on literary clues in our time. It has been pointed out that all these novels have impulsive, passionate heroines, whose fate is to suffer from forcing their own fantasizing vision on reality; that Meg Eliot is in their tradition and is, indeed, their heir. But there are germs of discomfort here. The novels are explicitly "an escape to the past"; Meg's identification with the heroines brings no access of wisdom, but a child-like evasion of present misery. David's literary work, like his boyhood pleasure in "the sad futilities of Emma Bovary's debts," is an evasion of reality. Is this like George Eliot's exposé of Dorothea's desire to dedicate herself to "Milton, when he was old," or is it a doubt about literature itself?

Literary references are also central, obtrusive and pervasive in *No Laughing Matter* (1967), but in different fashion. The Matthews family's Game deals with unpleasant realities by parody, pastiche, farcical mockery. The Game discovers, exploits, elaborates the sexual, political and aesthetic traits of the characters. It is a primitive, crude and vigorous form of the art of the writer, Margaret, the actor, Rupert, the twee "writings" of the self-deluded Susan, the high camp of Marcus. The characters use the Game, and the Game, directed by Angus Wilson, uses them. He derealizes them with overt manipulation, in lengthy parodies of Ibsen, Shaw, Chekhov, Bennett, framing them in a plurality of styles. The result is not realism, but is intimately and uncomfortably related to it. This is because, although Wilson's insistence on the "second-hand" quality of his people and their world renders them papery and insubstantial, they do nevertheless think and feel, and author requires of reader an imaginative response to thought and feeling which belongs with realism.[7] A reverberation is set up between their literary factitiousness and their own sense of this, corresponding to their author's sense of a similar problem in himself and his work, which produces a new, a novel kind of acute disorder and discomfort in the reading experience. This discomfort is intensified in *As If by Magic* (1973), to which I shall return. In that novel, as Raban says, the characters proceed by asking themselves "How would Birkin, or Myshkin, or Alice, or a Hobbit have felt about this . . .": their answers to these questions produce ludicrously parodic behaviour: the texture of the novel is insistent on its own farcical fictiveness, suggesting that all life is a ghastly fiction "behind" which stands no ratifying or eternal vision of a corresponding reality. When Alexandra declares "I know I am a fictive device" we are aware that we are out of the world of the realist novel and its norms and in the familiar world of the experimental novel, which proclaims its own artifice and comments on its own procedures. What I want to emphasize at this point is the curiously symbiotic relationship between old realism and new experiment, the way in which Alexandra as "device" grew out of Meg as typical humane reader.

III

. . . *As If by Magic* is also a "literary" artefact, symbiotically involved both in realism and in the modernist aspirations to the completeness of myth. The central theme of "magic" incorporates the economic "miracle" of the new rice, Magic, in underdeveloped economies, the new Oriental, Arthurian, astrological and Tolkienesque cults of the 1960s flower children; and sexual-Lawrentian magic, a rescuing of our culture by "good sex," transfiguring the Dark Gods into beneficent spreaders of sweetness and light. The novel proceeds by indiscriminate literary parody. Hamo, the rice geneticist with his servant, Erroll, is Frodo with Sam crossing Middle Earth; he is an Arabian Nights prince in search of The Most Beautiful Boy; he is a character from a Feydeau farce, or Victorian pornography, falling about, smashing things, disguising himself. Alexandra uses English literature to interpret life and also to plot the novel, rescuing the charlatan (at least nine-tenths) Swami from his incensed followers by recalling in quick succession Toad disguised as a washerwoman, and Panks exposing Casby in *Little Dorrit*. There are parodies of the Angry Young Men (in Alexandra's Father) and threadbare identification—Alexandra comes to see Hamo's clumsiness as Myshkin's divine idiocy.

The novel contains a collapsed myth, in the sense that all the characters are out to redeem the Waste Land with fertility magic: but Hamo's death at the hands of an incensed mob is neither Dionysian nor Orphic, his body is simply a "marionette," and the sex-magic of Ned, Roderigo and Alexandra, designed to redeem the aridity of Birkin's failure to love both Gerald and Ursula, produces a child who is explicitly not allowed to represent harvest or fulfilment. At the end of the novel, Alexandra rejects him as a symbol: unlike Helen's child at the end of *Howards End* he will neither reconcile opposites, close circles, inherit the earth nor play with the grain. "We've had enough of Forster's harvest predictions. Things may have turned sour for all of us, but we must not heap it all on *him*." Alexandra rejects both literature and stories. After her "plotting" success with Toad and Panks, she stops short of seeing her fatigue in terms of Frodo's. "She said to herself, enough of supersititious imagining. A story is a story is a story, even a good one, like the *Lord of the Rings*." And five lines from the end of the book, having become Shaw's millionairess, she cries "Damn English Literature!," as though brushing away mental cobwebs. Literature too is a magic spell, an illusion between men and reality.

As If by Magic is nihilistic, but it does not, like Nietzsche and Mann, open windows on blackness with a grim delight in reversals of meaning. It works by reducing everything to the ridiculous, in an intensely, inexorably, exclusively literary way. And it is not the absurd it indicates, it is simply the ridiculous. It is like an onion consisting of allusion, parody, interpretation, imitative plot and trumped-up analogy, but an onion encasing no green growing point, and putting out no roots. The comparison with Mann is instructive. Mann, writing *Dr Faustus*, discovered, he said, "my own growing inclination, which I discovered was not mine alone, to look upon all life as a cultural product taking the form of mythic clichés, and to prefer quotation to independent invention." Mann cannibalized the facts of Nietzsche's life, the forms of Dostoevski's fiction: his book has, as R. J. Hollingdale says "an airless, a horribly airless quality; it smells of the midnight, and worse of the *midday* lamp." An analogous airlessness permeates *As If by Magic*, but the differences are instructive. Mann was monstrously curious as a writer—he had to *know about* music, tuberculosis, syphilis, in heaped factual detail. Angus Wilson's rice, although clearly researched, was researched, one feels, as a *literary symbol*. Mann's book has an extraordinary vitality, however airless, even if it was, as he said it had to be, the vitality of *fleurs du mal*. Wilson's book is paradoxically less vital because of his residual liberal humanist warmth and duty towards his characters. He feels morally compelled to appreciate and understand Alexandra's true being, from the inside, and his display of this moral effort curiously vitiates the papery energies of his puppetry without really allowing the reader to care for that "fictive device" he has so respectfully put together. Further, the presence of this moral nostalgia for Forster's procedures curiously blurs Alexandra's rejection of Forster's metaphors. These moral confusions and formal blurrings are also characteristic of our time. . . .

Notes

1. See Rubin Rabinowitz, *The Reaction Against Experiment in the English Novel 1950–1960* (New York & London, 1967), p. 98.

2. *Ibid.*, p. 40.

3. B. S. Johnson, *Aren't You Rather Young to be Writing Your Memoirs?* (London, 1973), pp. 12 *et seq*.

4. Nathalie Sarraute, "Rebels in a World of Platitudes" in *The Writer's Dilemma: Essays from the TLS* (London 1961), pp. 35–41.

5. See Harold Bloom, *The Anxiety of Influence: A Theory of Poetry* (New York, 1973).

6. Jonathan Raban, "Angus Wilson: A Profile," *The New Review* I, 1 (April 1974), pp. 16–24.

7. There is a very helpful discussion of this aspect of *No Laughing Matter* in Malcolm Bradbury's *Possibilities*, to which I am indebted.

The Function of *The Idiot* Motifs in
As If by Magic   Jai Dev*

Although Dostoevsky "haunts" Angus Wilson,[1] so dissimilar are their
visions and temperaments that any attempt to relate the two writers or their
characters is bound to invite the charge of "relevance heresy." This seems to
be the case even with Wilson's *As If by Magic* which insists on its relation
with Dostoevsky's *The Idiot*. A. S. Byatt has described the literary parodies
in *As If by Magic* as "joky and papery." She sees little justification for Alexandra Grant's "threadbare" identification of Hamo Langmuir's clumsiness
with Prince Myshkin's divine idiocy.[2] This essay examines the two ways in
which Wilson postulates a connection between Hamo and Myshkin, and
then shows how the connection serves as a part of Wilson's characterization
strategy in the novel.

There is no doubt that at its worst, such a connection can be merely an
authorial insinuation, a case of self-indulgence or literary show-off. However, its relevance is not to be judged by its thickness or thinness, but in
terms of the function it serves in the overall design of the novelist. The novelist's commitment is ultimately to his own work and its characters, not to
the connection-source. Gilbert Phelps is right in his assertion that in English
fiction, Dostoevsky's influence "tends to resolve itself into a consideration of
separate aspects," but more to the point is his view that "an artist takes from
another what he needs . . ."[3] For example, Wilson's *The Middle Age of
Mrs. Eliot* not only connects Meg Eliot with Emma[4] but also takes from
Emma its pattern, theme, and several motifs; yet no one would regret that
there is not a more extended correspondence between the two novels.

Prince Myshkin is a highly adaptable figure. His shades can be traced
in the characters of writers as different as William Faulkner and Graham
Greene, Bernard Malamud and David Storey. Although among critics there
is much disagreement about his meaning — he has been viewed both as "one
of the supremely great 'good' characters in fiction" and as a "princely hum-
bug"[5] — writers have usually taken him as an archetypal figure of the holy
fool whose radical innocence makes him intuitively grasp the truths hidden
from the worldly wise. He approximates to the idea of a Christ-like man
and exemplifies the norm of becoming a fool so that one may be wise. An
adaptable figure, Myshkin has in him potential both for "interpretation by
invention"[6] and for interpretation through modification, parody, refrac-
tion, and even inversion. Wilson's adaptations of *The Idiot* motifs in his
characterization of Hamo Langmuir represent interpretation largely
through parody and inversion.

For the most part of the narrative, Hamo remains a diametrical opposite of Prince Myshkin. The very first thing one notes about the latter is his
quick, effortless success in gaining others' affection and trust. He returns to

*Reprinted with permission from *Twentieth Century Literature*, 29, No. 2 (1983), 223–30.

Russia as a stranger, but before the first day is over, he becomes intimate with all those he meets. By contrast, Hamo dreads intimacy. To him any personal touch becomes a prelude to the end of a relationship. A seeker of anonymous lovers, Hamo equates the emergence of a personality with the beginning of his own impotence. He craves beauty "unspoiled by muddying claims of human intimacy."[7] Although both ruin those whose lives they touch closely, lovingly, Hamo's stance towards others is antipodal to that of Myshkin.

Hamo's idiocy, too, is in sharp contrast to Myshkin's divine idiocy. Dostoevsky elevates Myshkin's idiocy above the wisdom of the wise. Myshkin is scandalized and insulted by Antip Burdovsky and his mates, but even as Burdovsky's story is exposed as fraud, Myshkin offers a substantial sum to him. When Burdovsky declines the offer, Myshkin is seized by remorse and self-disgust: he should not have made the offer in such a "coarse" manner. " 'I am at fault!' said the prince, going up to Burdovsky. 'I've wronged you, Burdovsky, but it wasn't sent in charity, believe me! I am to blame now, and I was to blame at the time.' (The prince was much distressed; he looked tired and weak, and spoke disconnectedly.) 'When I spoke of fraud, I wasn't referring to you. I was in error. . . .' "[8] Myshkin is called an idiot because he is irrational and unworldly, but his idiocy suggests grace. By contrast, Hamo lacks grace. In his scientific wisdom he regards the human aspects as irrelevant. More importantly, in his compulsive, "idiotic" escapades he achieves no transcendence. Each of his quests for the most beautiful youth in the world pushes him down into humiliating, disgraceful farces. When he is not a brilliant scientist-monster, he is an undivine clown. It is only towards his death that his idiocy rises above the level of ludicrous farce.

Unlike Myshkin who represents a developed heart and intuition, Hamo represents an overdeveloped intellect and undeveloped heart. The chaos that his quest for a dream youth and his Magic rice create is related to his exclusion of love and involvement from his scheme of things. Love to him is measurable in terms of the size of various body parts. In contrast to Myshkin's offer to Burdovsky, Hamo's gestures to the victims of his quest (£100 to each) are made impersonally, mechanically. Hamo is further contrasted with Myshkin in terms of the latter's humility, humanity, and compassion.

If Prince Myshkin hovers over Hamo like a contrastive shade, it is because both Alexandra Grant and the narrator, though each in a different way, connect Hamo with him. Towards the end of Book II, Alexandra makes a most explicit reference to Hamo as Prince Myshkin. In a Goa hotel she sees Hamo near the reception desk. He is indignant at the callous indifference of the local administration in the face of a riot. In exasperation Hamo bangs on the desk so that the inkwell falls down on the floor staining his neat white trousers. The sight of Hamo, the clumsy "big piece," "so tall and English and upright and indignant, at once so good and simple and so ludicrous" (p. 370), revives in her the memory of their previous encounter at her home in London. On that occasion Hamo's clumsy fall had resulted in the smashing of Zoe Grant's Nymphenburg Harlequin. Alexandra now connects the two episodes, connects them with Myshkin's smashing the china vase at the Yepanchins' party, rushes down towards him, jumps up to kiss Hamo, calls him Myshkin, and finally pulls him down.

> *She* pulled him down on the couch. *She* held his face in her hands lovingly. At intervals kissing him, she said, "You *are* Myshkin. Oh, damn! You've probably never even read Dostoevsky. We've got to find some means of communication. . . . You see all those other things—the Birkins and dandies and gurus—just won't do. But you've *never* bullied or cringed. And I need someone so much. I've been waiting for someone. It's you. You've acted with divine idiocy, just simply doing all the mad contradictory things that were right. I want," she ended, and she began to kiss his eyelids, "I want you to marry me." (p. 372)

The scene is wildly farcical. Feeling infected with what she judges to be Hamo's divine idiocy, Alexandra the Eng Lit student "takes" the role of Aglaia Yepanchin and "heterosexualizes" her homosexual godfather. On his part Hamo "homosexualizes" the potential of dream youth he wishfully sees in this boyish goddaughter: "He tried to remind himself that she had no cock, but then when had he ever cared whether the youths he fucked had cocks or not?" (p. 372).

The episode is a parody of the scene in which Aglaia insinuates Myshkin into asking for her hand. In each case, it is the woman who really proposes; and in each case, the reader knows, the proposed marriage is simply an impossible one. No sooner does Alexandra suggest marriage than Hamo realizes that "it was all wrong" (p. 372); and though, with a sinking heart, Myshkin does ask for Aglaia's hand, he is impotent, incapable of loving her in any but an abstract form. However the use of farce and mimicry in Wilson's adaptation of Dostoevsky's impossible-marriage motif produces effects contradistinctive to those achieved by Dostoevsky.

Unlike Hamo who knows nothing about Price Myshkin or his divine idiocy, Alexandra knows *The Idiot* well; but she knows Hamo only a little, and the little she knows she ignores while making her proposal. Her identification of Hamo's clumsiness with Myshkin's divine idiocy is flimsy, almost gratuitous. It signifies her compulsive tendency to make life into literature. She suffers from infection by fiction and distorts contingent reality by trying to fit it into pastiche patterns derived from fiction. That the identification is thin is precisely the point Wilson is making here; that it is thin is precisely how it should be for Wilson to direct his mockery at her. In other words, there is a definite moral, satiric design behind Wilson's making her draw thin, threadbare analogies and connections.

Alexandra makes too much of Hamo's clumsy fall. On the basis of this and some other tenuous details, she Myshkinizes Hamo. The narrator also singles out the clumsy fall motif from *The Idiot*, but overdoes it to such a degree that the reader becomes aware of the gap that separates Hamo from Myshkin. Hamo falls over and over again, but there is a persistent air of mockery in Wilson's descriptions of his falls.

> . . . he stumbled on a half buried rock and fell, arse over tip, deep into a stone hollow. Then, with his breath for a moment beaten from him, he rolled over painfully two or three times, suddenly, strangely to feel the firmness, the smoothness of another human body beside him. He opened his eyes to see two wide frightened dark eyes turned towards him with jungle alertness. There beside him on the sun-baked rock lay what seemed to him the most perfect, the most desirable youth he had ever encountered. Chest 30, hips 35. The measurements and lineaments of Hamo's ideal are sufficiently well known. (p.177)

Both in tone and in situation, the incident presents an absolute contrast to Myshkin's fall at the soirée. In *As If by Magic*, Wilson offers only parodies of Myshkin's fall, and these are all offered with a view to distancing the reader from Hamo. Of course, these parodies also indirectly prepare the reader to be skeptical about the connection Alexandra will draw between Hamo and Myshkin.

The recurring pattern in *As If by Magic* also offers a sharp contrast to the recurring pattern in *The Idiot*. In Dostoevesky's novel the pattern ensures an increasing involvement on the part of the reader with the divine idiot; in *As If by Magic*, the pattern increasingly alienates the reader from Hamo. Prince Myshkin every time starts from a low point, with everybody pitying and deriding him as an idiot, but ends off by achieving moral superiority over everyone else. Hamo every time starts from a high point, but ends off by touching low, humiliating depths. The first, long and eventful day for Myshkin ends with his being recognized as an extraordinary person, in spite of his idiocy. The first, long and eventful day for Hamo ends only after he has smashed Zoe's Nymphenburg Harlequin and also fallen full-length on top of a steward in the plane. Even those who initially take a dislike to Myshkin come to see him as a remarkable man. Ippolit, for example, claims to "hate" him, but admits in his "An Essential Clarification" that Myshkin is "a doctor, or he's truly a man of extraordinary intelligence, with remarkable insight (though there cannot be the least doubt that he is ultimately an idiot)" (II, p. 85). By contrast, the few friends that Hamo finds finally come to regard him as low, hopeless, and uncouth, if not worse. Mrs. Dissawardene's rebuke— "You have come among us without respect" (p. 290) — is one of the milder parting gifts he earns as the end of one of his visits in Asian countries.

There are certain similarities between Wilson's management of time and pace in *As If by Magic* and Dostoevsky's in *The Idiot*. The two novels, however, belong to two radically opposed fictional sub-genres. *The Idiot* is a grand tragedy; *As If by Magic* is close to farce. Wilson's novel is replete with Dostoevskian motifs, but these Wilson has adapted to suit his farcical design and mode. This is why, for the most part of the action, the reader never really identifies with Hamo. Hamo suffers, but his suffering does not quite touch the reader.

Though Wilson ridicules Alexandra's obsession with romantic literary figures, her identification of Hamo with Prince Myshkin occurs at a point where Wilson's irony is at its most complex. The identification is of a piece with her earlier infatuation with Lawrentian and Tolkienian figures, and is treated with irony as is her naïve adoption of the role of Aglaia. Yet there is much more to the proposal scene than just this. Alexandra is used here as a device (a fictive device?): her identification of Hamo with Myshkin serves as the first shrill, inescapable signal to the reader to attend to Wilson's farcical adaptations of *The Idiot* motifs as well. The identification thus sends the reader back to the scene where Hamo falls knocking down Zoe's Nymphenburg Harlequin *as well as* to Wilson's farcical descriptions of Hamo's falls. As a result of this backward glance, the reader is enabled to see through Alexandra's literary promiscuity. However, and this is most important, the reader is not allowed to rest satisfied with his grasp of Wilson's farcical intent. For, just before Wilson makes Alexandra issue that signal to the reader, he withdraws his mockery and farcical tone from Hamo. Except for the brief patch of sexual fantasy in which Hamo indulges, Wilson portrays him with an earnestness that is genuine and devoid of deflationary mockery or parody. Consequently the reader is required to adjust to a changed narrational tone while also being asked, through Alexandra's signal, to modify his former perceptions of Hamo. The reader is destabilized.

Wilson withdraws mockery and parody from Hamo a little too suddenly. While trying to relax at a pleasure resort, Hamo makes two shocking discoveries. He overhears an American tourist's remarks about the possibility of a riot in Goa: "A giant that was going to bring fertility or something to the crops, who turns out to be, would you believe it, some tall British scientist! And now he's disappeared and the poor bastards think he's being kept from them" (p. 360). Hamo thinks that it must be his sudden departure from Goa that has brought Panaji on the brink of a riot. This realization fills him with self-disgust but also goads him into an idiotic but courageous decision: "At least, if by his unconsidered, self-indulgent blabbing to the Press he had misled these poor men into believing that he could help, he must have the courage to go there and show them the god that had failed" (p. 360). As he is arranging to fly to Goa, he gets a second shock. The receptionist hands over to him a mail parcel containing the magic glasses, originally a gift from Alexandra, which he had given away to a pathetic voyeur in Goa. The voyeur was stoned to death while in the act of watching a naked American girl. The magic glasses, like his £100 cheques, have come back to him. The sight of the glasses completes his self-disillusionment. Both as an individual and as a scientist he has failed. Chaos has followed in the wake of his search for a dream youth as well as his revolutionary Magic rice.

In intense remorse and anguish Hamo takes the first positive action in the course of the narrative. He destroys one of the two reports he has written for submission to the Rapson Trust. This report was factual, scientific, but heartless, and treated the human issues as irrelevant. The report he dispatches is scientifically questionable (a little while ago he called it "the product of an hysteric emotionalism which has no place in scientific work" [pp. 358–59]) but it reflects a concern for the weak and is everywhere touched with compassion. Here he acknowledges that the human and moral issues must come first even in scientific work: "It is, indeed, a case of first things first, for our work on Magic, revolutionary though it has been, will never be complete until the human, to use a necessary word, the *moral* concerns involved are made clear to the beneficiaries; above all, until that acceptance of 'hopelessness' so endemic in these parts has been clearly and manifestly rejected" (p. 363). Back in Panaji, he makes a touching confession before Alexandra. The confession "takes" some of the most characteristic words of Myshkin and is made in a true Myshkinian spirit: "it's all been my fault. Magic, that's the rice I hybridized, had put a lot of people out of work and others can't grow it on their poor lands and so they've been ruined" (pp. 371–72).

Notwithstanding his individual differences and peculiar situation, Hamo, at this point, comes close to being a divine idiot. The remorse and self-abasement which are present everywhere in his confession suggest the transformation of this undivine clown into a divine idiot. Wilson does not subject Hamo to mockery or irony in these last, intense hours of life. He sends him down to a violent, "senseless" death but with a very humane, Dostoevskian suggestion: heroism and idiocy, even dangerous idiocy, are not incompatible. Hamo dies idiotically but dies in grace, redeemed, as it were.

To conclude, whether adapted for suggesting a contrast or a comparison, *The Idiot* motifs in *As If by Magic* serve Wilson well in his characterization of Hamo Langmuir. Remaining amenable to both a negative and a positive interpretation as they do, these motifs also serve as an integrating device in the novel. To the extent that the novel is Alexandra's story, the motifs enable Wilson to first calmly describe and then ironically deflate her tendency to fictionalize life and people. In playing up the thin identification which she establishes between Hamo and Myshkin, the narrator mimics her tendency, while at the same time stressing the inversion and contrast Hamo presents vis-à-vis Prince Myshkin. However, towards the end of Book II, *The Idiot* motifs are presented without mockery or irony. Freed from from these, the motifs naturally create sympathy for Hamo in the reader.

Notes

1. References to Dostoevsky's novels and characters abound in Wilson's fiction. See especially the meeting between Bernard Sands and Hubert Rose in Book III of *Hemlock and After*, where Bernard refers to Hubert as Lebedev, the professional clown, but denies Hubert's accusation that he himself is Prince Myshkin; and the pub scene in Chapter 8 of *The Old Men at the*

Zoo, where Simon Carter seeks to drown his anguish in drink and Dostoevskian depths-talk. *Hemlock and After* (London: Secker & Warburg, 1952), p. 205; *The Old Men at the Zoo* (1962; rpt. Harmondsworth: Penguin, 1966), p. 335. Wilson has also written admiringly of Dostoevsky's fiction, and in one of his essays he has suggested that the contemporary novelist should turn to him for assistance. "Diversity and Depth," *Times Literary Supplement*, 15 August 1958, Special Supplement, p. viii.

    2. A. S. Byatt, "People in Paper Houses: Attitudes to 'Realism' and 'Experiment' in English Postwar Fiction," in Malcolm Bradbury and David Palmer, eds., *The Contemporary English Novel* (1979; rpt. New Delhi: Arnold-Heinemann, 1980), pp. 27, 36. For a more sweeping, more damaging judgment, see "The Green and Brown Revolution," review of *As If by Magic*, *Times Literary Supplement*, 1 June 1973, p. 605.

    3. Gilbert Phelps, *The Russian Novel in English Fiction* (London: Hutchinson's Univ. Library, 1956), pp. 176, 65.

    4. Cf. Meg Eliot: "I'm a natural Emma, but luckily David's Knightley and Mr. Woodhouse rolled into one." *The Middle Age of Mrs. Eliot* (1958; rpt. Harmondsworth: Penguin, 1969), p. 322.

    5. Ernest Simmons, *Dostoevsky: The Making of a Novelist* (1940), and Robert Lord, *Dostoevsky: Essays and Perspectives* (1970); quoted in Elizabeth Dalton, *Unconscious Structure in The Idiot: A Study in Literature and Psychoanalysis* (Princeton, N.J.: Princeton Univ. Press, 1979), pp. 63, 64.

    6. The phrase "interpretation by invention" is Frank Kermode's who defines it (in the context of the Gospels) as "a way of finding in an existing narrative the potential of more narrative." *The Genesis of Secrecy: On the Interpretation of Narrative*, The Charles Eliot Norton Lectures, 1977–78 (Cambridge, Mass.: Harvard Univ. Press, 1979), pp. x–xi.

    7. *As If by Magic* (1973; rpt. Harmondsworth: Penguin, 1976), p. 74. All subsequent references are to this edition.

    8. *The Idiot*, trans. Julius Katzer (Moscow: Progress Publishers, 1977), 2 vols. I, p. 333. All subsequent references are to this edition.

"No Idle Rentier": Angus Wilson and the Nourished Literary Imagination
Margaret Drabble*

Angus Wilson is without question one of the most important British novelists writing today, and some would say the greatest. He has behind him a solid body of work: three collections of short stories, seven major novels, and a wide variety of critical and biographical studies. When one attempts to describe the quality of his achievement, one is almost daunted by its range, richness and diversity. He is a brilliant comic writer, with the keenest eye for social pretension and manipulation; he also writes of loneliness, doubt, breakdown and inner confusion. He dissects English society with a knowing familiarity, yet is widely travelled, and equally at home in foreign settings and with international themes. He loves extravagant set

*Reprinted with permission from *Studies in the Literary Imagination*, 13, No. 1 (1980), 119–29.

pieces — plays, crowd scenes, parties, public meetings — yet can also de-scribe the bewilderment of an elderly lady confronted for the first time by an automatic washing machine. He is fond of the macabre, the exotic, the bizarre and the camp, yet writes with deep sympathy of a Quaker's search for truth through self-abnegation. The moment one has decided that he is writing a comedy of manners with an edge of *haute-bourgeoisie* snobbery, he turns the whole book upside down and exposes the snobbery of the snobs. He castigates dullness, yet writes with respect and insight of the civil ser-vants and administrators of this world, battling on in face of the world's conviction that they are dull. A master of parody and pastiche, he has his own unmistakable centre. A "traditional" novelist, in the sense that he em-ploys elaborate plots, displays a great feeling for sociologically significant material decor, and fills his works with Dickensian "characters," he also uses a dazzling variety of shifts, tricks and fictive devices, a splendid (but rarely intrusive) display of literary allusions and echoes, and a highly sophisti-cated and complex narrative technique. Sophisticated in all ways, and im-mensely discriminating, his writing also embraces coarseness and relishes vulgarity in its many manifestations. Farcical, serious, malicious, compas-sionate — in short, a novelist for all seasons.

This multiplicity is not only evidence of his great talents; it is also at the core of his work. He is a writer who is never satisfied with the simple, or with the already achieved. He moves on, rejecting label after label, rest-lessly enquiring, balancing and reassessing, extending his range with each new work. The success of his first collections of stories, *The Wrong Set* and *Such Darling Dodos* (1949 and 1950), brought him fame as a social satirist, earning him such epithets as "merciless" and "savage," but like his own character Margaret in *No Laughing Matter* he soon found this kind of rec-ognition restricting and moved into larger fields, writing, with equal and increasing success, of wider themes, drawing together the random subjects of his stories into a more comprehensive portrait of British life. He has never abandoned his skill for spotting the eccentric, for exposing oddities and in-consistencies of speech, dress and attitude — in his latest novel occurs the wonderful and characteristic sentence, "I thought an entrée was what people like Mama call what people call starters" — [1] but these flashes have become part of the pattern of the whole, rather than the fabric itself, and in his later works he rarely allows himself the undisguised dislike manifested in such portraits as that of Gwen in "Rex Imperator":

> Gwen Rutherford did not reply, she was too busy settling herself on the sofa. It was a process acquired through years of competition for the best chairs in private hotel lounges and it took time. First a place had to be found for Boy, her white West Highland terrier, then there was her own ample body to be spread, next she had to put out on the seat beside her a jade cigarette holder, a shagreen cigarette case, her knitting and her Boots' library book; she would also have liked the newspaper, but Mr Ni-cholson had taken that. She sat bolt upright with her large bust and her

short thick arms held defiantly forward. Her fat face with its bulging eyes
was blotched from an over-hasty make-up, the lines of her plump cheeks
ran in a deep sulk at each side of her small pouting mouth. She looked like
the British bulldog at bay rather than a once beautiful woman soured by
seven years of legal separation. Long after most women had grown their
hair again, Gwen had retained her peroxide shingle and the rolls of blue
stubbled fat at the back of her neck added to the bulldog illusion.[2]

Not a pleasant caricature; his early experiences of private hotels stocked
Angus Wilson's imagination with some frightening visions.

His first two novels. *Hemlock and After* (1952) and *Anglo-Saxon Attitudes* (1956), both contain figures who are cruelly satirised: the pretentious,
manipulative, cultured, snobbish, sensitive, destructive Mrs. Craddock,
with her fancy geese and her tame son; the self-deluding Scandinavian
wife, Inge Middleton, with her ludicrous Christmas celebrations and her
ignorance of her own children; Ron, Vin, Larrie and Yves, an unpleasant
quartet of ineffective con-men; the historical novelist Clarissa Crane, who
is summed up so devastatingly by an elderly professor as a "time-waster";
the crazy and wonderful Rose Lorimer, an academic in fur coat and straw
hat with roses nourishing strange fantasies about pagan Christianity; the
mean, paranoid, wife-bullying Professor Clun (in fact a gallery of academic
portraits that surpasses Mary McCarthy's in *The Groves of Academe*); yet
they also contain much more. Both novels have male protagonists, successful novelist Bernard Sands and successful historian Gerald Middleton, both
ageing, guilty, introspective, pursued by a sense of failure, and anxious to
put right the mistakes of a lifetime, and neither seen through the eyes of
satire. The novels contain preoccupations with justice, evil, responsibility,
the possibility of self-knowledge. They raise the complex questions that
dominate Wilson's later works: the relationship between manners and morals, between the claims of the world and the claims of the self, between
activity and retirement, between town and country, the civilised and the
wild, between multiplicity and integrity, between (as a later character defines it) fun and duty. The comic effects are superb — on a large scale there is
the collapse of Sands' idealistic project for establishing a Writers' House,
Vardon Hall, which ends in a scene of operatic disaster; on a smaller scale
there is Middleton's attempt to vary his usual Christmas gift of a cyclamen
to his one-time housekeeper Mrs. Salad. Mistakenly he presents her with a
poinsettia, which she greets with disgust:

"Oh, it's a lovely foreign thing. Bright as blood," Mrs Salad said in her
old, croaking tremolo, and she peered at it through the haze of mascara'd
moisture that always clung to her eyelashes and stuck in little beads on
her black eye-veil. "I dare say it'll draw the flies. But lovely for them that
likes bright colours. Just like the stuff the girls put on their finger-nails
now. Like a lot of old birds giving the glad in the Circus, or the York
Road. Waterloo, more likely. Trollopy lot."

> And Mrs Salad's black-dyed curls and fur toque with eye-veil shook
> in disgust. . . .

The camp, the malicious and the macabre still flourish, but the novels are not primarily comedies.

The Middle Age of Mrs Eliot (1958) is neither comedy nor satire, though, again, it contains elements of both. Its structure is more traditional than that of its two predecessors, and unlike them, it is a journey into the future rather than a re-assessment of the past. Its protagonist is a woman, a choice which gives the author a well-judged distance from his creation (Sands and Middleton sound occasionally like apologists, even when most harsh on themselves). Like Mrs. Craddock, Meg Eliot is a cultured woman, but culture here is not subjected to mockery but to investigation. Her favourite novels include *Emma, The Mill on the Floss, The Small House at Allington* and *Daisy Miller*, a telling collection, and one of the novel's lovely subtleties is the varied way in which it demonstrates that the reading of novels (and the writing of them?) can be either an escape into the past or an attempt to make sense of the present. The plot, as Mrs. Eliot's reading matter might suggest, has a classic structure. At the opening of the book Meg Eliot is, like Emma, handsome, clever and rich, seeming to unite the best blessings of existence. She is, though childless, very happily married, has a wide circle of friends, and busies herself with voluntary social work and a pleasant if expensive hobby — she collects porcelain. Like Emma, she prides herself on her ability to manipulate others for their own good, and on her kindness to the less fortunate — notably to three women friends who have fallen on harder times, whom she thinks of as her "lame ducks." We see her in action, gracious, witty, seemingly self-aware, tying up her various obligations before departing with her husband, Bill, for a visit to the Far East. On the journey, disaster strikes. Bill is killed by an assassin's bullet on a foreign airport, and Meg Eliot returns to find that not only is she suddenly poor — her husband died in debt, unexpectedly to her but not to the reader — but that all her occupations have gone. Her change in status, and her growing awareness of that change, are charted with the keenest insight; she finds herself the victim of those she once patronized, a woman without place, fortune, protection or skills, a lame duck indeed. Her attempts to re-enter society, her false starts, her failures, her breakdown and slow recovery take us into many corners of English life — the world of decayed gentlefolk, the hard struggles of single professional women, the fringes of Bohemia, the grind of a shorthand-typing course, the respite of her brother's nursery garden in Sussex. The novel records the progress of a human being towards self knowledge and towards knowledge of the world she lives in, a world of which, as she admits, she had been dangerously ignorant.

I must confess that this seems to me an almost perfect plot, and perfect for Wilson's purposes. Through it, he explores the hypocrisies of society, displaying as he does so a profound sympathy with the lonely and the powerless, and a deep respect for the fighting spirit with which Meg Eliot faces the reality that has been thrust upon her. Like a true heroine, and a worthy successor to her fictional counterparts, she rejects the easy answers — marriage, a life of borrowing and sponging, a quiet life in the country with her brother, the comforts of religious mysticism — and battles on, determined to earn her own living, determining never to be taken by surprise again. At the end of the novel she is happily engaged as secretary to a Labour M. P., but thinking of moving on. Restlessness, or curiosity? A little of both, but certainly she recognizes that for her change and engagement with life are both essential.

The whole book is so solidly constructed and carefully accomplished that one might well wonder where the ever-restless Wilson himself might move next. He was in his mid-forties when it was published, an age when most novelists have found their voice and form, an age of consolidation. Here was a straight success, a moving story of triumph over tragedy, a story with a very wide appeal, restrained, balanced, apparently middlebrow, an apology to the middleclass reader for past satire at the expense of middleclass readers, a settling of accounts with womankind in general (for women had not shown too well in previous Wilson novels). A marriage of Virginia Woolf and Arnold Bennett, as Wilson claims the novel was described. Why not simply repeat the same formula?

But like his heroine, Wilson is not fond of repetition. His next novel, *The Old Men at the Zoo* (1961), is quite different — a not too fantastic fantasy, set in what was then the near future. *The Old Men* is about politics, about freedom and restraint, about responsibility and democracy. Its narrator, Simon Carter, is Secretary of the Zoological Gardens, and the Zoo's staff serve as a microcosm for government. (Wilson worked at the British Museum between 1937 and 1955, a member of the library staff, and in this novel he displays a useful familiarity with administrative problems and the administrative temperament that most novelists conspicuously lack.) Vanished are the polite archaic shades of Austen and Trollope: we are in a world of violent colour, of savage events, of bestiality (literally) and of war. Dickens? Zola? H. G. Wells? Men are seen and described in terms of the beasts they keep. They are corrupted by power, lost in the attempt to preserve a civilised balance between the ordered and the free, between the state and nature. "Limited liberty" is the slogan with which Carter and his colleagues attempt to establish a wild zoological park, a glorified Whipsnade, a project as idealistic and as doomed as Sands' attempt to provide a home for writers — for it is undermined not only by its own staff and their intrigues, but by the outbreak of European war. The plot sounds and is bizarre, but, as one might trust from Wilson, its symbolism is not disembodied (the descriptions of animal behaviour show how deeply he studied and felt for his subject), nor does it refuse the incidental delights of the other works, including a portrait of the Director's naive wife, Mrs. Leacock, whose favourite adjective is the schoolgirl "mouldy," and who hopes to pacify an outraged and contemptuous aristocratic neighbor with a little gift: "So I just popped a pot of bramble jelly I've made into a bag with a little note saying that it was a poor thing, but my own. You see with someone so rich there's nothing you can do for them. But I daresay they never think to give her anything homemade. . . ."

(Wilson is always hard on this peculiarly English brand of childishness: Mrs. Leacock insists on referring to her husband as "Daddy" even when no children are present, and despite the fact that her daughter, a nymphomaniac, is in her thirties; the daughter in turn complains that her father "still calls his prick his weewee." A similar regressive clinging to family talk can be found in many other ways — for instance, in the short story "Crazy Crowd" and in the character Susan in *No Laughing Matter*, who refers to her unfortunate youngest son as P. S., for Post Script. Wilson has little patience with this kind of whimsy.)

The Old Men at the Zoo is a sombre novel, showing a Europe which returns to the violence of the 1930's, where nationalism and neo-Fascism flourish. But even from this dark scene, there is no escape through withdrawal, no retreat into the quiet garden. Carter is a keen naturalist who likes to re-read *Tarka the Otter* and whose greatest joy is to watch badgers at play; yet through the fortunes of war he finds himself forced to kill the things he loves in order to eat them; his murderous task is aided, ironically, by a brutal village boy so far removed from natural life that he has never seen even a rabbit, and who can do little but lament the absence of "proper tinned stuff from Norwich." (For Wilson's own analysis of this scene, see his autobiographical study, *The Wild Garden*.)[3]

His next novel, *Late Call* (1964), is very far removed from fantasy; indeed, its subject matter is positively banal. It relates the story of a fat elderly woman, Sylvia Calvert, who retires as manageress of a hotel and goes to live with her son, Harold, headmaster of a comprehensive school in a New Town in the Midlands. The whole plot revolves round little domestic intrigues and disputes: her gambling husband, Arthur, is always borrowing money; her granddaughter, Judy, is in with the county set; Harold mourns his dead wife; grandson, Ray, doesn't seem to be interested in girls. Will Harold get together with big-bottomed Sally Bulmer? Will Arthur's courseness offend Judy's friend Caroline Ogilvie? Will Sylvia ever learn to use the Roastomatic? Will Ray and his friend Mr. Corney come up against the law? The whole thing is like a parody of the soap operas to which Sylvia herself is addicted. (Angus Wilson's pastiche soap opera about prison life, "Wardress Webb," was shortly followed in real life, if so it may be called, by a remarkably similar TV series called "Within These Walls," starring Googie Withers; thus does art imitate art. Similarly, I switched on a television programme about the Edinburgh Festival the other night to find myself watching a performance of actors portraying the tribal life of baboons that could only have been a continuation of the work of Ned's troupe in *As if by Magic*, whose previous dramas had included a drama called "Batteries," with chickens, and one called, "Territoriality," with elands and gazelles. Angus Wilson should beware of what he imagines next, for we are surely going to be watching it in three years time.)

In middleclass and lower-middleclass soap opera land, Angus Wilson boldly relinquishes all his familiar touchstones, for it is a world where echoes of Woolf and George Eliot and jokes about the reputations of Etty and Wilkie mean nothing — a world where almost all the cultural framework is drawn from Sylvia's own reading and viewing, apart from a fine account (through Sylvia's reactions) of a local amateur performance of *Look Back in Anger*, which horrifies her, when she wakes to pay attention, by Jimmy Porter's violent ranting about Alison's mother, "who ought to be dead." This is the focus of Sylvia's struggle — her sense of her own redundancy. Her struggle is not unlike Meg Eliot's, but she has none of her weapons, being ill-educated, old, and socially inferior to her relatives: her clever son is a characteristic product of the new post-war world, upwardly mobile, ambitious, deeply involved in community politics, proudly provincial, painstakingly progressive even to the extent of smiling with happy approval when ton-up boys with rowdy motorbikes shatter the peace of his neighborhood. Yet Sylvia's spiritual journey towards a new sense of purpose is treated with entire seriousness, and she emerges with great dignity, despite (or because of) the fact that she embodies many of the qualities that the earlier Wilson had found ridiculous: she is ignorant, has poor taste, and is fat. Obesity, in some of Wilson's satire, seems almost to be a crime in itself; Mrs. Curry, the procuress in *Hemlock and After*, is grotesquely fat and almost a personification of evil, as though appearance and morals held some direct correspondence. But Sylvia's size is a theme for sympathy rather than laughter. She waddles and puffs, even at the most dramatic moments of the action, and there is a shocking scene in which, on the way out for an evening's entertainment with her family, she slips and falls: "The pain and the shock were not enough to drive from her a dreadful picture of herself — a fat useless old woman dolled up to no purpose, a sprawling ugly furry mess on the pathway. She could sense that the cheap imitation hat had fallen rakishly to one side, and that the white hair straggling down her face was spattered with blood from her hand . . . she felt herself to be a huge sack of coals as they lifted her up from the ground and supported her back into the house."[4] In such scenes, Wilson's effort of imagination is triumphantly vindicated; he has entered into the mind and heart of a woman from a background utterly remote from his own, and in showing us the world through her eyes, he enlarges our sympathies as much as he has enlarged his own.

Predictably, *Late Call* was hailed as evidence of a new, mature compassion, and a sign that the novel of social realism was not yet dead. Equally predictably, Angus Wilson was not content to rest here. His next work, *No Laughing Matter*, which he described as his best, is yet again a new departure, and by far his most ambitious. When I first read it, despite my immense admiration, I must admit that I felt a slight regret that he appeared to have abandoned the traditional novel of which he had been a partisan, and with which I associated myself. He had seemed to stand as living proof that there was still life in the old forms, and that they could be adapted to the complexity of the post-Woolf, post-Joyce era; was he now to desert us for the avant-garde, for the barren wastes of intellectual play which literary critics so enjoy, abandoning through a desire for novelty the territory he has so decisively conquered? In fact my initial reaction to *No Laughing Matter* bears some relation to his own initial reactions to Woolf, which he described in *Studies in the Literary Imagination*[5] — a feeling that this was too rarified and literary for my taste, that it belonged to the realm of art rather than life — and like him, I have lived to change my mind. It is, as he says, his finest work, but it is of such richness that it requires many readings. (Having said that, I must record that when my husband went off with our new copy to work one Saturday morning when I was in the middle of my first reading, I took a taxi into town and bought another, poor though we were in those days, so anxious was I to continue it — so, even the first impact must have been considerable.)

On one level, *No Laughing Matter* is the story of a family and its fortunes, and a social history of Britain spanning more than fifty years of twentieth-century life: a thoroughly conventional project, and one that Thackeray, Trollope, Bennett and Galsworthy would all have applauded. (Indeed, in one of the novel's multiple ironies, one of the characters ends up watching *The Forsyte Saga* on television.) The six children of William and Clara Matthews (failed writer and faithless wife) occupy the centre of the stage, with supporting cast of grandmother, aunt, cook, husbands, wives, lovers, colleagues, grandchildren — but already we are confronted by the complexity of the novel's subject, and the corresponding complexity of Wilson's narration. For, from the first page, we are in a shifting world of theatrical effects, distorting mirrors, kaleidoscopic refractions, burlesques, imitations, shadows of shadows. The Matthews family is much given to posturing and self-dramatisation, and we see them, their actions and their views of one another through innumerable filters. Wilson's work had always emphasized the human need to play roles, to adopt manners and strike attitudes, but here that need becomes the texture of the book itself. The six children, in the early sections, find release and reconcile themselves to their painful and often squalid family life in a variety of ways; they daydream in solitude, composing their own future; they rearrange reality; they pursue solitary fantasies; and they also invent a corporate fantasy, The Game, in which each child takes on the role of one of the oppressive adults on whom they are dependent, and whose characters and destinies forge their own. The Game, which runs throughout the novel, centres on the favoured handsome son Rupert's impersonation of his weak and despised father, Billy Pop, the Billy Goat, the White Slug; and the impersonation by Marcus, the unwanted dark outcast changeling baby, of his mother, the Countess, the Black Bitch, the Tigress. (Rupert becomes a successful actor, whose professional progress is also a charting of the history of British theatre; Marcus becomes a homosexual with a flair for exotic decor and design, famous, as a minor character unkindly puts it, for his "green balls.") The Game is counterpointed by a succession of scenes from plays in the manner of dramatists as varied as Coward, Chekov, Shaw and, finally, Samuel Beckett, each shedding a different light on the characters and on the cultural milieu which they inhabit. And within this framework are dozens more variations, most notably, perhaps, those of Margaret, who becomes a successful novelist, (though she fears she is labelled as a "writer's writer," over-concerned with technique); her career is launched, as was Wilson's own, with short stories in which she takes revenge on her family for the embarrassments of her youth. One of them, produced at length, recounts in fictional terms the "real" wedding of Margaret's twin sister, Sukey, and is prefaced by a quotation from a review which reads "The ironies of Miss Matthews' stories expose our most cherished evasions." Irony indeed, and Margaret discovers that although writing can cure, it can also kill. Even Sukey, the dull, sensible, domestic member of the family, turns to fiction to solve life's problems, and writes little tales of domestic life for the BBC, carefully eliminating the uncomfortable and complex, with titles such as "How to Climb Snowdon Without a Tin Opener," "When Santa Left Too Many Cricket Bats" and "Why Can't We Take the Rhino Home." Quentin, the eldest, a disillusioned socialist, converts his personal and political despair into highly popular television cynicism and punditry. Gladys, an efficient business woman involved in a ruinous affair with an inefficient business man, comforts herself by seeing herself as Podge, the fat lovable Cockney. (Gladys, in fact, is a redeemed version of Gwen Rutherford, even to the point of imitating for her siblings a bulldog with such startling verisimilitude that they are all, despite their manifold anxieties, reduced to the laughter of childhood.)

Yet, despite the constant shifting of style and focus, the fictions within fictions, the multiplicity of echoes (in the first pages alone we are referred to cinema newsreels, films of the Wild West, Wordsworth, Bret Harte, Whitman, music hall and Marie Lloyd), there is nothing remotely confusing or artificial in the presentation of character and action. There is none of the arbitrary uncertainty and maddening fluid impermanence that haunts so many twentieth-century expositions of the multiplicity of personality. The major events of European history — the Great War, the rise of Fascism in Germany and London's East End, the Spanish Civil War, the growth of totalitarian tyranny in the Soviet Union, the Second World War, Aden, Suez — are woven into the family history with consummate artistry, yet with none of their weight diminished. The six protagonists and their supporting cast are not abstractions; they exist on every level of the self. They have faces, clothes, voices; they eat, they quarrel, they misunderstand themselves and one another, they grow old. In this novel, more than in any other I know, we see people — real recognizable people, in the most old-fashioned sense — in the act of becoming what they must ineluctably be, despite the shadow selves that they might have been, the impersonations that they carry with them. We seem to see into the heart of the family nexus, into the mystery of developing personality. It is a truly remarkable achievement, and seems to me to be, much more than *The Middle Age of Mrs Eliot*, a true fusion of the many traditions of British fiction. An inexhaustible book, and on so generous a scale that it can be re-read over a lifetime.

Of Wilson's last published novel, *As if by Magic* (1973),[6] I shall say little, largely because I know that I have not come to terms with it. Its theme is enormous — no less than the duties of affluence towards the Third World, and the possibility of individual engagement and responsibility within a capitalist society — and its form is extraordinary. Dickensian farce rubs shoulders with scenes from de Sade, dissertions on D. H. Lawrence and Tolkien mingle with Henry James and Shaw. On the last page the heroine, sick of her inescapable habit of seeing life through the spectacles of old books, cries "Damn English Literature! Damn the past and the future! I have enough to do making something of the present. But neither the past nor the future were escapable" — a cry of despair, of challenge, of acceptance of challenge. If anyone can make sense of the present, it is Angus Wilson. John Updike remarked recently that writing fiction in the seventies, this global decade, becomes increasingly difficult, a view which many novelists would endorse, and *As if by Magic* is an attempt at a global novel, ranging from London to Morocco, from Japan to Ceylon and Goa; its hero on his travels seems to hear "a high, distant overtone of perpetual woe. Could it be the natural noise of the world, as he began to fancy?" And if so, what fiction can cope with such knowledge?

But let me end on a more positive and more personal note. My respect for Angus Wilson's work will by now be evident; I hope I have also managed to indicate what a joy it is to read. His wit has been acclaimed by all his critics, but I would like to pay tribute to his immense store of sheer information, if that is not too dull a word for it. His books are packed with out-of-the-way facts about gardening, archeology, agronomy, educational theory, political history, esoteric religions, interior decor, Stonehenge, women's fashions and cookery. Mary McCarthy has said that the novelist has "a deep empiric love of fact," and that facts are part of the proper texture of novels. I agree. My son, having just finished *Anglo-Saxon Attitudes* for the first time (and watching him read it was almost as enjoyable as my own first discovery) said with a sigh of admiration as he finished it, "But how does he *know* so much?" "I suppose he finds it out," I replied vaguely — but how much he has found out, and to what use he has put it! What I have learned from him has become part of my own store of knowledge. I rarely see a rhododendron or a calceolaria without recalling his strictures upon these flowers in *The Middle Age of Mrs. Eliot*; I never rinse the rice without recalling that Harold's dead wife, Beth, used to rinse it three times. (In fact before I read *Late Call* I don't think I realised one had to rinse the stuff at all.) I am sorry to say that I used not to know that it was more chic to read novels than biographies, nor had I ever thought to enquire who designed the Raven's Cage in London Zoo. (Decimus Burton, of course.) In *As if by Magic* one character asks another how she knows that a certain kind of duck is called a mandarin, and she replies, "Oh, I've always known. Idle rentier women are like magpies. They collect any random fact in sight . . . I've got nothing but idle vision, but at least I must name what I see." Angus Wilson is no *idle rentier* (though he has created some memorable ones), but he too likes to name what he sees, and his readers are all in debt to his insatiable curiosity, to his conviction that the literary imagination nourishes itself in the real world of events, as well as in the world of fiction.

Notes

1. *As if by Magic* (London: Secker & Warbug, 1973), p. 202.

2. *Such Darling Dodos and Other Stories* (1950; rpt. London: Secker & Warburg 1959), pp. 12-13.

3. (London: Secker & Warbug, 1963), pp. 87-90.

4. *Late Call* (London: Secker & Warburg, 1964), p. 103.

5. See "The Always-Changing Impact of Virginia Woolf," *Studies in the Literary Imagination*, 11:2 (Fall 1978), 1-9.

6. Wilson's new novel, *Setting the World on Fire*, was published during the spring of 1980. — Ed.

Setting the World on Fire: Phaethon's Fall and Wilson's Redemption
Ted Billy*

Although widely recognized as a contemporary novelist of manners and morals, Sir Angus Wilson has maintained that self-realization lies at the heart of his fiction.[1] At the core of his own personality, Wilson sees an irreconcilable ambivalence that finds expression in most of his novels and short stories.[2] The most clearly defined manifestation of this "inner debate" takes center stage in his eighth novel, *Setting the World on Fire*. Wilson objectifies this complex dualism — order and chaos, tradition and revolution, civilization and nature, security and risk, method and imagination — in his tripartite dramatization of the lives of Tom and Piers Mosson, heirs to the Tothill estate. The triadic structure of the novel provides three significant glimpses of the brothers as children (Part I, 1948), youths (Part II, 1956-7), and as young adults (Part III, 1969). Each glimpse (especially the 200 pages of Part II) offers insights into their character formation as mutually coexist-

*This essay was written specifically for this volume and is published here with permission of the author. © Ted Billy, 1984.

ing opposing selves. Ultimately, Wilson rejects both extremes—unbridled freedom and protective constraint—in favor of a kind of wild civility that does not resolve the dichotomy, but rather holds these opposing forces in dynamic tension, making constructive use of life's ineluctable conflicts.

As the novel unfolds, Wilson links the brothers' contrasting personalities to the two seventeenth-century architects responsible for creating the majesty of Tothill House: Tom favoring the classic symmetry of Sir Roger Pratt, and Piers dwelling on the baroque Great Hall added by Captain John Vanbrugh after Pratt's death.[3] As tots at Tothill in the postwar atmosphere of 1948, the brothers develop opposing world views. Tom (nicknamed "Pratt" by his older brother) adopts the cautious conservatism of his grandmother (Jackie) and his Uncle Hubert, hoping that stability can be maintained in the face of chaos. Piers (called "Van" by Tom) identifies with the rash daring of Phaethon depicted on the painted ceiling of Vanbrugh's Great Hall; he also sympathizes with his blundering alcoholic mother (Rosemary) and his moody great-grandfather. As teenagers living in the shadow of the Cold War (1956–57), the brothers again take different paths: Tom desiring to preserve history as he prepares to become a lawyer, and Piers entering the theatrical world, first as the producer of a school production of *Richard II*, and then ambitiously planning to remake history by putting on Lully's opera, *Phaethon*, in the Great Hall. But the opera is postponed until 1969, when the rupture in family relations between Jackie and Rosemary has finally healed. The opera's success encourages Piers to stage a new play at the Tothill Stables. However, terrorist activities intrude upon the first night's performance, and in the melee that follows, Tom receives a fatal bullet wound in the act of saving his brother. On this poignant note of self-sacrifice and Piers' sudden isolation, the novel concludes.

I PRATFALLS AND VANITIES

The myth of Phaethon's fatal "dance through the clouds" provides the metaphor for Wilson's title as well as the inspiration for Piers' artistic aspirations. Wilson opens the novel with Piers' interior monologue as the little boy marvels at the spectacle immortalized on the ceiling of the Great Hall: "And, even if the young man did fall, you could see that he was in a delighted magic trance. He had made his shapes, he had danced through the sky. So the fall was only the last movement of the dance."[4] To Piers, Phaethon embodies youthful defiance of the rigidity of the established order. His perennial desire to stage the opera based on the hero's fatal bid for glory indicates his affinity for "the tragic defier of the gods' narrow dictates" (77). But Piers always maintains his awareness of the terrible aftermath of "Phaethon's glorious flight across the sky . . . Jove's thunderbolt thrown in the righteous cause of order and dull peace" (112). It reminds him that every noble enterprise entails considerable risk.

In childhood reveries, Piers stares in fascination at the great lantern suspended from the ceiling, dreaming that this magic lantern can lift him from the odious floor so he may sport among the clouds like Phaethon. Wilson associates Piers' swimming lessons with the necessity of Phaethon's daring ride: "If you were really happy, you couldn't be careful. If you had a need to fly in circles and twists and somersaults like the happy young man wheeling above him, you had no time to think of being careful. You *had* to do it" (4). Little Piers tries to emulate Phaethon's aerial dance by dancing naked in the Great Hall; after being reprimanded, he finds that he continues to dance inwardly. Ironically, Piers has lost his father, an aviator who, like Phaethon, "had been shot down over the sea" (6). Wilson evokes memories of Phaethon's fall and Piers' father's wartime death as the little boy mimics flights of glory throughout the open space: "he sought to glide across the Great Hall, his arms floating through the air, his legs parted in great leaps. He was nothing now but his dance" (7). Here Wilson objectifies Yeats' oft-quoted rhetorical question, "How can we know the dancer from the dance?" But more importantly, he establishes the groundwork for Piers' development as an artist who disappears in his work. Piers' artistic ambition is a curious blend of egotism and self-abnegation. In the course of the novel, he evolves from the adolescent producer of *Richard II* to the maturing professional who stages *The Master Builder*.

Piers reveals the embryonic spirit of a master manipulator in his dreams of producing the Lully opera: "He would so enter the very being of the actor who played Phaethon that the whole cast, the lantern itself, the great Solomonic columns would be shaped and ordered to his design, and Phaethon would fall at last in all his tragic wayward beauty to the terror and sadness and satisfaction of a fine tuned audience that would stagger from their seats amazed" (91). To the young artist who aspires to set the world on fire, Phaethon is both a doomed upstart and an innovative creator. Piers views Phaethon's role as constructive as well as daring: "His chariot ride is a brave gesture of defiance of the dismal routine life. But, of course, it *is* a tragedy and it turns out to be destructive. . . . But I don't think this makes Phaethon's gesture any less dramatic" (116). The youthful impresario who envisions Phaethon's glorious flight and tragic fall in the histrionic atmosphere of Vanbrugh's Great Hall, consciously affirming the freedom of transformation over the security of tradition, never shrinks from the hazard of leaping ahead on thin ice that might melt at any moment. Piers Mosson prefers "risk and sensation" to the "sleepy ease" of conventional living (149). Like the existentialists, he wants to maximize every moment — intensify each experience.

By identifying with Phaethon, Piers enacts the mythic role of all creators who dare to challenge the gods. But he also defines himself in his passionate affiliation with the miraculous grandeur of Vanbrugh's architectural imagination: "massive, eccentric, even brutal, but splendidly tragic" (196). Tothill, with its Great Hall and towers and battlements, presents a "magical stage" for the mythic role-playing of Piers' exuberant sensibility. For Tom Mosson, however, Vanbrugh's wild inventiveness has demoralizing implications. Conditioned by his grandmother and Uncle Hubert to distrust flights of fancy and drastic change, he identifies with Pratt's dignified decorum. Tom earnestly absorbs his uncle's monotonous tributes to Sir Roger's craftsmanship: "All regular and even. A marvellous sense of proportion. . . . Regularity in everything" (14–15). (Ironically, Wilson undermines these sage declarations later in the novel when Hubert's masochistic sexual predilection leads to his demise.) And although Wilson obviously admires calm order and radical innovation, he subtly burlesques the extravagance of stability in his description of the Tothill curiosities encased in Pratt's original Cabinet Room: "the *mummified* marmoset, the *petrified* lava from Etna shaped like a negro's thick lips, the caul taken from a Berber baby, . . . a sea-serpent *turned to rock* as it rose in spirals to strike, a mouse taken from the belly of a Chinaman, an anal fistula *bottled* in spirits, the *skeleton* of a great bat" (76; my italics). These grotesque images dramatize the fossilization of order and tradition in a stagnant culture. However, Wilson adds another turn of the artistic screw by implying that these convoluted shapes were a prophetic proclamation of Vanbrugh's future work (77). Whatever the function of these exotic knick-knacks, Wilson affirms the baroque art of "ordered disorder" — the wild civility that reaches out to embrace polarities, but only temporarily, not in a final (i.e., fatal) synthesis. So Wilson objectifies his artistic self by projecting the revolutionary impulse (Piers/Vanbrugh) and the reactionary recoil (Tom/Pratt) in intricate interaction.

Tom, who as a child wonders why Phaethon seems to be happy though he falls to his death, totally assimilates his uncle's simplistic formula for maintaining order and tradition: "the world isn't all Phaethons or Vanbrughs. The men that keep it safe and in order are the Pratts, the men who know how to keep themselves in hand, the blokes who do things well and regularly. If it wasn't for them, the ice *would* break, the flames *would* fly up into the sky" (15). Although quite "plucky" in other circumstances, little Tom lives in fear of Vanbrugh's Great Hall and the soul-searing panorama of Phaethon's tragic fall depicted on its ceiling: "Looking for his brother Piers to save him from these fears, to keep the sky from falling down upon him, to check the smiling young man from cruelly setting fire to the world, he had seen that Piers was not with them, had *turned to stone*, had *frozen into himself* like all these painted people on the ceiling, all these *marble people* by the walls" (7–8; my italics). Wilson's marmoreal imagery testifies to the petrifying power of fear as Tom, another Chicken Little, imagines that the painted Phaethon will bring the ceiling tumbling down (11). Tom grows to cherish his conservative world view, due in large measure to Hubert's monitory metaphor: "the world isn't altogether a safe place. It's a bit like an ice-covered pond" (13). Yet Tom intuitively recognizes the stultifying influence of his uncle's jeremiad against life's intrinsic incongruities. He grows up, nevertheless, reverencing Pratt's stand against chaos and dreading the danger threatening established order.

Even Tom's decision to become a gourmet cook stems from his passion to maintain order. He helps with the family cooking for three years after his mother suffers an arm injury. So the activity that becomes his principal creative outlet springs from his near-obsession to preserve stability. Yet when his resourcefulness fails him in a crisis, he psychologically recoils into a shell of childlike isolation, immersing himself in books or other solid objects of contemplation. In compensation for his sense of inadequacy, he turns "to the subtler certainties of mathematics and the wondrous flights of pure intellect" (112). Tom commits the genealogy of Tothill furniture to memory to show his grandmother that he values the reality and security of the family estate (159). She finds an appreciative listener in Tom when she sermonizes her aristocratic prattle: "Regularity and elegance. They are the important things. Especially when chaos is trying to take over. Keep beautiful things going" (160).

Wilson most dramatically depicts Tom's susceptibility to fear and trembling in the ominous scene foreshadowing the exile of their mother after the family lunch. Because Piers is preoccupied with his opera, Tom must meet his mother alone, though she asked them both to meet her at the station before seeing the rest of the family. As Tom walks along the riverbank, the sky seems to radiate protection and the perennial flow of the river appears to suggest that his "fears, all dangers of unrule or chaos, seemed remote" (178). But such sure signs of permanent peace abruptly abandon him as he walks across the bridge: "Then suddenly there was no road nor traffic nor people but water whose depths he could not see. And then, looking up, high, high above him the sky, across which some clouds were moving. At once the bridge's pavement beneath him was insecure, trembling. The clouds above him looming closer, threatening— the skies would fall in" (178). Without Piers to strengthen his faltering courage, Tom gives way to metaphysical vertigo, surrendering to the trauma of his perilous isolation: "he felt only himself, his own body totally alone, himself, Tom, and, high above, the sky, nothing, nothing between to save him from its fall, and below, the trembling bridge, the bottomless water" (178). Threatened by chaos without and emptiness within, Tom irrationally seeks a permanent escape from the vicissitudes of life: "no one was there but him, he felt, and nothing, nothing, would save him from finding safety in the depths of the river below, nothing could save him from throwing himself down where he would be cradled from all this frightening void above and around him" (178). Characteristically, Tom's confrontation with nothingness prompts his infantile recoil into the numbness of withdrawal. Beset by two dangers, the constriction of emptiness and the urge to leap over the parapet to the freedom of annihilation, Tom focuses his eyes on the shot tower as he runs across the bridge in panic. At last, he reaches the other side of the bridge and alleviates his anxiety before meeting his mother, ironically, at Waterloo Station. After his mother confesses her desire to move in with her married lover, Tom blames himself for the family strife that follows: "He, who was ever conscious of the ice cracking beneath us, . . . should have been on his guard. . . . But this had been the occasion for restoring order and civility and he, Tom, had failed to do it. . . . And all he could think of was that the pattern of order and civility he had set for himself was not an easy one; it often came near to contradiction" (218). Here Wilson not only prefigures Tom's death but also hints at the unnatural basis of established order. Tom's wish to freeze temporality into stasis is futile. Yet Tom, as a young adult, steadfastly clings to his conservative motto: "Everything in its place and order" (276).

II   THE WILD GARDEN

In addition to the Tom/Piers, Pratt/Vanbrugh polarity, Wilson engages in a more subtle dichotomy throughout the novel by contrasting images of the formal garden and anarchic wilderness. Hubert, the hypocritical spokesman for Tothill regularity, dreads the "invasion by the wild, by the untamed" (21), and for good reason. Tothill's "ravaged formal garden" testifies to its wartime use by the Coal Board (29). The "Woodwork" that flourished with the establishment of the Pratt house now looms as the "wilderness" that cuts off the mansion from the rest of London. And though it still retains its traditional name, the "Woodwork" has suffered the encroachments of the wilderness, turning its intricate maze of pathways into a rabbit warren. Overgrowth also typifies "Rosemary's famous wild garden," which evokes Rousseauistic impressions of the "noble savage." In contrast to her horticulturally ignorant sons, she makes a hobby-horse of gardening, resorting to the isolation of nursery affairs when she feels unable to deal with a crisis. Unlike the symmetry-loving Tothills, Rosemary identifies with organic images of spontaneous development: "And the wilderness that's grown up at the end of the garden. Such wonderful shapes the bushes have made, like those creatures that jump out at one in dreams. It's the sort of effect that I've tried to create with the shrub rose end of the nursery" (186). Piers even speculates that his mother carried her problems down to "the wild garden which alone in the great estate made any sense to her imagination" (210). Here Woodwork becomes webwork, as "the mazy paths wound and turned and turned sharply back again between hedges of holly and cypress and box and yew . . . in this compact, complex green labyrinth" (210).

Rosemary's retreat to the garden for therapeutic reasons reflects not only Wilson's fondness for gardening, but also a major motif throughout his fiction; it is an organic metaphor that lies at the root of his "symbolic view of life": "Tropical or subtropical gardens, indeed, have always stood for the 'garden or clearing in the wild' as opposed to the English 'wild garden,' a distinction of symbols which lies deep in the dichotomy of values that has troubled me so long. . . . The wild garden, of course, is the eighteenth century's attempt artificially to preserve the noble savage while taming him to fit into elegant surroundings."[5] The preceding passage, from Wilson's study of his own creative process, *The Wild Garden* (subtitled "Speaking of Writing"), makes a clear distinction between two different organic metaphors having psychological or spiritual connotations. Yet, in the same context, Wilson fuses the two symbols that lie behind "the major themes" of his work: "In seeking for an imaginative solution for the pressing human dilemma I have been led to both; indeed *in my imagination they have become one place*, for the wild garden and the clearing or garden in the wild are *one and the same place seen from different angles*, and they have the great advantages as moral symbols that each claims a completely opposite set of values."[6] If the "wild garden" or "garden in the wild" suggest a paradise lost in Wilson's imagination, the Tothill of Tom and Piers' early childhood constitutes a fictional embodiment of this fused dichotomy. The *Mosson* brothers are "garden blind" (95), ironically because their polarized personalities embody the "wild garden" conglomerate tended by their mother. Tom and Piers are the "wild garden" anthropomorphized and nurtured at Tothill, where the "architectual union of opposites" stands as a permanent tribute to the creative merger of contraries.

As a moral symbol, Tothill represents freedom and constraint, formal order and imaginative disorder, and perhaps even unity in disunity. (Wilson has stated that the location of Tothill House is a tribute to his early education at Westminster School.)[7] Certainly nostalgia plays a role in the author's polarization of his personality into two fictive brothers who mature in the confines of a magic mansion of glorious paradox. And since the Great Hall is a monument to Vanbrugh's eccentric genius, the Library becomes the favorite boyhood room of Tom and Piers: "They had called it the Van-Pratt room, not only for its intricate, almost paradoxical entwining of their beloved architect heroes, but in *its union of themselves*" (76; my italics). The Library, therefore, serves as a microcosm of Tothill House itself, with its fusion of contrary styles into a higher order of art. Piers intuitively senses this anomalous merger of opposites: "it was impossible for him to breathe the air of the Library without feeling Pratt [Tom] there, in busy, orderly, methodical reading" (76). Tom and Piers are the descendants of the House of Tothill, which includes "two very different men, Thomas Tothill, essentially a slow-moving, hard-headed man of affairs, and Francis Tothill, essentially a quick witted, graceful courtier, in turn, took the risk of choosing architects who were not easy, safe bets and were rewarded by the wonderful results" (134). Thomas and Francis Tothill, Pratt and Vanbrugh, Tom and Piers Mosson, the wild garden and the garden in the wild — each duality functions as a manifestation of the dialectic of creation and conservation in Wilson's own personality.[8] Tothill House stands as a palace of enchantment — created by architects of opposing visions — fostering Tom's desire to preserve its majesty and Piers' ambition to expand its grandeur throughout the world. These are conflicting responses to Tothill's splendor, yet "the house was the enchanter that brought them all together in pleasure" (126).

III   TOTHILL TRANSFORMED

Wilson most vividly defines the contrasting sensibilities of the brothers as they react to the element of change in their lives. Tom, whose sense of the precariousness of existence dictates his defense mechanisms, views their ancestral home as an inheritance that must be treasured and guarded with great vigilance: "a great house is a shape and it is also the way people have lived in it over centuries and what they filled it with. That's what makes it a *strong fortress* instead of a weak shell" (109; my italics). Piers strongly disagrees with his brother's "hold fast" attitude toward life: "I think you'll become a slave to history that way. One must break the mould of what *actually* happened by what might have been. That's why this avenging of Sir Francis Tothill by staging *Phaethon* is so satisfactory. We're not just gradually changing the inside of the house with different artifacts as all our ancestors have done, we're going to make a new work of art out of an old one — or rather I am" (109–10). Rather egotistically, Piers identifies with the forces of drastic change, believing that art depends on transformation, not on static conceptions of reality. As a child, in the enchanted Great Hall, he had played the role of Phaethon in his imagination countless times, boldly unafraid of the "green turned to fire" in the great bowl, and regardless of the "silly marble girls" whose "legs were turning into stalks of plants — trees, . . . willow trees" (4). Piers grows up believing that fear only exists as an obstacle to achievement, hardly a valid reason for assuming a futile position.

Throughout the novel, Tom has difficulty adapting to change, particularly the odd metamorphosis in his grandmother (formerly the exponent of Tothill traditionalism). Even prior to her transformation, she evinces a willingness to accept the impermanence of life: "There is no need to be afraid of change. God made a changing world. He does not want us to turn our backs on the future" (219). (Of course, Jackie says this before Rosemary announces her intention to live with her married lover, Jim. This apparently proves too much of a change for Jackie to handle, and the brothers become victims of the estrangement between their mother and their paternal grandmother.) Jackie undergoes a complete transformation of personality in 1969, several days after a stroke leads to her hospitalization. When her grandsons visit her, Tom cannot acclimate himself to Jackie's new image: "She's born again, . . . and a jolly good rebirth it was proving. . . . [B]ut then, again as always, he found himself shivering slightly — was this really any longer his grandmother?" (266). Tom attempts to join his brother in rejoicing over their grandmother's newfound happiness, but he is appalled by "the sense of almost macabre pantomime her new, so much welcomed personality gave him. She who had been so rock-like, hard, egotistic if you like, but reliable, firm in the knowledge of the things she valued, appeared to be like a feather on top of a wave" (267). Viewing his grandmother as the embodiment of the inevitable ravages of time, Tom examines her face to find tell-tale evidence of human frailty: "the stroke had pulled her mouth down slightly at the right side, her eyes had lost their old steely look and danced now, glinting yet gentle. But, to him, she seemed like a pretty but battered old doll" (267). Tom views his grandmother's new outlook on life as a compromise of her integrity, a sign that Tothill House is as susceptible as any other human contrivance to the winds of change. When Jackie remarks that "it is such fun breaking down barriers," Piers agrees with her, "But Tom said nothing; the concept did not seem to suit the grandmother he had once so respected" (272). Tom's reluctance to adapt to change indicates that he lacks the quality that Piers has in abundance: imaginative empathy, the talent that permits Piers to enter the various personalities in *Richard II*, *Phaethon*, and *The Master Builder*. (If "Sir Piers" becomes a histrionic master builder, Tom assumes the role of historical preserver, as Wilson's finale demonstrates.) As the brothers walk back from the hospital, Piers comments on the happy change in their grandmother's disposition. But Tom does not share his brother's confident viewpoint: "I don't really *like* the idea of people being changed. It seems to make nonsense of life" (274).

But Tom *does* change, and in a most significant way, during the final act of Wilson's tragic-comic novel. For in their final appearances, Tom and Piers exchange roles. As the police raid interrupts the performance of Ralph Tucker's play at the *Tothill Stables* (an ironic location for the play, which is a cover-up for a modern day Guy Fawkes plot by anarchists), Piers asks Tom to escort the audience into the house for an early supper while the police round up the terrorists: "The ground of a whole wonderful dream had sunk beneath his feet, but it was what he had expected for so long; his calm was automatic" (293–4). Suddenly recalling that his Uncle Hubert's ex-fiancée, Marina, was in the audience and might be one of the "crazy ladies" backing the terrorists, Tom pushes his way back through the crowd. Ominously, Lord Beale warns him, "Mosson, keep your head" (294). Tom "looked everywhere for Marina and there she was, still seated, but now collecting her bag and programme. Not a crazy lady, but a lady who'd kept her head. He ran up the steps onto the stage" (294). Ironically, in the final scene of his brief life, Tom (for a fatal instant) plays the sacrificial role of the impetuous Phaethon, accepting the bullet directed at his brother: "Piers saw only a Medusa face with arms gesticulating, hair streaming—but Tom saw the hand's movements. He rushed towards his brother and, saving himself from tripping, knocked him over" (295). Tom, who devoted his undramatic life to order and tradition, dramatically and poignantly gives up his life to save Piers, the heir to Tothill House. In the ambulance, while Tom's consciousness flickers prior to its eclipse, Piers promises his brother that he will not allow terrorism to put to rout "art and shape." Piers, the histrionic modern-day Phaethon, vows to preserve and protect the order and tradition that Tom revered.

After Tom's death, Piers leaves the hospital and momentarily assumes his brother's character:

> It was only when he was walking across the bridge that panic seized him. Every step that he took, every step that those around him took, seemed to shake the bridge, seemed to shake the world. The water flowing below, the starred sky above him, seemed ready to meet, to burst upon the human insects, upon him, in one shapeless flow of eternity. Tothill in front, Pratt dead behind. How could he go on to deal with Tothill, . . . all the disorder to put right, . . . all the management and order to keep going. What good were his wonderful Vanbrugh inventions in a dead chaotic universe? (296)

In this dark night of the soul Piers retrogresses spiritually to his childhood self, the one Wilson pictures at the opening of the novel: a small boy who imagines himself the tiniest beetle dwarfed by the "twisting black marble pillars" in the Great Hall (3). But Piers recovers from his moment of psychological constriction, deciding that the show must go on, even though he has vicariously experienced a Phaethon-like death. Just as Vanbrugh accepted the challenge of completing Tothill's architecture after Pratt's death, Piers dares to take up the challenge of living and growing without his brother at his side: "Go up, Master Builder, go up! Now. Lest delaying, you lose the power to ascend the towers of imagination" (296). Piers dramatically evolves from a self-indulgent, adolescent Phaethon to a self-diffusing, maturing Master Builder of the Ibsen mold in Wilson's symbolic birth of the artist. At the close of the novel, Piers adopts a posture similar to his attitude as a spectator of his production of the opera: he "must not let the scene, the realised wonder of Tothill Transformed, distract him from the producer's eye" (243). The "producer's eye" displaces the Phaethon-like egotism in Piers' sensibility. He has assimilated the value of his brother's life and death, and at last, Tom and Piers are one.

Wilson's tale of two brothers may have been inspired by his own relation to an older brother, as he describes in *The Wild Garden*: "As a child I was much with my brother next in age—thirteen years old when I was born. He was a youth of *exceptional histrionic powers*, strangely combining sharpness of wit and tenderness of heart, extremely effeminate, with *deep powers of creation that were never fulfilled. His wit and his fantasy* have both strongly influenced the texture of my free imagination, giving it an unusual quality of severely moral chi-chi and camp."[9] *Setting the World on Fire* may be Wilson's elegy for the unrealized potentiality of his older brother. It may also chart the metaphorical course of action leading to his decision to become a creative artist (i.e., to accomplish what his brother might have accomplished). In any event, Wilson endows the artist with the capacity to deal with the perils of mutability. Rejecting the extremist measures of radical force and reactionary caution, Wilson portrays the artist as the agent of transformation, the enchanter of adaptation whose creation is orderly disorder. Art is the only redeemer in a mutable world of fire and ice.

Notes

1. In *The Wild Garden; or Speaking of Writing* (Berkeley: Univ. of California Press, 1963), Wilson denotes self-realization as the theme of his first four novels (p. 29).

2. Wilson speaks of the "opposite poles" of self-inquiry and self-deception in the characters of Bernard and Ella Sands, Gerald and Ingeborg Middleton, and Meg Eliot, though he denies that any of these characters have a basis in his own personality (*The Wild Garden*, pp. 43–44).

3. The fictitious Tothill House has an historical counterpart in Fonthill Abbey, commissioned in 1795 by William Beckford, author of the Gothic extravaganza *Vathek*. Fonthill was an architectural chaos, featuring a host of excesses, including a Great Hall 120 feet high. See Diana Hirsh, *The World of Turner: 1775–1851* (New York: Time-Life Books, 1969), p. 43.

4. Angus Wilson, *Setting the World on Fire* (New York: The Viking Press, 1980), p. 6; hereafter, cited in the text.

5. *The Wild Garden*, pp. 60–61. In "An Interview with Angus Wilson," conducted by Betsy Draine, *Contemporary Literature*, 21, No. 1 (1980), 1–14, Wilson speaks of Kipling's sense of "the lure of the wild and at the same time the desire to make some point of contact between the wild and the civilized" (p. 7). Wilson asserts that he shares this attitude toward "the problem of nature versus civilization, the country versus the city" (p. 7).

6. *The Wild Garden*, p. 62; my italics.

7. See Michael Barber, "An Interview with Angus Wilson," *New York Times Book Review*, 16 November 1980.

8. In his pioneering study of *Angus Wilson* (Edinburgh: Oliver & Boyd, 1964), Jay Halio observes that two history masters exercised considerable influence on the formation of Wilson's personality: John Edward Bowle, an energetic and perceptive teacher who enthusiastically urged Wilson to write novels; and Lurie Tanner, the "carefully balanced" scholar who "taught his pupils the virtues of decorum and good sense" (pp. 5–6). Halio affirms that "the alternation of such opposite dispositions as theirs appears to form the basis of Wilson's own character and of his wit" (p. 6). These two early influences seem very much in evidence in *Setting the World on Fire*. When interviewed by Michael Barber, Wilson openly admitted his novelistic strategy: "Tom and Piers represent the two sides of me. Part of me wants to take enormous risks, experiment with form, let my imagination rip, dazzle people. But then there's another part that says, 'Steady on, the ice is beginning to crack.' That's Tom. He stands for method and order and regularity."

9. *The Wild Garden*, p. 140; my italics.

Sources and Analogues in Angus Wilson's *Setting the World on Fire*

Michael O'Shea*

Angus Wilson's *Setting the World on Fire* describes the lives and fates of two boys possessed of an edifice complex. Piers Mosson, the heir-presumptive to a baronetcy, and his younger brother, Tom, share an extraordinary passion for their ancestral home, Tothill House. As the author explains in a prologue, Tothill is a great mansion built on the ruins of monastic buildings of Westminster Abbey, and it exhibits two principal and contrasting styles: the Palladian style, in the basic structure designed by Sir Roger Pratt, and an elaborate baroque style, in the Great Hall designed by Sir John Vanbrugh. Piers adopts, along with the nickname "Van," a view of life and art derived from the extravagant Vanbrugh hall with its ceiling painting of Phaethon, by Antonio Verrio; on the other hand, his brother Tom, nicknamed "Pratt," adopts a regulated, decorous demeanor inspired by the order and symmetry of the Pratt architecture. As the author says at the end of his prologue, "It only remains to say that the house and its history are of course the inventions of the author."[1]

Invention though it may be, Tothill has been crafted with Wilson's keen historian's sense for coherence. He has made a virtually imperceptible tear in the fabric of history and London geography, and expertly rewoven it to accommodate Tothill, its history, and his characters' lives. Although more than one earlier reviewer quibbled with the literal credibility of a mansion of Tothill's size, complete with grounds, squeezed between Westminster Abbey and St. John's, Smith Square,[2] Tothill stands as an essentially convincing illusion, an elaborate frame within which Wilson casts his tale of two brothers. The architectural complexity of Tothill adumbrates the complex texture of the entire novel: like Tothill House, *Setting the World on Fire* is constituted of, and subsumes, numerous disparate elements to yield a complex, yet synthesized, whole. It is a work of fiction which yokes together Ovid's myth of Phaethon and Ibsen's *Master Builder* to tell a single story, using the techniques and language of architecture and drama. Moreover, by using the twin artistic paradigms of architecture and drama, this novel partakes of a tradition that includes not only Ibsen's play, but also Jane Austen's *Mansfield Park*. This essay considers how some of these artistic sources and analogues interact in *Setting the World on Fire*, and how they inform a reading of the novel.

I

The myth of Phaethon, told in Ovid's *Metamorphoses*, is an important subject in Western art. While not specifically as central as the Judeo-Chris-

*This essay was written specifically for this volume and is published here with permission of the author. © Michael O'Shea, 1984.

tian myth of the fall, or such myths as Faust, the story of Phaethon is of the same archetype. Wilson's use of Phaethon in *Setting the World on Fire* is strikingly similar to the use of another classical myth of the fall in another "portrait of the artist as a young man": Joyce's use of the Icarus and Daedalus myth in *A Portrait*.[3] Although Wilson does not go so far as to name his character "Piers Phaethon," the myth's central place in the novel is reinforced in other ways (not the least of which is its title, which refers to the outcome of Phaethon's hubris). The two principal vehicles for the myth are the Verrio painting with which the young Piers is fascinated, and Lully's opera, *Phaethon*, that Piers aspires to produce (and ultimately does).

The Tothill "Phaethon" is not a real painting, but, as a study of its analogues reveals, it very nearly could be. Located on the lanterned ceiling and adjacent walls of the Vanbrugh Great Hall in Tothill, this "Phaethon" is a sprawling work, depicting on the ceiling Phaethon's progress from his taking the reins of the chariot of the sun, through his fall, which by an illusion terminates in a malachite bowl (112-13). On either side of the bowl, "two silly marble girls . . . wept their tears . . . their legs . . . turning into stalks of plants [young Piers' perception of Phaethon's sisters, turning into poplars]" (4). While Verrio did not paint a Phaethon ceiling that was as inclusive as the Tothill ceiling, the painting does sound similar to a work executed by Verrio for Charles II in Windsor. Kerry Downes describes what Verrio's painting (destroyed in the nineteenth century) in the Queen's Staircase at Windsor probably looked like, and links it to a similar painting in Vanbrugh's Castle Howard:

> The walls to the left and right had "square niches" with Ovidian scenes, the transformation of Phaethon's sisters into trees and of Cygnus into a swan. . . . This introduced into a fictive scheme a real spatial experience and one which was only taken up again by Vanbrugh in the arches between the stairs and hall at Castle Howard, a building which has other links, both formal [e.g., the use of a lantern to admit exterior light] and iconographical, with the Windsor stair . . . In its roof was a painting of Apollo permitting Phaethon to drive the Chariot of the Sun; in the ceiling below were the winds and the signs of the Zodiac, with the Four Elements in the corners or pendentives.[4]

As the connection between the Windsor and the Castle Howard *Phaethon* suggests, and as any reader familiar with Wilson's blending of history and fiction in earlier works like *Anglo-Saxon Attitudes* and *No Laughing Matter* might expect, the artist and architect of the Tothill Great Hall have not been selected casually. Wilson's choice of artists places the Great Hall in a very specific time and social milieu. *The National Trust Guide* describes the proliferation of structures like the Vanbrugh portion of Tothill in precisely the manner of Wilson's fictitious Great Hall:

> Then suddenly, between 1690 and 1710, we come upon a bouquet of National Trust houses, representative of what to many people is the climax of English domestic building, our only truly indigenous style apart

from the Elizabethan. Some call it loosely "Queen Anne," others "Wren," but it is misleading to label it as an architectural period at all, since it was highly diverse and boldly experimental, the period of Vanbrugh and Hawksmoor, of huge wall-paintings and Grinling Gibbons, of the Baroque and a strong influence from France. . . .[5]

As is clear in the reference above, the playwright and architect Vanbrugh and the sculptor Grinling Gibbons (whose carvings ornament the fireplace in Tothill's dining room [185]) figured prominently in this period of extravagantly opulent baroque residences, as did Antonio Verrio. The post-Restoration royalty set the trend, employing both Verrio (who was court painter to Charles II) and Gibbons not only in Windsor, but also in Hampton Hall. Verrio might be worthy of the scant praise offered him by various characters in *Setting the World on Fire* (as an adolescent, Piers admits, "I wondered at the beauty of the Verrio ceiling as a small kid. It's not very good, I know now . . ." [132]); he seems to have been competent enough to decorate the ceilings and staircases which were his métier, but his artistic greatness had its limits. In his *Anecdotes of Painting in England*, Horace Walpole called Verrio "an excellent painter for the sort of subjects on which he was employed; that is, without much invention, and with less taste, his exuberant pencil was ready at pouring out gods, goddesses, kings, emperors and triumphs, over those public surfaces on which the eye never rests long enough to criticise and where one should be sorry to place the works of a better master: I mean ceilings and staircases."[6]

In the same discussion, Walpole later adds his belief that Verrio painted the great stair at Hampton Court "as ill as if he had spoiled it out of principle." Pope gently mocked the painter in his *Moral Essay* entitled "On the Use of Riches": "On painted Ceilings you devoutly stare,/Where lounge the Saints of *Verrio*, or *Laguerre*" (ll. 145–46). Pope's second reference is to Louis Laguerre, erstwhile apprentice to Verrio, thought by many to have surpassed the talent of his somewhat mediocre master. This latter sentiment was reflected in the remark of the twentieth-century wag who said of a Verrio ceiling, "C'est magnifique, mais ce n'est pas Laguerre."

Whatever his artistic limitations, however, Verrio was highly successful at his job, and was much in demand as a painter of precisely the type of work which Wilson's Vanbrugh assigns to him in the fictitious Great Hall: when Sir Francis Tothill (the Mosson ancestor responsible for the Great Hall) commissioned the painting, the "real" Verrio had already painted a "Phaethon" (at Windsor); and the "real" Vanbrugh later designed a lanterned ceiling featuring a "Phaethon" (Pelligrini's, at Castle Howard). Moreover, at the time of his death, Verrio was preparing to undertake the painting of another Vanbrugh edifice: Marlborough's Blenheim.[7] Of particular significance to Wilson's use of Verrio is the painter's fame as an "illusionist" painter. The type of illusion at Tothill, where the "artistic" space of the paintings merges with the "real" space of the room (e.g., the "apparent" fall into the malachite bowl), was precisely Verrio's specialty. Downes describes Verrio as a major force in the emergence of interior architecture relying on *trompe-l'oeil* art:

> Between his arrival in 1672 and about 1720 at least fifty painted staircases were executed in new and existing private London houses and country mansions; ceilings and walls appeared to show, through an illusionist architectural skeleton, buildings, landscape and sky as a background for allegorical and historical figures. A smaller number of entrance halls and saloons also had walls painted as well as ceilings, for instance Verrio's stories of Hercules in the saloon of the first Montagu House (1682–3); in many other cases staircases and rooms had only painted ceilings.[8]

Probably the most famous Verrio painting of this sort is the "Heaven Room" at Burghley, where the room seems to give way to a (painted) colonnade, and various painted figures seem to overstep the limits of the painting, as if entering the room. This merger of physical and artistic space is crucial to Piers' production of the Lully *Phaethon*, in which he used light to shift his narrative from the players to the painted fall of Phaethon.

While Sir Francis Tothill employed a painter later immortalized by Pope, his architect, Sir John Vanbrugh, would be lampooned by Swift: "Van's genius, without thought or lecture,/Is hugely turned to architecture" ("The History of Vanbrugh's House"). Wilson gives 1688 as the year in which Sir Francis undertook renovation of Tothill; the project is, for the novel's purposes, Vanbrugh's first architectural commission. Just as some might question whether the soldier, playwright, and sometime herald would have been capable of such a project so early in his career, many have indeed questioned whether he was up to taking on Castle Howard when he received that commission in 1699. It is generally believed that Vanbrugh was not competent in either draftsmanship or management, and that he relied on Nicholas Hawksmoor for handling the essential details of building Castle Howard.[9] As several characters in the novel note, however, Vanbrugh did not undertake Tothill until returning from his four-year imprisonment in France (1688–92). Meanwhile, after 1688 (the year of the Glorious Revolution), Verrio, a Roman Catholic, found himself out of courtly employment. Consequently, the fictitious work at Tothill would be contemporary with Verrio's work in other private great houses, including Burghley and Chatsworth. One character notes that the Verrio ceiling had just been completed in 1697 when Vanbrugh attempted to produce Lully's *Phaethon*; given that Verrio would not return to courtly painting until 1702, and that only Verrio's death prevented his working with Vanbrugh on Castle Howard, Verrio's Tothill commission seems as historically consistent as it is aesthetically consistent.

Impressed as a child with the Verrio ceiling, Piers Mosson is obsessed with the Phaethon myth, and adopts it as the centerpiece of his sensibility and aspirations. As an eight-year-old boy, Piers sees the subject of the Verrio ceiling as joyous rather than tragic: "So happy . . . that he left his golden cart and the horses to fly on their own, and, turning and wheeling, now feet first, now head first, he floated through the sky, dazzling all with his sudden dives and plunges and somersaults . . ." (4). He sees Phaethon's fall as not so much a fall, but a flight: "And, even if the young man did fall, you could see that he was in a delighted magic trance. He had made his shapes, he had danced through the sky. So the fall was only the last movement of the dance" (6). Piers' conception of Phaethon, then, contains elements of Camus' conception of Sisyphus: one whose doom is accepted, not with mere resignation, but with happiness.[10]

In Part II of *Setting the World on Fire*, an older Piers (in 1957) attempts to give form to his dreams of Phaethon by producing Jean-Baptiste Lully's opera, *Phaethon*, in the Great Hall. As plans for the production develop, he explains to Ralph Tucker, a groundsman at Tothill, his existential (and somewhat Byronic) conception of the Phaethon legend: "His chariot ride is a brave gesture of defiance of the dismal routine life. But, of course, it *is* a tragedy and it turns out to be destructive. The Earth is in danger of a ravage by fire as his horses get out of control. In the opera, the Earth, that is, appeals to Jove to save her people from burning. But I don't think this makes Phaethon's gesture any less dramatic, less exciting" (116).

Piers' youthful fantasies — and, subsequently, his adult aspirations — involve distinguishing himself in as extravagant a fashion as Phaethon: as a child, he imagines that he "would make shapes and turns as he wanted when he grew up, but it would not be so that the people he loved became angry or afraid. Everyone he loved, no, perhaps everyone everywhere would be happy at what he did, and, like the Vicar read at church, 'stand amazed' " (6).

Wilson's treatment of the Phaethon motif in *Setting the World on Fire* illustrates the complex, multivalent use of myth and symbol that defines the novel's texture. The myth supports Piers' dreams and aspirations for himself, while simultaneously functioning in many more complex ways. Nor does it only act in a parallel manner to its significance for Piers: it also moves contrapuntally, acting in antithesis to its common associations. While to the young Piers, his father Jerry (a pilot killed in World War II) is Phaethon, to Piers' Uncle Hubert (Jerry's brother), Hitler is Phaethon. In "The First Performance," Marina Luzzi, Uncle Hubert's fiancée, becomes Phaethon to Grandmother Mosson's Zeus: as the noise of Marina's arrival becomes audible, Tom looks at his grandmother "expecting that she might hurl a thunderbolt . . ." (52). At "The Family Lunch," even Great Grandfather Mosson becomes a Phaethon in Piers' eyes, as the old man reminisces about his life: "Of course, it wasn't a firework illumination, a real baroque, *Phaethon* affair. A bit of a Victorian magazine story really. . . . But for all that, the old man had had his moment of flight and, more important, he'd allowed himself to remember flying and to crown that memory by making a shape out of it. For that's what the story was—Great Grandfather's only work of art" (201–2).

The characterization of Piers as Phaethon, naturally, is the most consistent use of the myth, and parallels the Vanbrugh side of the novel's duality. At one point, Marina casts Piers as Phaethon, predicting that "In the theatre you would set the world on fire." Piers agrees, " 'Oh, I shall!' he said. 'It's my intention' " (55). Tom asks his mother, who (like Phaethon's mother, Clymene) has expressed her ambition for her son, "Would you mind if [Piers] set the world on fire?" She replies, "No, of course not. It's just what I know he *will* do" (98).

As Piers' explanation to Ralph of Lully's opera suggests, he has a slightly eccentric view of the Phaethon myth, one which is rooted in two illusions. The first is the illusion of the happy Phaethon in the Verrio painting (even Tom points out to his Uncle Hubert that the allegedly unfortunate young man is smiling: "He *looks* happy" [13]), and the second is the illusion of the triumphant Phaethon which is central to Lully's opera.

First produced in 1683, Lully's *tragédie lyrique*, with a libretto by Philippe Quinault, consists of a prologue and five acts. Magda Sczekerny, a researcher in the Tothill library, describes *Phaethon* as "of all Lully's work the people's opera" (85). This reputation is due to popularity resulting, in large part, from the opera's extravagant machinery and effects, including (in addition to Phaethon's elaborate chariot), the spectacular Temple of Isis, and the transformations of Proteus. Originally performed in Versailles (6 January 1683) without the machinery, it opened in Paris with the effects on 27 April, and was a tremendous success. In his 1962 biography of Quinault, Étienne Gros states that the success was such "qu'on appela *Phaëton* 'l'opéra du peuple', comme *Atys* était 'l'opéra du roi.' "[11] While not standard fare in anyone's opera season, the Lully/Quinault collaboration created sufficient interest to inspire at least five parodies,[12] and was used as an opera-within-an-opera in the revised version of Paul Hindemith's *Cardillac* (1926; revised 1952), the third act of which takes place at a performance of Lully's opera at the Académie Royale.

Of the opera's five acts, four concern Phaethon's pride and ambition and his move toward driving the chariot of the sun. The fourth act ends in a *divertissement*, an elaborate spectacle of celebration, song, and dance, in which the characters anticipate Phaethon's triumph. This illusion of triumph is the basis on which Piers sees Phaethon as "constructive." It is only an illusion, however; for in the final act, of course, Phaethon falls. Michael Robinson summarizes the final two acts, noting

> [Phaethon's] good fortune continues in the first part of Act V when he appears in the sky in his father's chariot and triumphantly proclaims his superiority over his mortal enemies. However, this period of celebration and happiness is simply a prelude to tragedy, for the chariot then goes off course and he is pitched out and killed by Jupiter's thunderbolt. To seven-

teenth-century audiences, who would have known their classical legends and therefore the ultimate fate of Phaethon well, the festivities before his downfall must have appeared as a fine piece of dramatic irony, a quality which effectively occurs in opera for the first time in Lully's work.[13]

Piers elects to emphasize the illusion of glory more than the irony, interpreting *Phaethon* positively. His reflections on Phaethon during the performance of "The First Night" emphasize the extent to which he has yielded to his illusion: "Suddenly, the irony of Phaethon's dreadful end compared to his own sudden unlooked for inheritance of Tothill's magnificence made Piers squirm with embarrassment, even fear. No! Nonsense! All the more reason why he should show the hero's tragedy as fated yet glorious" (247). The dramatic irony of Piers' evasion (preceding, as it does, the conflagration in his own life) is heightened by Tom's thought that "Van had played down Earth's plea to Jove when the world was in danger of being set on fire" (251); as a director, Piers has succumbed to the illusion to which he had succumbed as a person, and of which the Phaethon-like conflagration at the novel's end disabuses him.

The parallels with the character of Phaethon in the Quinault libretto are particularly striking in "The First Night," as specific attention to Quinault's characterization shows. Gros remarks that Phaethon alone, of all Quinault's heroes, places any value above love; while not characterizing Phaethon as loveless, he notes that Phaethon places personal glory above love. First he renounces his fiancée, Theone, in the hope of a more auspicious marriage to Lybie, the daughter of Epaphus, the king. In the Quinault treatment, Phaethon's need to demonstrate his godly origin to Epaphus is the occasion of his chariot ride, and thence of his fall.[14]

The parallel between the Lully/Quinault Phaethon and Piers is clear; even as the Lully/Quinault *tragédie* unfolds in the Great Hall, Piers reflects on his renunciations of human love (first, with his wife, Kate, and then with George, an actor) for the theatrical glory which is of paramount importance to him.

II

The Phaethon motif in *Setting the World on Fire*, pervasive as it is, stands as one side of the novel's central duality. Tothill is a union of two contrasting styles, and the Phaethon side is associated with the Vanbrugh architecture, just as the dramatic, flamboyant life that Piers/Van espouses is one side of the brothers' personal duality. On the other side is the Pratt sensibility, espoused by Piers' brother Tom. In this view of the house, and of life, the architect Pratt's symmetry is associated with a sense of order and proportion, and is extended to a moral stance. The boys' Uncle Hubert, who ultimately proves to be anything but regular in his personal life (in his bizarre death, he is revealed to have been a devout practicing masochist), nevertheless introduces the moral connotations of Tothill's architecture early in the novel. Discussing Pratt's original design of the house, Hubert deplores the "scandalous" modification of the structure by Vanbrugh. Hubert comments, "Of course, Francis Tothill should never have allowed it. But a man who let his life become a public scandal! — " (14). Hubert asserts a preference for the virtue that Tothill's original Palladian style supposedly exemplifies: "Now there's a real building for you. All regular and even. A marvellous sense of proportion. Count those windows on the ground floor" (14).

Ultimately, it becomes clear that Hubert merely gives lip service to the orderly norm which he attributes to the classical style of Tothill ("But we don't have to worry. . . . The men that keep [the world] safe and in order are the Pratts, the men who know how to keep themselves in hand, the blokes who do things well and regularly" [15]). His nephew, Tom, on the other hand, to whom Hubert's remarks are addressed, adopts the "Pratt" style of living, both in terms of his aesthetic tastes and the sense of moral proportion which he associates with them.

If Piers/Van is Phaethonic, Tom/Pratt is anti-Phaethonic. He sees the Phaethonic flights of which his brother is enamored as the prelude to "breaking the ice," which is his vision of all types of catastrophe and destruction. The ice motif is planted in young Tom's apprehensive imagination by his Uncle Hubert in Part I, when Hubert describes the world as not "altogether a safe place. It's a bit like an ice-covered pond — even a skater should never play the giddy ox, in case he falls through the ice" (13). Tom's aversion to the ice-breaking Phaethons of the world emerges frequently throughout the book, as at the party after *Richard II*, he reflects that by her behavior, Marina was "breaking the ice beneath them all . . ." (56). Tom's quietist, anti-Phaethon posture is burlesqued at one point by the boys' Uncle Eustace, who tap-dances around Tom, singing "I don't want to set the world on fire, I just want to be sitting alone" (105). Tom's conception of Phaethon differs markedly from Piers': "Looking for his brother Piers to save him from these fears, to keep the sky from falling down upon him, to check the smiling young man from cruelly setting fire to the world, he had seen that Piers was not with them . . ." (7–8). What is a joyous, affirmative flight to Piers, is to Tom an awful, fatal fall, an object of menace and terror.

The imposition of the contrasting Vanbrugh portion on the Pratt foundation of Tothill is a precise representation of Piers' view of life and history, as opposed to the Pratt view espoused by his brother. Tom/Pratt sees the house as an accumulation of its traditional elements: expressing his admiration for the State Bedroom ("it's a Pratt master-piece . . ."), he adds, " 'But all the same I *am* beginning to realise that a great house is a shape and it is also the way people have lived in it over the centuries and what they filled it with' " (109). Piers counters from his Vanbrugh stance, "I don't know about all that. I think you'll become a slave to history that way. One must break the mould of what *actually* happened by what might have been" (109).

Numerous motifs in *Setting the World on Fire* — most notably, the dramatic sensibility versus the solid values of the great house, and the conflict between the formal garden and estate "improvements" — suggest a relation between Wilson's novel and Jane Austen's *Mansfield Park*. Many novels and poems in English literature share the "great house" tradition operative in Austen's novel; among modern English novels that might be mentioned are Forster's *Howards End*, Woolf's *Orlando*, and Waugh's *Brideshead Revisited*. None of these, however, is as precisely evocative of *Mansfield Park* as *Setting the World on Fire*, which not only incorporates the house motif of Austen's novel, but also the important and (in the case of *Mansfield Park*) controversial playacting motif. Margaret Drabble perceptively suggested the parallel between the two novels in a review of *Setting the World on Fire*.[15] In Austen's novel, the playacting instigated by the shallow, worldly Crawfords stands in opposition to the moral order which the great house, Mansfield Park (like Tothill, the home of a baronet), embodies. Fanny Price's inability to "act" (in the sense that she cannot dissimulate) is emblematic of her essential virtue. In *Setting the World on Fire*, the playacting sensibility of Piers/Van stands in contrast to the solid Tom/Pratt sensibility. Unlike Mansfield Park, however, Tothill is large enough to embody both sides of this dichotomy.

It is in this uniting function that Tothill comes into its own as a character; for Tothill *is* virtually a character. A typical instance of the house's presence is Tom's comment, after the catastrophe of "Rosemary's Confession," that his Great Grandfather could have set matters right: "Even Grandma said that he has authority because he sees Tothill and himself as one" (233); or Piers' thought at the end of "The Family Lunch": "Oh, it was an enchanting afternoon and the house was the enchanter that brought them all together in pleasure" (216).

Like Vardon Hall in Wilson's *Hemlock and After*, and Meg Eliot's home in *The Middle Age of Mrs. Eliot*,[16] Tothill is pervaded by a *genius loci*; but in the case of Tothill, this spiritual force is so pervasive as to differ from the houses in Wilson's earlier novels, both in kind and in degree. Tothill as a whole embodies the spiritual union of the two brothers, in the same way that the library room does: "They had called it the Van-Pratt room, not only for its intricate, almost paradoxical entwining of their beloved architect heroes, but in its union of themselves" (76).

Another motif which extends the architectural dichotomy of Tothill, and which also links the novel to *Mansfield Park*, is the wild garden, a metaphor which has occupied an honored niche in all of Wilson's fiction. Tothill features an extensive formal garden, but having fallen into disrepair during World War II, it resembles a wild garden more than anything else. This "ravaged formal garden" (29) thus embodies the type of dichotomy which Wilson attributes to those wild gardens which were "the eighteenth century's attempt artificially to preserve the noble savage while taming him to fit into elegant surroundings."[17] The garden in *Setting the World on Fire* functions like the Palladian/baroque house, serving as a touchstone for identifying the novel's characters with either side of its basic duality. The boys' Uncle Hubert is first seen commenting on the need "to get the formal garden into its old order" (17). Hubert is threatened by the fall from grace of his formal Eden: "At that moment, nearby Big Ben's loud boom sounded four o'clock. For Hubert, it emphasised the enormity of this anarchic retrogression, this invasion by the wild, by the untamed. They had the place in Sutherland for shooting and that sort of thing" (21).

Piers and Tom are both horticulturally illiterate, even though their mother runs a nursery. Most of the other characters, however, align themselves squarely with some type of horticultural sensibility which parallels the boys' architectural viewpoints: each character tends either toward the side of the formal garden (analogous to the Pratt architecture), as do Hubert, his mother, and Rosemary's brother Eustace, or toward the wild garden (analogous to the Vanbrugh architecture), as do Rosemary and Marina. In "The Family Lunch," when Rosemary praises Tothill's "wilderness," Jackie corrects her reference ("They called it the Woodwork . . ." [187]) and makes a note to clear the overgrowth. Rosemary and Eustace also divide along ideological gardening lines; Eustace remarks, "Rosemary, you know I can't face your wonderful wild garden at the best of times," and adds, "It's all too Rousseau and noble savage for me" (103). Eustace prefers formal gardens. Conversely, Marina objects to Jackie's formal garden sensibility, arguing for a "baroque garden," with beds in "amusing shapes" (170).

The various schemes for Tothill's Woodwork, falling into either a formal or a wild rubric, evoke another echo of the moral and aesthetic vocabulary of *Mansfield Park*. In *The Wild Garden*, Wilson comments on the basic dichotomy of Austen's novel, delimited by "the declaredly 'solid' values of Fanny and Edmund Bertram against the witty, declaredly meretricious rootlessness of the London Crawfords."[18] One level on which this opposition is articulated in Austen's novel is with regard to estate "improvements": Henry Crawford encourages Tom Rushworth in his scheme of substituting an eighteenth-century wild garden for the formal garden at Sotherton. While the connotation of the wild garden for Hubert is that of *Mansfield Park* (that is, the absence of proportion, and, by extension, of morality), the garden duality of *Setting the World on Fire*, like its architectural duality, admits to the reconciliation of two opposites implicit in the "ravaged formal garden." Piers, who defends a revisionist view of history consonant with the Vanbrugh modification of Tothill, approves his mother's scheme of adding some modern (and therefore strictly anachronistic) varieties of roses to the Tothill gardens: Piers remarks, "Of course it doesn't matter. History's there for us to create the shapes we want out of it" (211). At the same time, Eustace is devising a scheme to eliminate all horticultural anachronism in the garden: he advocates "Species and varieties of flowers suitable for planting in the parterre beds of the late seventeenth century; all to be found in Thomas Hanmer's notebook of 1659" (213). In an interesting accommodation to the "opposing camp," Piers selects a formal garden as the backdrop for the Palace of Astrée in Lully's *Phaethon*: "not pale woody groves and temples of Claude, as had been urged upon him, but the most formal, sedate brilliance of tulip beds and the sharp symmetry of statuary and urns and oddly shaped myrtle bushes — this was the glory of Louis' *real* Versailles gardens, not the figment of the painter's imagination of classic pastoral Elysium" (242).

While using the two aesthetic ideas connected with the Crawfords of *Mansfield Park* — playacting and estate "improvements" — Wilson uses them without insisting on the moral connotation attached to them in Austen's novel. Piers' artistic, dramatic flights of fancy are upheld equally with Tom's more practical, "Pratt" sensibility, just as the *de facto* wild garden of Tothill is symbiotic with its formal setting. Thus Piers is able to argue for the "order" underlying his conception of baroque, revealing what Tom sees as his brother's "Pratt-like" side, and he is able to prefer the formal garden over the pseudo-pastoral for the setting of Lully's *Phaethon*.

In addition to sharing the architectural/dramatic motif of *Mansfield Park*, *Setting the World on Fire* also shares the architectural motif of Ibsen's *The Master Builder*. The identification of drama with architecture in Piers' mind is an equation which occurred to Ibsen. Halvard Solness has been seen as an alter ego of Ibsen for several reasons, including a reply made by Ibsen to a question concerning his interest in architecture: "Yes; it is, as you know, my own trade."[19] *The Master Builder* is nearly as central to the novel as the Phaethon myth, and it is similarly linked to the novel's title. Ibsen's play, like the Phaethon myth, is rooted in the archetypal myth of the fall. Moreover, Halvard Solness' career begins, as Phaethon's ends, with a conflagration: he is able to achieve architectural success as a result of events following the destruction by fire of his wife's ancestral home. Finally, like Phaethon, Solness' career ends with a fatal fall at a moment of symbolic achievement.

Like the Phaethon myth, the *Master Builder* analogue pertains most significantly to Piers, who at one point produces Ibsen's play (264). While the allusions to Ibsen's play imply a shadow structure parallel to Piers' aspirations, achievement, and fall, they simultaneously point in other directions, as do the allusions to the Phaethon myth. Halvard is analogous not only to Piers, but also to Tom, who, having come to an awareness of his failure to see the aesthetic significance of life around him, brings about his own death in a final affirmative act — in Tom's case, while trying to save Piers' life. At one point, even Magda Sczekerny becomes part of the analogy to *The Master Builder*, when Piers, meeting her for the first time, casts her (in his mind) as Hilde Wangel, Solness' temptress. The allusion is not casual, since Magda is a major agent in bringing about the events which set Piers' world on fire (i.e., she persuades Piers to become involved in Ralph Tucker's play, which occasions the novel's tragic denouement).

Another sense in which Wilson's use of *The Master Builder* illustrates the architectonic complexity of *Setting the World on Fire* has to do with the close relation between theme and technique in this novel. *Setting the World on Fire* shares with *Hemlock and After* the presence of an Ibsen play as incidental reference and shadow structure: in Wilson's first novel, several characters attend a performance of Ibsen's *Ghosts*, a production that is discussed by various characters at various times. As the idea of *Ghosts* is elaborated upon at the novel's surface, certain parallels emerge between the marriage of the Sandses and that of Captain and Mrs. Alving, and between the grand plan of the Alving Orphanage and Vardon Hall. Further ghosts appear in the *genii loci* of Vardon, and in the relationship of Bernard's daughter with his former lover, Terence.

In a more involved way, *The Master Builder* is the shadow structure of *Setting the World on Fire*: not only does the play become a contrapuntal commentary on the Phaethon myth and Piers' life, it also reflects the architectural and dramatic themes and techniques central to the novel. In many respects *Setting the World on Fire* aspires to the condition of a well-made play: its exposition consists primarily of dramatic set-pieces—brief episodes, within fixed locations—propelled principally by dialogue. Wilson even provides a "List of Principal Characters," a device he has used in earlier novels. Furthermore, through *The Master Builder*, Wilson invokes Ibsen's equation of drama with architecture. Finally, in its coordination of the numerous threads of myth, symbol, history, and artifice, the novel aspires to the condition of the integrated mansion, Tothill, which joins the novel's essential dualities (Palladian and baroque art, pragmatic and dramatic sensibilities, tradition and innovation).

As in the *tragédies lyriques* of Lully, the synthesis of numerous themes and techniques (musical, dramatic, poetic, and architectural) in *Setting the World on Fire* moves toward a moral point as well as an aesthetic one. The novel's moral point of view does not reside in either the artistic "Van" sensibility, or in the opposing practical "Pratt" sensibility, but rather in the inadequacy of either point of view without the balance of the other. Even Hubert seems sensitive to this synthesis, when, slightly misquoting T. S. Eliot and/or Mary, Queen of Scots,[20] in his speech in "A Marriage Has Been Arranged," he says, " 'This Great Hall of Vanbrugh's built into, even extending Pratt's splendid house, has always seemed to me to explain that otherwise mysterious saying 'In my end was my beginning' " (136).

Although Piers/Van resides in the world of artistic flights of fancy, and Tom/Pratt resides in that of the empirical and practical, each nevertheless exhibits aspects of the other, and each recognizes his need for his opposite. Tom, for instance, his aversion to Phaethonic flights notwithstanding, at one point contemplates his future in suspiciously Phaethonic terms: "He saw a lifetime of complimentary stalls for 'glittering' first nights and a lifetime of standing in a corner with a glass of champagne fighting off the threatening din of the meaningless chatter of celebrities in dressing rooms. He *must* do his own thing. He turned back to his book, to the subtle certainties of mathematics and the wondrous flights of pure intellect" (112). Conversely, Piers, at one point, argues with Marina concerning the essence of baroque, borrowing his brother's "Pratt" vocabulary: " 'Baroque is based upon order. It must be. Even Vanbrugh at his most fantastic. That's what gives the Great Hall its powers. What allies it to Pratt's work' " (70).

Piers recognizes the essential symbiosis in his relationship with Tom, as represented in the Pratt/Vanbrugh fusion in Tothill, as he reflects on the eclectic library room: "He looked at [the library room, or the Van-Pratt room] now and thought how little he could have achieved without his brother's cautioning voice, ironic curbing and loyal devotion, and hoped that those looks of excitement, of delight that he evoked in return were sufficient repayment" (76). Finally, just before the tragic denouement of the novel, Piers reflects on his symbiotic dependence on his diametrically opposite brother: "And the success [of Lully's *Phaethon*] was all heightened by the circumstances. By Vanbrugh's exuberant, splendid fancy of the Great Hall, all firmly based upon Pratt's order and sobriety. As his own career owed so much to his dependable brother" (249).

The moral point of *Setting the World on Fire* has to do with the failure of each of the two brothers to recognize fully the limitations of his chosen world view, rather than the utter failure of either view. Piers consistently places artistic realities over any other type of reality; even on those occasions, such as the aftermath of his uncle's rift with Marina, when he must come face to face with the circumstances around him, he does so only after he can convert the imbroglio into dramatic parody: "Piers had reduced the whole scene now to surrealism mainly in the form of dialogue. . . .   There seemed no other way of banishing its horror" (174). Any form of reality outside of his dramatic art — his marriage to Kate, the terrorist assaults upon the French theaters — is consistently subordinated to his aesthetic imperative; even when the terrorist plot at Tothill is discovered, Piers' response is to complain petulantly that "these fanatical idiots have got in the way of art" (293).

Piers' narrow vision of life is analogous to that of Hamo Langmuir in *As If By Magic*, who posits his faith in the supposed magic of science and sexuality. Only when Hamo is on the point of death does he realize the vacuity of his life and the impotence of his supposed magics. As Angus Wilson explained in a lecture on *As If By Magic*, "people have taken refuge in all sorts of magics because they cannot solve the meaning of their own existence there, let alone any kind of attempt to reach a connection with other human beings around them."[21]

Piers has fallen into the habit of granting to illusion (the illusion of Verrio's ceiling, of the *divertissement* in Lully's opera, and that produced in his own art) a value in life equal to that he accords it in his art. In the novel's tragic conclusion, Piers is forced to confront realities outside of the fragile boundaries of art. Yet Piers' education is not equivalent to learning that art does not matter; Tom has come to the reverse of Piers' revelation immediately before the bombing. Having been rooted in the realm of the practical and orderly, Tom is so oblivious to beings and events outside his "Pratt" universe that he finds that he cannot read Ralph Tucker's play, because his chosen view of life cannot accommodate fiction. Tom comes to lament his lack of artist's insight on the last night of his life: "How could he have lived all these years noticing so little of the creature world surrounding him?" (289). This moment resembles the moments of discovery in *As If By Magic*, when both Hamo and Alexandra discover that they have been blind to the world around them.

Thus the point of this novel is not to affirm either side of its dual views of life and art over the other, but rather to point out the inadequacy of any single point of view without its dialectic antithesis. Finally, like so many aspects of this elaborately structured novel, its thematic significance is a function of its technique. The synthesis of the numerous mythic and artistic sources for *Setting the World on Fire*, like the juxtaposition of the opposing architectural styles of Tothill House, is a paradigm for the blending of viewpoints of which life is constituted. In recognizing the reality of his brother's death, while realizing his need to carry on, Piers for the first time in his life recognizes the coexistence of external reality with his sense of aesthetic reality. While neither type of reality is subordinated to the other, circumstances force a full affirmation of their interdependence, an affirmation which has hitherto eluded Piers. Like Bernard Sands, Gerald Middleton, Hamo Langmuir, and many of Wilson's earlier protagonists, Piers discovers a new sense of his responsibilities, and at the end of the novel he turns from self-pity to concern for the old actor, Tim Pleydell. In the final passage of the novel, he evokes the image of Halvard Solness, who affirms his own artistic essence in the same gesture which brings him face to face with his own mortality: "Go up, Master Builder, go up! Now. Lest delaying, you lose the power to ascend the towers of imagination" (296).

Notes

1. *Setting the World on Fire* (New York: Viking, 1980), p. x; hereafter cited in the text.

2. Angela Carter, "Illusory Flames," *Guardian*, 10 July 1980, p. 8: "[The novel's] core is a deliberate distortion of the familiar world in such a blatant way that anyone who rides the 77 bus route is struck by the fraudulence of the illusion." See also, David Holloway, "While Phaethon Drove," *Daily Telegraph*, 10 July 1980, p. 12: "virtually all the action takes place in a privately owned great residence, Tothill House, situated in large grounds between Westminster Abbey and St. John's, Smith Square. This staggers the imagination."

3. Other similarities between these works might be noted; although Piers Mosson does not stand in as close relation to Wilson as Stephen Dedalus does to Joyce, it is noteworthy that Piers is an alumnus of Westminster School, like his creator, and that he also shares Wilson's deep interest in acting and history; after a brilliant performance on his history exams (Mr. Brownlow remarks that "the Christ Church examiners consider Van's papers to be the most impressive they'd seen since the war" [p. 43]), Piers goes on to Oxford (like Wilson, who belonged to the Oxford University Dramatic Society).

4. Kerry Downes, *English Baroque Architecture* (London: A. Zwemmer Ltd., 1966), pp. 19–20.

5. Robin Fedden and Rosemary Joekes, *The National Trust Guide* (London: Jonathan Cape, 1973), p. 38.

6. Horace Walpole, *Anecdotes of Painting in England* (London, 1862), II, 467.

7. Michael Foss, *The Age of Patronage: The Arts in England, 1660–1750* (Ithaca: Cornell Univ. Press, 1971), p. 115.

8. Downes, *English Baroque Architecture*, p. 55.

9. Ibid., p. 75; see also *A Biographical Dictionary of British Architects* (New York: Facts on File, 1978), p. 849.

10. Albert Camus, "The Myth of Sisyphus," in *The Myth of Sisyphus and Other Essays* (New York: Vintage Books, 1955), p. 91: "The struggle itself toward the heights is enough to fill a man's heart. One must imagine Sisyphus happy."

11. Étienne Gros, *Phillippe Quinault: Sa Vie et Son Oeuvre* (Paris: Librairie Ancienne, 1926), p. 143.

12. Alfred Loewenberg, *Annals of Opera: 1597–1940* (Geneva: Societas Bibliographica, 1955), p. 73: "Arlequin *Phaéton*, by J. Palaprat, 4 February 1692; *Parodie de Phaéton*, by Macharti, 11 December 1721; *Arlequin Phaéton*, by P. F. Dominique and J. A. Romagnesi, 22 February 1731; *Arlequin Phaéton*, by F. Riccoboni, 21 January 1743. A fifth parody, by G. Bailly, was published in 1758."

13. Michael Robinson, *Opera Before Mozart* (New York: Morrow, 1966), p. 94.

14. Gros, *Phillippe Quinault*, p. 677: "Phaëton est, en effet, le seul personnage de Quinault, pour qui l'amour n'est pas le plus important des devoirs et la première des vertus. Non pas qu'il soit absolument insensible: un héros insensible était inconcevable à l'opéra. Phaëton a aimé, il aime peut-être encore; mais il place la gloire au-dessus de l'amour" ("Indeed, Phaethon is Quinault's only character for whom love is not the most important duty and the supreme virtue. Not that he is utterly insensitive; an insensitive hero would be unthinkable in opera. Phaethon has loved, perhaps he still loves; but he places glory above love").

15. Margaret Drabble, "Angus Wilson's New Novel," *Listener*, 10 July 1980, p. 51.

16. In Wilson's first novel (*Hemlock and After* [London: Martin Secker & Warburg, 1952]), the *genii loci* of Vardon Hall are among the forces which thwart Bernard Sands's "high project of a writer's country home" (p. 30). At several points it is remarked that Vardon Hall's ghosts would not allow the future which Bernard envisions for the house, first, by Bernard's brother-in-law (p. 157), and later, by Mrs. Rankine: "I could never settle down, I'm afraid, . . . in a place so full of ghosts — ghosts of happiness and miseries. Personality, and especially a family personality like the Vardons', is so persistent" (p. 162)

In *The Middle Age of Mrs. Eliot* (New York: Viking, 1958), Meg Eliot likewise sees her house as inhabited by a spiritual force, in this case a benign one; she thinks of the house as "the centre of all the life she had made for herself" (p. 32). Later, Meg seems at times to mourn the loss of her house as profoundly as of her husband: after an argument with Lady Pirie, "Tears came to her eyes; but it was for her house that she was weeping, not this time for Bill" (p. 283).

17. *The Wild Garden* (Berkeley: Univ. of California Press, 1965), p. 61.

18. Ibid., pp. 115–16.

19. Michael Meyer, Introduction to *The Master Builder*, in *Ibsen: Plays*, trans. Michael Meyer (London: Eyre Methuen), 237.

20. "In my end is [not "was"] my beginning" was the motto of Mary, Queen of Scots, and is the final line of Eliot's "East Coker," the second of his *Four Quartets* (in *Collected Poems, 1909–1962* [New York: Harcourt, Brace & World, 1970], p. 190). To which of the two Hubert might be referring is anybody's guess.

21. Lecture on *As If By Magic*, in *Dutch Quarterly Review of Anglo-American Letters*, 6 (1976), 264.

In Defense of Imagination: Angus Wilson's Three Critical Biographies   Hans-Peter Breuer*

When in 1897 Samuel Butler announced to the world that he had identified the true author—or rather authoress—of the *Odyssey*, he was proud to confess in characteristically cocky fashion that a simple commonsense assumption had guided him to his discovery: "For after all it is not the outward and visible signs we read, see, or hear, in any work, that brings us to its feet in prostration of gratitude and affection; what really stirs us is the communion with the still living mind of the man or woman to whom we owe it, and the conviction that that mind is as we would have our own to be. All else is mere clothes and grammar."[1] What draws us to a work, in other words, is our sympathetic identification with the creator whose lineaments we fancy we detect in the details of his creation. It was an assumption that allowed Butler to cut through the muddle of critical canons and scholarly exegesis enshrouding the epic and claim certainty for what in fact his intuition and keen sensitivity to detail and nuances of language had suggested to him. But he had always believed in what C. S. Lewis would refer to as the "personal heresy," the principle that art is essentially an extension of the creator and his times, a document really, his surviving "Karma,"[2] and hence explicable and decipherable in terms of his personality and the experiences that had shaped it.

The delightful mixture of fact and fancy marking his study of the *Odyssey* was Butler's own, but it reflected a growing critical trend, noticeable in the latter half of the nineteenth century, of linking art and artist to social realities, as we see brilliantly done, for example, by John Ruskin in his attempt to discriminate between the artistry of Turner and Giorgione in terms of the cultural realities each experienced in their boyhood. In our own time, a literary work is often regarded as a puzzle for leisured intellectuals; and the most recent literary theorists share with more orthodox Freudians and Marxists this task of triumphing, as it were, over the written work, only more destructively, by dissolving its substance to self-obliterating process, to empty referentiality, to semiotic signals—if they do not annihilate it entirely in the name of some sterile ideology or fixed formula. The result of this tortured, hollow cerebration is a subversion virtually of our primary experience of a work, of our naive, unmediated but reflective absorption into its magic and richness.

To realize the virtues of Angus Wilson's three critical biographies— quite apart from the solidity and sureness of the scholarship—we should consider them in the context of this modern critical climate. In his approach to Zola, Dickens, and Kipling, Wilson is unabashedly "personalist"; he relies considerably on Freud, more remotely on Marxist social analysis. Hence

*This essay was written specifically for this volume and is published here with permission of the author. © Hans-Peter Breuer, 1984.

he uses biographical and historical fact to explain and justify works of his chosen trio and plumbs the works for whatever light they may shed on the writers' personalities. His purposes, however, are entirely different from what we might expect, for two reasons. First, not being primarily (and only) a scholar, he prefers not to explain a work from an extraneous theoretical position but is intent on understanding the connection between life and fiction as he, himself a creator of fictions, experiences it — from within. He brings to his studies the "feel" (not merely the intellectual awareness) that only a writer (and a very particular kind) can possess of how novelists transform the smallest detail into aspects of a fictional vision, and it is this he wishes to communicate. To paraphrase Samuel Johnson's poet-philosopher,[3] every writer by examining his own mind may guess what passes in the minds of other writers, especially if he has a close affinity for them. Wilson's interpretation of the significance of biographical events to fictional devices is in the end, as in Butler's case, a creative act of understanding and not simply an explanation. It owes its persuasiveness less to theoretical assumptions than to a thorough acquaintance with, and extraordinary sensitivity to, the details and nuances of the entire oeuvre.

Secondly, he also has the writer's feel for the independence of a literary creation from the contingency of history and private experience. At the lowest level of creativeness, as in Butler's *The Way of All Flesh* (a novel which gave such great encouragement to the flowering of the autobiographical novel in England), the gap between experience and fiction is often small, and the unconscious element, the power of transformation, participates less markedly in the act of creation. The writers Wilson has chosen, however, were driven by demons and possessed by a creative urge they did not always understand; hence, in their case the unconscious element in the transformation of the nonfictional material is more profound. Wilson does not assume that personality is open to psychological "invasion" in any helpful way,[4] nor does he suggest that the deepest creative urges are less mysterious than personality itself. As he points out in *The World of Charles Dickens* (1970), many people have shared Dickens' compulsions and obsessions without therefore becoming creators of living fictions. The psychological and sociological analyses he makes are clearly intended to illuminate the inherent significance of the work: "What matters about [Dickens'] public and private life," he writes in the preface to *Dickens*, "is the way in which they both fed his great fiction; what matters about his opinions is their relation to, sometimes their conflict with, the measuring of his fiction."[5] He states here his principle of organization: he deals only with such matters in the lives of the three writers as can assist in a fuller appreciation of this independent meaning. Rather than seeking to treat the work as a document of a particular time, place, and personality, as yet another transcript of a time-bound "value system," he wishes instead to pay homage to it as a gift that has permanently enriched the spiritual atmosphere in which we live.

II

The relative brevity and sparseness of *Émile Zola: An Introductory Study of His Novels* (1952) lets us see most clearly Angus Wilson's approach to literary analysis. The major thrust of the study is to demonstrate that the novels of Zola owe their dark power to his emotional conflicts and sexual frustrations—an essentially Freudian thesis. Wilson begins, consequently, by sketching in that most fundamental of Freudian axioms, that the character traits of the adult (and in this case the contours of his art) are a flowering of what is planted deeply by traumatic experience of childhood and adolescence: "Upon the stresses and strains, which fuse the personality in these [youthful] years, will depend in great degree not only the force of the liberation of the explosion which gives the imaginative expression its power, but also the vitality" and energy so necessary to enduring the hard work of writing.[6] Later adult experiences are not as crucial to the depth of a writer's art; therefore, Wilson looks closely at the significant details of the early years for clues that may explain the quality and substance of the novels. Zola's implacable hatred of all sections of society (especially for the pretentious ruling class and the bourgeoisie with its *souplesse* and *mollesse*) and, by contrast, his Balzac-like admiration for the ruthless striver who manipulates the social currents of his time to his advantage; his compassion for the down-trodden; the general vision of society as an arena of bleak Darwinian struggle; his vivid sense of wasted human energy and the unstable weakness of the human will — all are traced to the humiliations endured by a sensitive youth experiencing his family's decline after his father's death. The deep shame of the social isolation that followed amid the bourgeoisie of Aix-en-Provence, moreover, led to Zola's firm determination to escape penury at all costs. During these early years of bitterness were implanted the inevitable tensions between the outer world and inner hopes, between paradisaical retreats and harsh reality without which a profound sense of the world is impossible. This is a conclusion, as we shall see later, central to Wilson's understanding of the nature of fiction.

Once the connection is established, Wilson focuses on the most formative personal relationships and sexual encounters and, by moving with remarkable ease and mastery of detail across the whole of Zola's works, shows us how the conflicts in these relationships reappear in the patterned character configuration of the fictional worlds and in Zola's thematic preoccupation. Most significantly, when Zola married his second wife, he found the happiness denied him during his first marriage; but the tensions of his life dissolved, old memories receded, he subscribed to an optimistic Fourierist socialism; and though his radicalism remained intact, the fierce fire that had kindled his imagination flickered out. His last novels, for all their careful realism, lack the vitality that would breathe life into the details of their texture.

Furthermore, Angus Wilson is at all points careful to place Zola into a sociological context, but this is usually only briefly sketched in, as when he reminds us of the milieu of the Second Empire, and after: "The optimistic, cocksure bourgeois world of the 'forties and 'fifties was giving way to fin-de-siècle melancholy and ennui; all but the most obtuse felt the rotten boards creak beneath their feet, saw the scaffolding tremble above their heads."[7] He shows little sympathy for the world Zola attacks; he identifies so completely with his spirit that from this partisan angle Zola appears as the great advance warrior battling for justice in dialectical opposition to a moribund social order, who forces the conventional reader to see how "his sacred bourgeois creeds were being recited backwards, his angels of virtue revealed as seven deadly sins, and the very Host of his self-esteem spat upon."[8]

We see that ready-at-hand categories are made to stand for complex realities. In this enthusiastic endorsement of Zola's mission we can detect a tone suggesting that the greatness of the novels is gauged not a little by the sheer force of their rebellious negation and the carefully detailed undermining of traditional values and institutions. In this, no doubt, Wilson reveals his intellectual background, the anticonservative radicalism he shared with many English intellectuals schooled at Oxford and Cambridge who entered into their majority during the fateful 1930s.

Even so, such strictly intellectual constructs and the strong emphasis on Freudian analysis remain in the background, and recede even further in his next studies. In *The World of Charles Dickens* and *The Strange Ride of Rudyard Kipling* (1977) he retains his method: indeed, we are made aware of remarkable parallels in the lives of the three authors. There is the centrality of Dickens' sudden expulsion from his idyllic life at Chatham into the desolation of Hungerford Stairs; there is Kipling's forced endurance of the lonely misery in the boarding school at Southsea after the "safe delights" enjoyed as a young, indulged sahib in Bombay. Then there are the first romances and the marriages that shape the writer's understanding of the opposite sex; there is the same atmosphere of deep iniquity in the social fabric that engages the fury of each writer; and so on. But now we have more understanding, less mere explanation, for these links are now fashioned in dense detail drawn from fact and fiction and with an enlarged sympathy for those aspects of characters and events — especially in Kipling's case — not entirely congruent with Wilson's sensibility. This rendering of fact and fiction is fused into an imaginative amalgam that has the palpable three-dimensionality of a novel and is not simply a chaste, dry, and accurate account of what is known — as, for example, Dudley Barker's biography of John Galsworthy, *The Man of Principle*. Summarizing the middle-class world of Dickens' earlier novels, Wilson writes:

> This is a newly emerging middle class coming out of the obscure subordination of the eighteenth century — where attorneys and ushers and doctors and curates still rank low, where merchants and apprentices had only just separated from living together over the shop; a money-grubbing society, narrow, suspicious, worshipping mammon, sometimes

with an indefinable cant of high-mindedness like Mr. Pecksniff's that is
not markedly religious yet certainly not secular, crude and generous in its
appetite for pleasure yet disguising this greed with increasing gentility
and prudery, intensely individual yet huddling together like some under-
ground creatures not yet finally dug out of their burrows.[9]

The Dickensian cadence of the sentence shows us how fully Wilson has entered into the fictional world and how deeply he feels it and its historical
counterpart on his pulse; he is so thoroughly soaked in his material that his
rendering of it has the force of experience and intuitive revelation. In his
study of Kipling he also relies on his impressions of the chief places of
Kipling's sojourn — Bombay, Lahore, Vermont, the downs and pastoral
weald of Sussex — as well as on memories of his childhood and adolescence,
for providing greater density to the historical background: "This Delhi
Gate is still today a tattered, blotchy, rubbish-filled nook and cranny end of
Lahore City. The great Wazir Khan Mosque in Moslem Pakistan seems
crumbling and damp-heat-stained beside the memory of the great show-
place tourist-filled Moghul mosques we have left behind in India. The road
runs here by day, noisy, crowded with bazaar stalls between which tongas
clatter even now."[10] And again:

> I remember seeing this world in top hats and frock coats, in picture
> hats and slightly dowdy smart dresses, at the Royal Academy Summer
> Exhibition when I was a London school-boy in the late twenties — it was,
> by then, their swan song. The men bronzed, some of the women evident
> ex-memsahibs, all, as my brother showed me, touched with "county,"
> making their way across the road to Fortnum's to shop, but not, as they
> would even by the late thirties, returning that night to their homes by
> train or motor car.[11]

Wilson's suspicions of categories is apparent in his unwillingness to regard, as is fashionable, Dickens as a modernist prophet, or Kipling as the
spokesman for the British Empire. We are informed that Dickens' radicalism is based upon the impercipient simplification of the journalistic outsider: his anarchic dismissal of Parliament, his easy mockery of legal clerks
(and the entire judiciary) rest upon a complete ignorance of the real work
politicians and civil servants did. For their depiction of women, at times
bordering on tiresome cliché, both writers come in for some sharp rebukes.
In fact, Wilson's sympathetic, almost chivalric defense of the women in the
lives of Kipling and Dickens, his rescue of them from unsympathetic assessment and a bad press, is surely one of the characteristic aspects of the later
studies. Dickens' own estimate of his mother — she is Mrs. Nickleby for
Wilson — is put in question, and rather more than conventional blame is put
on John Dickens' shoulders for the sad fortune of his family. Of course,
Dickens is not spared for his inexcusable treatment of his wife Kate; but
even the young Maria Beadnell is seen as a prisoner of her youth, her class,
and her parents:

> Although in later years when he was famous and she was a respect-
> able stout matron, Maria implied romantically that she had always loved
> him and if only he had pressed . . . it is surely more likely that her youth-
> ful attraction to an unusual, lively, talented youth from outside her own
> usual circle was dissipated as her parents sensibly expected by a change of
> scene, a bit of mischief-making by her girlfriend, and perhaps a little in-
> fluence of the worldly advice of her parents.[12]

By delving into Mrs. Holloway's background, Wilson shows that she, too, is
far less the monster that young Kipling experienced. Most remarkable of all
is Wilson's freeing — here the authority of the writer is decisive — of Carrie
Kipling from the usual charge that she was a domineering, restrictive
battle-ax; no, she was more likely the helpmate who quite properly protected the privacy so absolutely essential to Kipling's creative work, and
who furthermore shielded him from the distractions of the practical affairs
of the household.

Proof of Wilson's capacity for *tout comprende* is his patient review of
Kipling's belief in Great Britain's imperial mission, more especially of the
radically conservative opinions Kipling uttered during the Boer War, and
more shrilly still, during the Great War. Wilson confesses that if he had had
to share the political views of Kipling, the study would never have been
written.[13] But his sense of the man lets him penetrate beyond these doctrinaire views to the moral and psychological grounds that prompted them.
The warning note sounded in the famous "Recessional" derives its larger
resonance from Kipling's "almost superstitious apprehension of disaster
brought on by taking for granted, by failing to recognize that all hopes and
all securities rest upon the thinnest of ice."[14] This apprehensive fear runs like
a ground bass through *Kim* (it informs the whole notion of "the law" and
the "game") and so much of his finest stories; it is a tone with which Wilson
is completely in tune.[15] It shows us that Wilson is fully alive to the important
fact that Kipling's political views are no more crucial to his artistry than
Dostoevsky's strange mixture of mysticism and chauvinism is to his. It is a
tribute to his critical faculties that Wilson has moved so far beyond the radicalism that occasionally breaks through his studies of Zola and Dickens to
praise the artistic expression of its opposite, the other side of what he calls
the "gypsy" impulse.

In thus distinguishing between Kipling's political views and the deeper
level of his art, Wilson focuses sharply on the autonomous appeal of a
work — despite his at times breathless movement between fact and fiction.
Precisely because, as in his discussion of "Recessional," he seeks to isolate the
experiential substance in a work, he always distinguishes, at times radically,
between those aspects of a work, or its background, that are ephemeral and
contingent on specific conditions, and those aspects and qualities that transcend both the author and his time and thus constitute the basis for the
work's continued power. We need not, in weighing *The Authoress of the
Odyssey*, share Butler's conviction that the author was indeed the charming

young woman disguised as Nausicaa in Book VI to appreciate that his reading of the epic pin-points real qualities in it. So, too, we need not agree with
Wilson's argument — that the failure of many stories written after the turn
of the century is due to Kipling's having exhausted his Indian material — to
realize that they do lack the strong evocative power of the Indian stories.
Wilson rarely commits the error — as many critics do with mostly a thesis
for their qualifications — of praising what is dead (his assessment of *Hard
Times* is instructive) to bolster a theoretical conclusion formed outside the
works. The thrust of all the learning he brings to bear on his subject is to
define the tone, the peculiar atmosphere, as the reader will encounter it and
thereby to discriminate among the novels and not indulge in sweeping generalities. In this vivid recording of his own enthusiastic responses he is rivet-
ing and convincing.

III

Since his success in these studies depends upon a sympathetic identification with the authors, we might ask what in them has captured Wilson's
affections. In all three cases Wilson seems to be righting a balance, rescuing
the writers from false impressions: Zola from the general neglect into which
he had fallen by mid-century; Kipling from unsympathetic attitudes of
many critics; and the popular Dickens from the solemn theories with
which, since Edmund Wilson, scholarly critics have obscured the true
source of his magnetism. Angus Wilson is, as we have seen, aware of many
parallels in the artistic and very different lives of his trio. All three were
gifted journalists, restless and acute observers in full contact with the dust
and sweat of life, a fact which helps explain the colorful plenitude of their
fictional worlds, the great diversity of vivid characters, the often panoramic sweep of the visions, the vital energy suffusing them. All share a
strong awareness of the fragility of the rational world, of the "skull beneath
the skin," a bleakness which informs even the happiest fictional evocations
(in Dickens especially) and provides an often heart-wrenching poignancy.
All exude a relish for the variety of life. All owed their peculiar world to
traumatic experience of violent contrasts early in life. Dickens and Kipling,
in life and art, also never lost touch with the child within them — a trait
particularly endearing to a novelist who began his writing career by re-cre-
ating the world of neglected children.
        This surely brings us to the most significant similarity: that the value of
their works lies not in ideas, in the moral philosophy they might reflect, but
in the accomplished conjuring up of place and character with an at times
nightmare intensity. As a writer, Wilson is aware (as rarely a critic is allowed to be) of how little an idea carries a writer, how easily the conscious
message, the imposed didacticism, can sink a novel, or at least in the case of
a Tolstoy, direct its appeal to another, chiefly intellectual plane. What
Wilson cherishes in his three writers is their "enveloping" world and their

"clarity of direct vision," a world, that is, whose first appeal is to our imagination.

However much Zola may have prided himself on his adherence to scientific materialism, however cocksure he was about his modernist beliefs and "patent-leather up-to-dateness,"[16] Angus Wilson dismisses all that as superficial lumber. Had Zola relied on his naturalist creed for inspiration, his novels would today be mere period pieces preserved in amber by intellectual historians. He was not a naturalist, but a great mesmerizing impressionist in the grips of a dark imagination to which his theoretic learning hardly had access. By contrast, writers like Galsworthy, Bennett, and Thomas Mann lacked "those vast childhood reserves with which their predecessors had filled their vast bottles. . . ."[17] To link Thomas Mann's work to the pale, dated sentimental lyricism of Galsworthy is instructive, if not entirely just. Mann was a novelist of ideas; his first novel, *Buddenbrooks*, was apparently inspired by Morel's now exploded psychological theory of degeneration;[18] but quite obviously its vitality—it is in debt to Zola and the epic Tolstoy—suggests that it too owes its strength to the vividly realized memories of Mann's Lübeck youth. Whatever we may think of this Freudian view, Wilson is correct in insisting that if ideas are to serve fiction, they must disappear in its rich imaginative particularity; the work must, to paraphrase James Dickey, reduce "generalities to local fact."[19]

Even the Jamesian doctrine of realism, virtually an orthodoxy today, is not decisive in locating a novel's true quality. Kipling was no "realist" any more than the poetic Zola or Dickens. He could not even think of the Empire except in terms of specific heroic acts. Kipling's forte "was the creation of his own world out of his impressions of the real world. The facts—accurate or inaccurate of the real world—are only important in so far as they impress the reader with the truth of the created world."[20] Fiction tells lies to tell the truth—the old adage describes the ancient purpose of storytelling—and both Kipling and Dickens were essentially raconteurs. No doubt Wilson would have jibed at a recent essay that castigates R. L. Stevenson's Scott-like distortion of the historical realities concerning divided Scotland in *The Master of Ballantrae*.[21] But *Kim*'s greatness lies in its poetry, in its imaginative (and not entirely factual) evocation of India's atmosphere. Because Wilson is not affected by doctrinaire opinions regarding fiction, he is free to do full justice even to the *Just So Stories* and to the best tales dealing with Mowgli, his animal friends, and the man-pack: for in them Kipling has achieved a magnificent interplay between the world of children and that of adults. To be able thus to refrain from ordering particular appreciations to theoretical conclusions is indeed to place the primary experience of reading at the center of all critical concerns.

The studies of Zola and Kipling are related, in this matter of fiction-making, as two pendants to a centerpiece. *The World of Charles Dickens* is written with unflagging zest from one end to the other, reflecting certainly the most complete act of identification. Dickens seems most completely to fulfill Wilson's ideal of a writer: for he was one in whose work, from *Boz* to *Edwin Drood*, ideas as such have no role; he possessed an inexplicably powerful intuition of character and an almost neurotic sensitivity to the impressions of place. If intellectual propositions hold these rich worlds together, then they are Dickens' belief in the necessity of Christian charity and of the importance of the imagination in keeping the human heart alive — rather pale platitudes outside the rich context of the novels, whose appeal is first of all aesthetic. The novel is, as it was for John Cheever, a great — if not the greatest — source of refreshment; and just as for Cheever, its magic derives from a force of memory which is comprehended only gradually as the writer moves away from his formative impressions. Its substance, whatever else it may reveal beneath its surface, is the convincing evocation of place and character fused into a vision by some effable, poignant resonance.

Wilson is reluctant to take the moral measure of the novel; he does not evaluate its truth, the element of *dianoia*, directly as the traditional Aristotelian critic would. But he does not neglect it: he is aware that the artistic vision is a moral act. In praising his favorite works, or finding the weakness of others, he suggests that, after all, the novel constitutes at its best a heritage of meaning. So *Little Dorrit* owes its profundity to Dickens' depiction, not just of the Victorian rich exploiting the Victorian poor, but to the larger insight into the effect of cynicism, despair, and self-pity on all characters. In *Great Expectations* we see the mature Dickens dramatize the corruption inflicted by that most human desire for respect and success; it is, though Wilson is reluctant to give his full approval, a moving realization and summary of Christ's Beatitudes; in it, as throughout the work, Dickens retains his strong sense of the evil, as mysterious ultimately as the saintly idiocy of Jo Gargery. Finally, in *Kim* the lama and the little friend of all the world share a relationship to each other that can symbolize the conflicting paths to the central meaning of life. Quite clearly, Wilson expects the novel to reflect his own humanistic conception of man: he cannot quite approve of Kipling's masculine world of Stalky & Co., or the cruel punishment Kipling rains upon those who disobey the law, or Dickens' strange fascination with criminals. In these aesthetic responses we detect a moral norm that guides his critical judgment. But as if to say that fiction does capture so much better the ineluctable flux of life than our intellectual and moral categories and that therein lies the real justification of novels, he prefers to lay the stress on storytelling as an enrichment created by the play of a refined and deeply nourished sensibility that it should be the critic's endeavor to explore. Wilson's unwillingness to apply a more sullen and rigorous standard may be regarded by some as a weakness; but it is enormously invigorating and reassuring in these times — when the novel is often pronounced dead, when every aspect of fiction has been put in question, when we have dug with so much cerebral self-consciousness about the foundations of our being until we fancy that we see through everything and find a blank — to encounter an informed and richly stored mind that so convincingly bears witness to the lasting validity and significance of every form of storytelling, and that has not unlearned the naive pleasure of participating in the experience of imaginary worlds.

Notes

1. *The Shrewsbury Edition of the Works of Samuel Butler*, ed. H. F. Jones and A. T. Bartholomew (London: Jonathan Cape, 1923–26), XII (*The Authoress of the Odyssey*), 279.

2. *Ibid.*, XX, 7.

3. *Rasselas*, Chap. VI.

4. *The World of Charles Dickens* (Harmondsworth: Penguin Books, 1970), p. 292.

5. *Ibid.*, p. 8.

6. *Émile Zola: An Introductory Study of His Novels* (New York: William Morrow & Co., 1952), p. 69.

7. *Ibid.*, p. 52.

8. *Ibid.*, p. 52

9. *Dickens*, p. 80.

10. *The Strange Ride of Rudyard Kipling* (Harmondsworth: Penguin Books, 1979), p. 60.

11. *Ibid.*, p. 200.

12. *Dickens*, p. 102.

13. *Kipling*, p. 218.

14. *Ibid.*, p. 202–3.

15. *Setting the World on Fire* (1980) is proof enough. This is what he is quoted as saying in a recent interview: A sense of " 'precariousness is in all my books.' It is as though 'people are walking on cracking ice. Life is always like that for me' "(*News Journal*, [Wilmington, Delaware], 8 December, 1983, pp. D2, D12).

16. *Zola*, p. 38.

17. *Ibid.*, p. 59.

18. Karl Stern, "Literature and Psychiatry," in *Love and Success* (New York: Farrar, Strauss & Giroux, 1975), p. 4.

19. James Dickey, *Babel to Byzantium* (New York: Grosset & Dunlap, 1971), p. 201.

20. *Kipling*, p. 280.

21. Andrew Noble, "Highland History and Narrative Form in Scott and Stevenson," in *Robert Louis Stevenson* (London: Vision Press Ltd.; Totowa, N.J.: Barnes & Noble Books, 1983).

SELECTED
BIBLIOGRAPHY

The following is a list of the principal publications by Angus Wilson. A full bibliography of primary and secondary materials is available in Robert J. Stanton, *A Bibliography of Modern British Novelists* (Troy, N.Y.: Whitston, 1978), II, 997-1071, 1110-23, updated and corrected by J. H. Stape in *Twentieth Century Literature*, 29, No. 2 (Summer 1983), 249-66). Paperback reprints of books are generally not included below but are chiefly available in Britain through Granada-Panther and in the U.S.A. through Academy Chicago.

The Wrong Set. London: Secker & Warburg, 1949; New York: Morrow, 1950.

Such Darling Dodos. London: Secker & Warburg, 1950; New York: Morrow, 1951.

Émile Zola. London: Secker & Warburg, 1952; New York: Morrow 1952; rev. ed., London: Secker & Warburg, 1964.

Hemlock and After. London: Secker & Warburg, 1952; New York: Viking, 1952.

For Whom the Cloche Tolls. London: Methuen, 1953; New York: Curtis, 1953; rev. ed., Harmondsworth: Penguin, 1976.

The Mulberry Bush. London: Secker & Warburg, 1956.

Anglo-Saxon Attitudes. London: Secker & Warburg, 1956; New York: Viking, 1956.

A Bit Off the Map. London: Secker & Warburg, 1957; New York: Viking, 1957.

The Middle Age of Mrs. Eliot. London: Secker & Warburg, 1958; New York: Viking, 1959.

The Old Men at the Zoo. London: Secker & Warburg, 1961; New York: Viking, 1961.

The Wild Garden; or, Speaking of Writing. Berkeley: Univ. of California Press, 1963; London: Secker & Warburg, 1963.

Tempo: The Impact of Television on the Arts. London: Studio Vista, 1964.

Late Call. London: Secker & Warburg, 1964; New York: Viking, 1965.

No Laughing Matter. London: Secker & Warburg, 1967; New York: Viking, 1967.

Death Dance: Twenty-Five Stories. New York: Viking, 1969. A reprint of stories from *The Wrong Set, Such Darling Dodos, A Bit Off the Map*.

The World of Charles Dickens. London: Secker & Warburg, 1970; New York: Viking, 1970.

As If by Magic. London: Secker & Warburg, 1973; New York: Viking, 1973.

The Naughty Nineties. London: Eyre Methuen, 1976.

Writers of East Anglia. Selected and edited by Angus Wilson, poetry adviser, John Holloway. London: Secker & Warburg, 1977.

The Strange Ride of Rudyard Kipling. London: Secker & Warburg, 1977; New York: Viking, 1978.

Setting the World on Fire. London: Secker & Warburg, 1980; New York: Viking, 1980.

The Portable Dickens. Edited with an introduction, by Angus Wilson. New York: Viking, 1983.

Diversity and Depth in Fiction: The Critical Writings of Angus Wilson. Edited by Kerry McSweeney. London: Secker & Warburg, 1983.

INDEX